MEXICAN AMERICANS AND SPORTS

MEXICAN AMERICANS AND SPORTS

A Reader on Athletics and Barrio Life

EDITED BY JORGE IBER
AND SAMUEL O. REGALADO

TEXAS A&M UNIVERSITY PRESS
College Station

COPYRIGHT © 2007 BY TEXAS A&M UNIVERSITY PRESS
Manufactured in the United States of America
All rights reserved
First edition

The paper used in this book meets the minimum requirements
of the American National Standard for Permanence
of Paper for Printed Library Materials, Z39.48-1984.
Binding materials have been chosen for durability.

"The Foot Runners Conquer Mexico and Texas: Endurance Racing, *Indigenismo,* and Nationalism," appeared in *Journal of Sport History* 31(1) (Spring 2004): 1–31.

"*Peloteros* in Paradise: Mexican American Baseball and Oppositional Politics in Southern California, 1930–1950," appeared in *Western Historical Quarterly* 34(2) (Summer 2003): 191–212.

"Wearing the Red, White, and Blue Trunks of Aztlán: Rodolfo 'Corky' Gonzales and the Convergence of American and Chicano Nationalism," appeared in *Aztlán: Journal of Chicano Studies* 29(1) (Spring 2004): 83–117, UCLA Chicano Studies Research Center. Reprinted with the permission of the Regents of the University of California. Not for further reproduction.

"On-field Foes and Racial Misconceptions: The 1961 Donna Redskins and Their Drive to the Texas State Football Championship," appeared in the *International Journal of the History of Sport* 21(2) (March 2004): 237–56.

Library of Congress CataloginginPublication Data

Mexican Americans and sports : a reader on athletics and barrio life / edited by Jorge Iber and Samuel O. Regalado.— 1st ed.
   p. cm.
Includes bibliographical references and index.
ISBN-13: 978-1-58544-551-6 (cloth : alk. paper)
ISBN-10: 1-58544-551-7 (cloth : alk. paper)
ISBN-13: 978-1-58544-552-3 (pbk. : alk. paper)
ISBN-10: 1-58544-552-5 (pbk. : alk. paper)
   1. Mexican Americans—Sports. 2. Mexican Americans—Recreation. 3. Mexican American Athletes. 4. Mexican American Athletes—Social conditions. 5. Sports—United States—History. I. Iber, Jorge, 1961- II. Regalado, Samuel O. (Samuel Octavio), 1953-
GV583.M48 2006
796.0868'72073—dc22
                                    2006005168

CONTENTS

Acknowledgments   vii

Introduction: Athletics and Chicano/a Life, 1930–2005   1
JORGE IBER

The Foot Runners Conquer Mexico and Texas: Endurance Racing,
   Indigenismo, and Nationalism   19
MARK DYRESON

Peloteros in Paradise: Mexican American Baseball and Oppositional
   Politics in Southern California, 1930–1950   50
JOSÉ M. ALAMILLO

Los Heroes del Domingo: Soccer, Borders, and Social Spaces
   in Great Lakes Mexican Communities, 1940–1970   73
JUAN JAVIER PESCADOR

Wearing the Red, White, and Blue Trunks of Aztlán:
   Rodolfo "Corky" Gonzales and the Convergence of American
   and Chicano Nationalism   89
TOM I. ROMERO II

On-field Foes and Racial Misconceptions:
  The 1961 Donna Redskins and Their Drive to the Texas State
  Football Championship   121
  JORGE IBER

Read All about It! The Spanish-language Press, the Dodgers, and
  the Giants, 1958–1982   145
  SAMUEL O. REGALADO

Raza Boxing: Community, Identity, and Hybridity in the 1960s and
  1970s in Southern California   160
  GREGORY S. RODRÍGUEZ

Beating the Odds: Mexican American Distance Runners in Texas,
  1950–1995   188
  ALEXANDER MENDOZA

Advance at Your Own Risk: Latinas, Families, and
  Collegiate Softball   213
  KATHERINE M. JAMIESON

Invisible Identity: Mexican American Sport and Chicano
  Historiography   233
  SAMUEL O. REGALADO

List of Contributors   247

Index   251

ACKNOWLEDGMENTS

As with all book projects, many people have helped to bring this undertaking to its conclusion. I would like to thank Dr. Larry Gerlach of the University of Utah for introducing me to the field of sports history. I thank the many people involved with the North American Society for Sport History (NASSH) who, over the years, served as mentors and commentators on my research and earlier versions of this manuscript. I also thank the members of the 1961 Donna Redskins and the Lerma and Cavazos families for allowing me to research the lives of an extraordinary group of Mexican American athletes and coaches.

Thanks also go to my colleagues at Texas Tech University, whose encouragement made it possible for me to complete this project: Gretchen Adams, Randy McBee, Julie Willett, Paul Carlson, Alwyn Barr, Don Walker, Monte Monroe, Jane Winer, and David Snead. Finally, I thank my coeditor for his effort, sharp editorial eye, and, most important, his friendship and support.

The final acknowledgments are the most meaningful and heartfelt of all. To my father, Manuel Iber, who engendered in me a love for sport through his wonderful stories of the Havana Leones, Almendares Alacranes, Havana Sugar Kings, and the glories of prerevolutionary Cuban baseball. To my wife,

Raquel, and our son, Matthew: I can never repay you for the joys that you have brought to my life; thank you both for everything.

—JORGE IBER

First and foremost, Jorge Iber, my friend and colleague, deserves my greatest thanks for having brought me on board to coedit the essays in this important anthology. His scholarly intuitiveness and dogged determination to bring this work to fruition speak to his commitment to incorporating the essential role of Mexican American sports into the larger picture of U.S. history. Mary Lenn Dixon, editor in chief at Texas A&M Press, because of her constant support, professionalism, and the expediency with which she guided the early versions of the text through the cumbersome protocol that is part of the publication process, also merits high praise. In addition, I am appreciative of my colleagues in the Department of History at California State University–Stanislaus. Their professional camaraderie and appreciation of my work have been invaluable components of my career. Other colleagues such as Richard Crepeau, Larry Gerlach, Steve Gietschier, Patrick Miller, Steve Riess, and members of the North American Society for Sport History have contributed, in one manner or another, to the development of this work. Finally, I honor the memory of my late uncle Gregory Regalado, an exceptional ballplayer who, along with his many contributions to East Los Angeles Mexican American adult baseball, so graciously gave me, as a boy, an opportunity to be a part of that wonderful world.

—SAMUEL O. REGALADO

MEXICAN AMERICANS AND SPORTS

INTRODUCTION
Athletics and Chicano/a Life, 1930–2005
JORGE IBER

On September 4, 2002, an exposé appearing on the ESPN website probably caught many auto-racing fans throughout the country by surprise. The title of Jerry Bonkowski's article "NASCAR Aims to Attract Hispanics" is simple, yet it describes the new demographic, social, economic, and sporting realities of life in the United States in the twenty-first century.[1] The article details the attempt by "a sport with roots steeped in the South" to engage a whole new fan base. The numbers Bonkowski cites are difficult for marketing executives to dismiss: Spanish speakers are projected to constitute approximately 20 percent of the national populace by 2020, and, by 2050, that figure is expected to reach 25 percent. The potential benefits of increasing the attraction of auto racing to this population are spelled out by Eddie Gossage, chief overseer of the Texas Motor Speedway (in the Dallas–Fort Worth area): "It's very important to us to make our sport more open and aggressively promote to the minority community.... So, we do things like produce press releases in Spanish, produce ads for Hispanic newspapers, have promotions with local Hispanic businesses, work with all of the Spanish media outlets.... We've identified the Hispanic market as a very key market."[2]

According to Bonkowski, NASCAR has taken a two-pronged approach at the corporate level in order to increase its Hispanic fan base. First, management hired Dora Taylor, a Cuban American, as senior manager for diversity affairs. Her responsibilities include increasing the number of Latinos in three key areas: spectators, drivers, and team owners. Taylor has a proven track record in working with organizations such as the previously scandal-plagued Denny's Restaurant chain, which at one time had dealt unsuccessfully with its minority customers. Second, in 2000, NASCAR formed an internal diversity council, whose members include some of the most recognized names in the circuit: Winston Cup champion Jeff Gordon; team owner and coach of the Washington Redskins, Joe Gibbs; and former driver and now broadcaster Ned Jarrett. It is their responsibility to "formulate strategies to get more minorities involved in the sport, be they Hispanic, African American, Asian, or female."[3]

A critical first step in this process is to get more Latinos behind the wheel at NASCAR events. Cuban American Félix Sabates, the first Spanish-surnamed person to own teams in the Busch and Winston Cup tours, argues that, until there are more participants, auto racing will continue to lag behind other sports in the drive to increase the number of *fanáticos* (fans). "The potential is there, but you have to have the drivers. You have to have the Martinezes and Gomezes and Gonzaleses. But, if you could change Jeff Gordon's name to, say, Jaime Gordino, that would be good. That would bring a lot of attention."[4]

Track manager Gossage agrees: "It's not realistic for us to expect minorities to attend races when no minorities are participating. The first step is to get some minority participants in our sport, and it can grow and take off from there." Another Cuban American involved in auto racing, Mike Vázquez, a team owner in the Busch Series who recently hired Colombian-born driver Roberto Guerrero for his squad, argues similarly: "Up until now, NASCAR has been ignored by the majority of the Hispanic community. Even when I was a kid, I'd tune out after the first 10 or 15 minutes because I couldn't see a[n Emerson] Fittipaldi or [Ayrton] Senna or even Roberto Guerrero. I had no Hispanics to identify with. I've since come to respect names like Petty and Yarborough, but back then it didn't mean squat."[5]

Whether NASCAR ultimately succeeds or fails in its quest to attract significant numbers of our nation's Spanish-surnamed population as observers and on-track participants remains to be seen. Although NASCAR has traditionally ignored the vast majority of Spanish speakers, its attempts to branch out and deal with the nation's new demographic and economic realities has considerable ramifications for the broader study of sport.

During the 1980s and 1990s historians and others who are interested in minority populations produced voluminous research on sport's impact on neighborhoods and schools throughout the United States. The majority of these works focus on the white/black dichotomy. Researchers such as Robert Ruck, David K. Wiggins, John M. Carroll, the late Arthur R. Ashe, Jeffrey T. Sammons, Eliott J. Gorn, and Sandy Tolan (to name just a few) have commented on how success in athletics has impacted the perception of this population by both African Americans and the broader society.[6]

Students of the Native American experience have generated similar works. In a 2001 article on the Carlisle Indians, for example, David Wallace Adams argues that success on the gridiron has helped some of the squad's members believe that, if they can succeed on the playing field, then they can achieve in other aspects of American life as well.[7] Gerald R. Gems's fine study of Native American and African American football players similarly notes that such competition (at all levels) has "allowed subordinate groups to challenge the social Darwinian beliefs and stereotypes that characterized them as 'others.'. . . . [These] social evolutions took place on the high school teams . . . as disparate groups found some common ground in the popular culture of football."[8]

Similarly, Roberta J. Park, Samuel O. Regalado, Susan G. Zieff, and Joel S. Franks have cited the impact of sport upon Asian Americans living in the American West. They have described how people of Japanese, Chinese, and Pacific Islander heritage in the United States used their success on the baseball diamonds, football gridirons, and basketball courts to challenge the majority population's notion that Asian people were naturally "unathletic" and specifically that Asian males were "unmanly."[9] Further, Peter Levine, Steven A. Riess, and William M. Simons studied the communal and personal implications of athletic accomplishment among the children of Jewish immigrants, primarily in the large metropolitan areas of the Northeast.[10] Finally, authors such as Gary Ross Mormino, Wes Singletary, and Anthony A. Yoseloff have summarized the impact of sport on Italian American neighborhoods from New York City to St. Louis and Tampa (the Florida materials examine both Italian American and Cuban American neighborhoods, such as Ybor City).[11]

Given the population changes that have taken place over the past few decades, it is imperative that scholars break new ground and add the Spanish surnamed (the nation's largest minority group as of 2000), and in particular Mexican Americans (the most numerous of the various ethnic groups among Latinos), to the analysis of U.S. sport history.

It is not surprising that few scholars of Mexican Americans have focused their inquiries on the story of athletic participation in the barrios (neighborhoods); indeed, the majority of the field's specialists do little more than provide a passing glance at sport within the communities they study. An excellent example of such oversight is found in the 1990 article "Recent Chicano Historiography: An Interpretive Essay" by Alex M. Saragoza.[12] In this important discussion, Saragoza calls for new directions in the field of historical research. He argues for an expansion of the geographical focus (beyond Texas and California), as well as an examination of the impact of U.S. popular culture on the lives of barrio dwellers. Among the stimuli he suggests as deserving of academic inquiry are the "influence of advertising, the mass media, fashion, consumerism," and similar issues.[13] In the years since this call, numerous writers have answered Saragoza's challenge and produced works on identity formation and maintenance, music, clothing, glamour magazines, and marketing.[14] Saragoza provides researchers with an extensive array of subjects for scrutiny but fails to note the possibility that an analysis of sport could yield positive contributions to an understanding of Mexican American existence.

Although the Saragoza article provides an effective and thorough synopsis of major trends in Mexican American history through 1990, it is now somewhat dated. Surely one might anticipate that, since the year that article was published, scholars of the historiography of this field (seeing the substantial amount of work done on sports and other minority groups) might have recognized the potential of incorporating athletic endeavor as part of the totality of the Mexican American historical experience. Unfortunately, for the most part they have not.

An illustration of such an omission is found in a discussion by Antonio Rios-Bustamante in *Voices of a New Chicana/o History,* edited by Refugio I. Rochín and Dennis N. Valdés.[15] Rios-Bustamente's chapter, titled "A General Survey of Chicano/a Historiography," presents a list of twenty thematic subfields (and a description of numerous theoretical models) of Chicano/a scholarly study; among the subjects he finds worthy of historical inquiry are immigration, politics, gender, regional identities, Mexican American/Mexican relations, and the depiction of Latinos in film and art. Unfortunately, nowhere in this exceptional essay is athletic endeavor by people of Mexican descent in the United States mentioned as a topic worthy of academic study.[16]

One final example of such oversight occurs in Matt García's 2001 work,

A World of Its Own: Race, Labor, and Citrus in the Making of Greater Los Angeles, 1900–1970. In this well-written and exhaustively researched project on life in citrus *colonias* (communities) such as Claremont, La Verne, and Pomona, García sheds light on a wide range of group activities that influenced the lives of the Spanish-speaking men, women, and children there. In particular, he focuses on labor organizing, educational initiatives, identity formation, youth culture, and social and recreational pastimes. Given the book's format, it would seem that an examination of sport in the various locales would add to his description of the texture of colonia reality, but García does not thoroughly develop this topic. While he includes a photograph of a "Mexican baseball team" and spends about one paragraph listing various teams from the area's "Mexican league," García mentions them mainly to note the role of women's auxiliaries in supporting the teams during their trips to "away" games. This topic, although worthwhile, disregards any other impact that the baseball circuit has had on the colonias.[17]

Lest we be accused of placing the blame for this omission in the intellectual ballpark of scholars of Chicano/a history, academicians who specialize in sport history have also failed to address this topic. For example, in *Sports: The First Five Millennia,* in the sections dealing with sports in the United States, Allan Guttmann makes only one pithy reference to Mexican Americans. He asserts that, in the Lone Star State, the gridiron "separates manly young Texans from alleged effeminate soccer-playing Mexican Americans."[18] While correct in noting that whites in Texas have not always looked upon Mexican Americans as their athletic (or intellectual or social) equals, as some of the chapters in this collection demonstrate, it is incorrect to assume that Texas' population of Mexican descent plays (or has played) only soccer. Spanish-surnamed people in Texas and elsewhere participated in a wide variety of athletic endeavors during the twentieth century. Indeed, they have "used" sport in many of the same ways that other ethnic Americans have: to derive personal and communal enjoyment, to forge neighborhood and working-class bonds, and to refute the racist stereotypes held by many in the majority population.

Another example of the failure to notice the Mexican American presence (indeed, that of all Hispanics) in athletics in the United States is evident in an inspection of the index of the *Journal of Sport History.* This publication, which has featured many articles on the sporting experiences of African Americans, Italian Americans, Jews, Native Americans, Asian Americans, and other ethnic groups, has barely broached the subject of Hispanic (and specifically Mexican American) participation in sports in the United States. Among the journal's few items on Hispanic issues are two works by Mary Lou LeCompte on vaqueros and their influence on rodeo, one article by Jodella K. Dyreson examining sporting pursuits in Mexican Texas, and an overview by Mary Lou LeCompte and William Beezley of pre-1900 sporting activities by Germans, Anglos, and tejanos in San Antonio.[19] All of these works, while significant, do not delve into the sports and time period covered by the chapters in this book.

Although this area of inquiry has not received sufficient scholarly consideration, the cupboard is not totally bare, for a few people have recently—and clearly—demonstrated the potential of adding sport to the historiographical mix of Mexican American studies. First and foremost is Samuel O. Regalado. Beginning in the early 1990s, he introduced the story of *peloteros* (ballplayers) to the academic community by studying athletic achievement and the way in which major and minor leaguers have influenced the perception of Spanish-surnamed people by society at large. Regalado's investigations scrutinize issues such as the significance of baseball *ligas* (leagues) to barrio life in Los Angeles, the social consequences of the Los Angeles Dodgers' Spanish-language broadcasts, and the majority population's view of Spanish-speaking athletes such as the late Pittsburgh Pirate great, Roberto Clemente.[20]

Two works by Richard Santillán and Douglas Monroy have followed up on Regalado's pioneering studies. In an article titled "Mexican Baseball Teams in the Midwest: The Politics of Cultural Survival and Civil Rights," Santillán focuses on the longevity, extent, and importance of ligas (industrial, community, and Catholic) to colonias in places such as Emporia, Kansas; Flint, Michigan; Aurora, Illinois; Omaha, Nebraska; and Des Moines, Iowa. Through an extensive use of oral histories, Santillán records the birth and durability of these leagues and focuses on the way in which sports have benefited Latinos living in Midwestern states. Not surprisingly, on-field ability frequently facilitated a worker's employability since "being an outstanding player was oftentimes a ticket to employment for Mexicans. . . . Companies went out of their way to find outstanding Mexican players." Sport was also a vehicle for community celebrations, a way to demonstrate pride in ethnic and religious heritage, and a welcome diversion after a week of back-breaking work. Significantly, "other benefits of athletics have been the leadership skills and survival tactics that young people developed by participating in team sports—skills that have been useful in the political arena and in the fight for social justice." Santillán argues that the worth of such ligas is evidenced by their continued existence into the 1990s and beyond. Long after the end of "legal" segregation in schools and communities, Mexican Americans continue to sponsor teams in associations such as the Liga de Béisbol Mexicana in Oklahoma City, as well as the Aztec and Mayan leagues in Chicago.[21]

While the Regalado and Santillán contributions are noteworthy, they are confined to baseball. One scholar who moves beyond this limitation is Douglas Monroy. In his 1999 book, *Rebirth: Mexican Los Angeles from the Great Migration to the Great Depression,* he encapsulates aspects of colonia life, including what he terms the "passions of *México de afuera*" (Mexico outside of Mexico). Among these are food, religion, music, and politics. Monroy also notes at least three ways in which sports were important to the community's (primarily, the male's) psyche. First, it provided an opportunity for competition and success for men and boys who faced difficulties at work and in school. "It was one way for the various people from south of the border to forge an identity as Mexicans . . . and a public reinforcement of the traditional manly values of forceful, dynamic activities."[22] Second, sports permitted Spanish-surnamed males to pit themselves against other minority groups, such as Japanese Americans. Victory in such tournaments did much to reinforce barrio pride. This is quite evident in a quotation from *La Opinión,* the most important Spanish-language newspaper of early twentieth-century Los Angeles:

> "The most important baseball event that has registered in the bosom of the Mexican colony in the past years will take place tomorrow afternoon in White Sox Stadium, when the Mexicans of the mighty El Paso Shoe Store Club battle the orientals [sic] of the Los Angeles Nippons for the 'foreign championship of baseball' of the United States." I do not know how the Japanese press portrayed the series of games, and the americano [sic] press remained predictably silent about the matter, but the Mexican press proclaimed that the "Mexican stars" won "the championship" by a score of ten to five on May 12, 1929. Sports writers have always embellished their articles with such rhetoric . . . but we can be sure that they expressed some truth when, after the Mexicans won the first game in April, *La Opinión* reported that the El Paso Shoe Store team "established themselves as [the] idols of the hundreds of aficionados of our *raza* [race] who attended yesterday."[23]

Finally, it was believed that success on the baseball diamond (and elsewhere) helped dispel some of the negative perceptions of Spanish speakers in the broader society. Every triumph by the El Paso Shoe Store team was important because "'The task these boys are undertaking on the sports field, which is the most appreciated among the American people, [was] to elevate the good name of our *raza,* [and this] should not be overlooked.'"[24] My own work appeared in the *Southwestern Historical Quarterly* in 2002 and focused on high school football in South Texas, which is predominantly Mexican American. It supports this contention: "While athletic competition, and the ties created thereby, did not eliminate all racist preconceptions about Spanish speakers . . . [the athletes'] success did present Anglos in southern Texas with a different archetype of the Mexican American. Instead of the stereotypical views which many Texans [held with regard to] persons of Mexican descent, here were . . . men succeeding on the gridiron and bringing athletic glory to their hometown and schools."[25]

Although baseball was an important aspect of male existence, Monroy asserts that no "events so consistently excited the appetites of so many Mexican men as the fights. . . . The Mexican boxers quickly became an important presence . . . and provided a central means by which men's ethnic consciousness was formed."[26] As with other groups (most notably the children of Irish and Jewish immigrants), this violent undertaking provided an opportunity to display personal and communal value and strength.[27] For a select few, it also offered an opportunity to escape the economic poverty of barrio life: "Boxing gave youths a particular and Mexican notion of manhood to think about, or more likely, a demeanor to emulate. . . . But since nearly all fights must have a loser, many youthful fighters proved their fortitude by being able to take a punch, by enduring beatings. We see here how, consistent with virtually all cultures in which men engage in combat sports, Mexican culture, as its men defined and experienced it, came to associate physical prowess (in victory or defeat) with the quality of character for its men. Boxing has provided a path to success for young men, one that affirmed in a public arena these masculine values of aggressiveness, forcefulness and immunity to pain."[28]

A limited number of other studies on the significance of Latino participation in various sports in the United States have appeared since the early 1970s. *Practice! Practice! Practice!: The History of the King Ranch Cowboys Baseball Team,* a slim volume written and published by Donovan López, examines the impact of a mostly Mexican American team (although a few of the players were white and African American) on social relations at the legendary King Ranch and in the nearby city of Kingsville, Texas. López sums up the importance of the Cowboys' games by stating that athletic endeavor created "an environment that allowed ranch hands, councilmen, blue-collar workers and corporate [ranch] managers to mix and mingle in the realm of sport." Further, López cites a 1997 *San Antonio Express-News* story that argues that baseball games often acted as "male icebreaker[s] and leveler[s] of class, race, and age. It's the democratic elevator conversation, the anonymous coffee shop exchange. . . . It's what many men who [otherwise] have little in common have in common."[29]

Three other publications—Jorge Prieto's *The Quarterback Who Almost Wasn't,* Mario (Mike) de la Fuente's *I Like You, Gringo—But!,* and Lee Treviño's *They Call Me Super Mex*—provide firsthand accounts of Spanish-surnamed people who used sports to break down stereotypes and achieve athletic, academic, and professional success. The stories by Prieto and de la Fuente are particularly interesting because these men achieved success during an era (the 1930s) in which few members of the raza in Texas or elsewhere in the West and Southwest even graduated from high school. A final contribution is Mario Longoria's thoroughly researched book, *Athletes Remembered: Latino Professional Football Players, 1929-1970,* which focuses on the careers of Hispanic players in the National Football League (NFL) and the Canadian Football League (CFL), as well as notables from the collegiate ranks.[30]

Since the early decades of the 1900s, then, in places such as the Rio Grande Valley of South Texas, metropolitan areas of the Midwest, and California, Spanish speakers have actively participated and excelled in community-based, interscholastic, and professional athletic competition. The men, women, and children of many barrios used sports in much the same way as other minority populations—for recreation, leisure, community bonding, identity creation and maintenance, and proof of their worth to an often-skeptical broader society. The chapters in this book, which are written by historians and authors from other disciplines, document some of the varied aspects of the extensive, colorful, and significant history of Mexican Americans and sport.

The chapters that follow are arranged roughly in chronological order and cover the late 1920s through the present. They provide a survey and analysis of sporting experiences and organizations and their impact upon communal and individual lives from diverse areas: South Texas, the Midwest, and

California. The chapters spotlight various fields of athletic endeavor—baseball, football, soccer, boxing, track, and softball—by both men and women who are primarily, but not exclusively, of Mexican heritage or birth. Through all of the chapters run the myriad issues (recreation, community bonding and empowerment, and identity creation and maintenance) that scholars of other minority groups and sports highlight in their works but which academic writers who focus on the Mexican American experience have almost completely ignored.

Before moving on to a synopsis of the chapters, it is important to mention that we have made every effort to solicit contributions from scholars who are researching issues relating to Latinas. While pleased that we were able to acquire one article dedicated to this topic, we renew our assertion that it is imperative for more work to be done on topics relating to the participation of Spanish-surnamed women in sports.

The first chapter is, surprisingly, not about people of Mexican descent born in the United States but rather about a group of Tarahumaran *indios* whose abilities astonished the world in the late 1920s. Mark Dyreson does an effective job of establishing key themes that the other chapters develop: for example, the significance of sports in the creation of national and ethnic identity and the use of athletic prowess to counter certain racist assumptions. Dyreson focuses on the exploits of a number of Tarahumaras who accomplished extraordinary feats in distance running and demonstrated their superb abilities in Mexico and the United States. These indigenous people brought international recognition and national pride to Mexico and its recently installed revolutionary government. Not unexpectedly, once the indios' efforts became known in the United States, critics asserted that white runners could run longer and faster than this bunch of "savages" (if only the Caucasians would train properly).

The Tarahumaras and the Mexican government accepted the challenge, and a contingent of runners came to *el norte* to demonstrate their prowess. The men in the group (three women participated in a shorter race) agreed to run an extreme marathon of more than eighty miles (from San Antonio to the capitol building in Austin). In an examination of papers from throughout Texas, Dyreson clearly demonstrates the attitudes of most white Americans toward brown-skinned peoples. Simply put, the mexicanos were damned if they did and damned if they didn't. If the indios succeeded, their success would be attributed to the fact that they were uncivilized, lived in a pristine state, and therefore were closer in abilities to certain animals than to humans. If they failed, it would be proof that the Mexican "race" was weak, inferior, and given to exaggerating their puny accomplishments. Many Texans and other Americans assumed that people of such weak "stock" could not possibly compete at the same level as whites.

Such assertions, as readers will see, were not new in the 1920s. As Arnoldo de León notes in his important work, *They Called Them Greasers: Anglo Attitudes toward Mexicans in Texas, 1836–1900*, the notion of Mexican inferiority (both physical and intellectual) has long been a part of the psyche of the American West, especially in the Lone Star State.[31] Beginning in the early decades of the twentieth century, people of Mexican descent took to the baseball diamonds, gridirons, tracks, and boxing rings of the United States to battle against such perceptions of weakness.

The second chapter, by José M. Alamillo, is *"Peloteros* in Paradise: Mexican American Baseball and Oppositional Politics in Southern California, 1930–1950." Here Alamillo describes how players in various ligas used "our national pastime" to foster working-class unity and community pride through athletic achievement. He then explains how success on the diamond (some of the players from these leagues even had tryouts with major league organizations) was used to challenge Anglo assumptions about Mexican Americans' character, intellectual ability, and personal accountability.

Alamillo also briefly illustrates how such competition reinforced macho behavior, which, unfortunately, was often used to curtail opportunities for women of Mexican descent, thereby helping to sustain "a rigid gender hierarchy." Still, in conjunction with the chapter by Kathy Jamieson later in the collection, he provides insight into how some mexicanas utilized sports to challenge patriarchal behavior and to carve out their own athletic space.

Juan Javier Pescador's *"Los Heroes del Domingo:* Soccer, Borders, and Social Space in Great Lakes Mexican Communities, 1940–1970" focuses on the genesis and history of soccer leagues in Detroit and Chicago and examines how, in these soccer fields "mexicanos adopted outdoor leisure activities and sport rituals prevalent in U.S. cities. . . . At the same time . . . [they] mexicanized the urban landscape and manifested their right to public facilities."

Pescador challenges the notion that mexicanos used soccer as a way to maintain the traditions of their homeland. Instead, he asserts, the Spanish-surnamed people of the Midwest's largest cities utilized *fútbol* to demonstrate that mexicanos could organize and maintain community organizations, challenge (and defeat) other ethnic groups in vigorous athletic competition, and make use of these associations to organize a myriad of other activities such as schools for English as a second language, dances, and various mutual aid projects. Finally, he examines the way in which entrepreneurs (both ethnic and white) who catered to the needs of Mexicans used soccer matches to promote a wide variety of products and services. This trend, Pescador asserts, helped advance the integration of people of Mexican descent into the developing consumer culture in the United States, not by totally eliminating their "Mexican-ness" but rather by creating a culture of consumption based on the blending of Mexican traditions and American values.

Next, by Tom I. Romero, is "Wearing the Red, White, and Blue Trunks of Aztlán: Rodolfo 'Corky' Gonzales and the Convergence of American and Chicano Nationalism." In this fourth chapter Romero traces the boxing career of this Chicano-era icon and describes how Denver-area newspapers constructed their representation of his amateur and professional pugilistic career.

Gonzales's depiction in the print media, Romero argues, changed over a roughly twenty-year span from that of a minority youth who made good (and helped save boxing in Denver) to that of a young entrepreneur (who hoped to achieve the American Dream) to Democratic Party operative (used by the party to gather Mexican American votes) to a civic activist working to implement aspects of the national War on Poverty among Denver's poor. However, by the mid-1960s, as Gonzales's politics became radicalized, the mostly positive descriptions by Colorado newspaper editors disappeared and were replaced with a totally different assessment of the former pugilist. After 1965, gone were the days of Gonzales as a "young man on the make." Now he was portrayed as a troublemaker who was responsible for mobilizing Mexican Americans in "inappropriate" ways, thereby increasing racial tension within the city and the state. In summary, through his extensive use of newspaper articles, Romero examines the way in which the mainstream media depicted the sporting, entrepreneurial, political, and radical activist phases of Corky Gonzales's career, thereby demonstrating "the limits of the language of Americanism with regard to Chicano and Chicana nationalists."

The fifth chapter, "On-field Foes and Racial Misconceptions: The 1961 Donna Redskins and Their Drive to the Texas State Football Championship," by Jorge Iber, shifts the focus to South Texas and, in particular, to the area known as "the Valley" (the Rio Grande Valley, composed of Cameron, Hidalgo, Starr, and Willacy counties). While the majority population of these jurisdictions has always been Mexican American, the Anglo minority controlled the economic, social, and political power for most of the twentieth century.[32]

Because of the high percentage of Mexican American players in the Valley, many football coaches in the state considered an appointment to a school there as toiling in the "graveyard of coaches." When Charlie Williams arrived in 1962, colleagues warned him that "the Valley was 80% Mexican American and everybody knew that Mexican Americans were poor football players."[33] Pigskin prognosticators throughout Texas agreed that the Valley could never produce a state champion in football. Well, "the impossible" has happened only once, but the story of the Donna High School team that accomplished this remarkable feat provides important insight into the significance of sports for an oppressed community.

Samuel O. Regalado's chapter, "Read All about It!: The Spanish-language Press, the Dodgers, and the Giants, 1958–1981," offers an off-the-field perspective of the importance of sports to Mexican Americans. Regalado argues that, since the mid-nineteenth century, *periódicos* (newspapers) have performed a vital function for their colonias. For the editors, writers, and owners of such publications, one of the primary reasons for their existence was to "highlight the positive aspects of both Mexican and Latino culture" for their readers and, they hoped, the greater community. This trend spilled onto the sports pages of newspapers such as *La Opinión* of Los Angeles. For years, while the Dodgers failed to produce Spanish-surnamed stars (with the possible exception of Dominican pinch hitter extraordinaire, Manny Mota), the Giants' farm system up the coast generated numerous all-star-caliber peloteros. This spawned a serious dilemma for *La Opinión*. How should the paper treat the *estrellas* (stars) of the "hated" Giants, while trying to maintain the positive imagery of players like the Alou brothers? Through an extensive analysis of *La Opinión* and other Spanish-language papers, Regalado examines this balancing act up to the arrival of Fernando ("El Torito") Valenzuela on the major league scene in 1981.

The seventh chapter, "*Raza* Boxing: Community, Identity, and Hybridity in the 1960s and 1970s in Southern California," by Gregory S. Rodríguez, provides a rich tapestry detailing the role of boxing in the "continuing evolution of 'identity' and 'community' among Mexicans, Mexican Americans, Chicanos, and other less-powerful groups . . . that formed the fabric of Southern California." Rodríguez effectively integrates critical studies theory into an analysis of the shifting allegiances visible in Southern California's diverse population. He explains how, through boxing and support of individual pugilists of varied (e.g., Mexican, Cuban, Mexican American, African American) backgrounds, it is possible to forge "an extension of cultural communication and collaboration" with which to resist white social, economic, and cultural hegemony.

The eighth chapter, by Alexander Mendoza, "Beating the Odds: Mexican American Distance Runners in Texas, 1950–1995," affords, to the best of our knowledge, the first overview by an academician of the significance of this sport for a Spanish-speaking population. Mendoza examines the exploits of track stars such as Lee Montes of Nacogdoches, who won a state championship in the mile in 1937, as well as the career of historian Ricardo Romo, a thinclad from San Antonio's Fox Technical High School, who triumphed at the Southwest Conference championships in the mile, three-mile, and cross-country competitions during the 1960s while attending the University of Texas. Mendoza conveys the connection between this sport and the Mexican American community when he states that running "had a significant impact on . . . Mexican American runners in the state" as they witnessed athletes "with a similar background succeeding at the collegiate level."

In the final chapter, "Advance at Your Own Risk: Latinas, Families, and Collegiate Softball," Kathy Jamieson examines the impact of collegiate competition on the players—as well as their families' expectations of their daughters. In many ways, this study mirrors some of the issues presented in the chapter on the Donna Redskins by asking certain questions: Are sports a viable alternative for social advancement? What is the impact on these women's culture of playing softball in mostly white institutions? Do sports offer a way to maintain their culture, or is the result a redefinition of culture? Jamieson asserts that the "fluidity of identities, the valuing of multiple cultures, and the ability to cross borders both enabled and constrained [these women] as they made their ways to collegiate softball."

A word about terminology is necessary at this point. The term "Mexican American" is used in this book to refer to people who were born or reared in the United States but who trace their ancestry to Mexico. From the 1930s to the 1950s, the term "Latins" (or simply "Mexicans") was commonly used in Texas (mostly in a derogatory manner) to refer to these people. At certain points, when referring to the era or the literature of the Mexican American civil rights struggle of the 1960s and 1970s, the term "Chicano" is used. Finally, the terms "Hispanic" and "Latino" (currently the most commonly accepted expressions in the United States) are used to refer to works or situations that mention Spanish-speaking peoples of a variety of backgrounds (e.g., Cuban American, Puerto Rican, and other Central or South American citizens living in the United States).

As these chapters and the conclusion by Samuel O. Regalado—"Invisible Identity: Mexican American Sport and Chicano Historiography"—make clear, an analysis of athletic endeavor is a potentially profitable vein of Mexican American history that scholars are only now beginning to mine. The chapters presented here serve as an introduction to this subject. Some of them are theoretical in nature, while others focus on interesting (and mostly overlooked) snippets of Mexican American life. Still, the editors and contributors to this volume always kept two main goals in mind: They wanted to demonstrate how people of Mexican descent have used sport in the United States to build community and challenge the majority population's notion of Mexican American intellectual, athletic, and cultural weakness; they also wanted to reconstruct a neglected part of barrio and colonia history in order to demonstrate the potential for this line of study. Over the past two decades, students of African American, Native American, Asian American, Jewish, and Italian American history have revealed the value of sports to minority populations in both large and small communities throughout the United States. We hope that this collection will mark a first step toward a more complete inclusion of Latinos—and Mexican Americans specifically—into sports history and will also act as a call to insert sports into future investigations by historians of the Mexican American experience.

NOTES

1. Jerry Bonkowski, "NASCAR Aims to Attract Hispanics," http://www.freerepublic.com/focus/news/748696/posts.
2. Ibid., 3.
3. Ibid., 2.
4. Ibid.
5. Ibid., 3.
6. Rob Ruck, *Sandlot Seasons: Sport in Black Pittsburgh* (Urbana: University of Illinois Press, 1993); David K. Wiggins, *Glory Bound: Black Athletes in a White America* (Syracuse: Syracuse University Press, 1997); John M. Carroll, *Fritz Pollard: Pioneer in Racial Advancement* (Urbana: University of Illinois Press, 1992); Arthur R.

Ashe Jr., *A Hard Road to Glory: The African American Athlete in Football* (New York: Amistad, 1993); Jeffery T. Sammons, "'Race' and Sport: A Critical, Historical Examination," *Journal of Sport History* 21 (Fall 1994): 203–78; Elliott J. Gorn, ed., *Muhammad Ali: The People's Champ* (Urbana: University of Illinois Press, 1995); and Sandy Tolan, *Me and Hank: A Boy and His Hero, Twenty-five Years Later* (New York: Simon and Schuster, 2001).

7. David Wallace Adams, "More than a Game: The Carlisle Indians Take to the Gridiron, 1893–1917," *Western Historical Quarterly* 32 (Spring 2001): 25–53. For a similar argument, see John Bloom, *To Show What an Indian Can Do* (Minneapolis: University of Minnesota Press, 2000).

8. Gerald R. Gems, *For Pride, Profit, and Patriarchy: Football and the Incorporation of American Cultural Values* (Lanham, Md.: Scarecrow Press, 2000); see especially chap. 4, "The Huddle: Multicultural Football," 140.

9. Joel S. Franks, *Crossing Sidelines, Crossing Cultures: Sport and Asian Pacific American Cultural Citizenship* (Lanham, Md.: University Press of America, 2000); Joel S. Franks, *Whose Baseball?: The National Pastime and Cultural Diversity in California, 1859–1941* (Lanham, Md.: Scarecrow Press, 2001); Roberta J. Park, "Sport and Recreation among Chinese Americans of the Pacific Coast from the Time of Arrival to the 'Quiet Decade' of the 1950s," *Journal of Sport History* 27(3) (Fall 2000): 445–80; Samuel O. Regalado, "Incarcerated Sport: Nisei Women's Softball and Athletics during Japanese American Internment," *Journal of Sport History* 27(3) (Fall 2000): 431–44; and Susan G. Zieff, "From Badminton to the Bolero: Physical Recreations in San Francisco's Chinatown, 1895–World War II," *Journal of Sport History* 27(1) (Spring 2000): 1–30.

10. Peter Levine, *Ellis Island to Ebbets Field: Sport and the American Jewish Experience* (New York: Oxford University Press, 1992); Steven A. Riess, *Sport and the American Jew* (Syracuse: Syracuse University Press, 1998); and William M. Simons, "The Athlete as Jewish Standard Bearer: Media Images of Hank Greenberg," *Jewish Social Studies* 44 (Spring 1982): 95–112.

11. Gary Ross Mormino, "The Playing Fields of St. Louis: Italian Immigrants and Sports, 1925–1941," *Journal of Sport History* 9 (Summer 1982): 5–19; Wes Singletary, *Al López: The Life of Baseball's El Señor* (Jefferson, N.C.: McFarland, 1999); Anthony Yoseloff, "From Ethnic Hero to National Icon: The Americanization of Joe DiMaggio," *International Journal of the History of Sport* 16 (September 1999): 1–20.

12. Alex M. Saragoza, "Recent Chicano Historiography: An Interpretive Essay," *Aztlán* 19 (Spring 1988–1990): 1–77.

13. Ibid., 44–45.

14. Some of the most important contributions on these topics include George J. Sanchez, *Becoming Mexican American: Ethnicity, Culture, and Identity in Chicano*

Los Angeles, 1900–1945 (New York: Oxford University Press, 1993); Vicki L. Ruiz, "Star Struck: Acculturation, Adolescence, and the Mexican American Woman, 1920–1950," in *Between Two Worlds: Mexican Immigrants in the United States*, edited by David G. Gutiérrez (Wilmington, Del.: Jaguar Books on Latin America, Scholarly Resources, 1996), 125–48; Manuel H. Peña, *The Texas Mexican Conjunto: History of a Working-class Music* (Austin: University of Texas Press, 1985); David Reyes and Tom Waldman, *Land of a Thousand Dances: Chicano Rock 'n' Roll in Southern California* (Albuquerque: University of New Mexico Press, 1998); Arturo González, *Mexican Americans and the U.S. Economy: Quest for Buenos Días* (Tucson: University of Arizona Press, 2002); and Arlene Dávila, *Latinos, Inc: The Marketing and Making of a People* (Berkeley: University of California Press, 2001).

15. The specific chapter is "A General Survey of Chicano/a Historiography," by Antonio Rios-Bustamante, in *Voices of a New Chicana/o History*, edited by Refugio I. Rochín and Dennis N. Valdés (East Lansing: Michigan State University Press, 2000), 258–73.

16. Ibid.

17. Matt García, *A World of Its Own: Race, Labor, and Citrus in the Making of Greater Los Angeles, 1900–1970* (Chapel Hill: University of North Carolina Press, 2001), 73–74.

18. Allan Guttmann, *Sports: The First Five Millennia* (Amherst: University of Massachusetts Press, 2004), 151.

19. The term "tejano" was used by people of Spanish and Mexican descent who lived in Texas prior to the state's incorporation into the United States. At present the term is used by those who are descendents of these early pioneers. Mary Lou LeCompte, "The First American Rodeo Never Happened," *Journal of Sport History* 9 (Summer 1982): 89–96; Mary Lou LeCompte, "The Hispanic Influence on the History of Rodeo," *Journal of Sport History* 12 (Spring 1985): 21–38; Jodella K. Dyreson, "Sporting Activities in the American-Mexican Colonies of Texas, 1821–1835," *Journal of Sport History* 24 (Fall 1997): 269–84; and Mary Lou LeCompte and William H. Beezley, "Any Sunday in April: The Rise of Sport in San Antonio and the Hispanic Borderlands," *Journal of Sport History* 13 (Summer 1986): 128–46.

20. Samuel O. Regalado, *Viva Baseball!: Latin Major Leaguers and Their Special Hunger* (Urbana: University of Illinois Press, 1998); "Baseball in the Barrios: The Scene in East Los Angeles since World War II," *Baseball History* 1 (Summer 1996): 47–59; "Dodgers Béisbol Is on the Air: The Development and Impact of the Dodgers' Spanish-language Broadcasts, 1958–1994," *California History* (Fall 1995): 282–89; "'Image Is Everything': Latin Baseball Players and the U.S. Press," *Studies in Latin American Popular Culture* 13 (1994): 101–14; all three of the preceding articles are by Samuel O. Regalado.

21. Richard Santillán, "Mexican Baseball Teams in the Midwest: The Politics of Cultural Survival and Civil Rights," *Perspectives in Mexican American Studies* 7 (2000): 131–52.

22. Douglas Monroy, *Rebirth: Mexican Los Angeles from the Great Migration to the Great Depression* (Berkeley: University of California Press, 1999), 47.

23. Ibid.

24. Ibid., 48.

25. Jorge Iber, "Mexican Americans of South Texas Football: The Athletic and Coaching Careers of E. C. Lerma and Bobby Cavazos, 1932–1965," *Southwestern Historical Quarterly* 55 (April 2002): 616–33, 632.

26. Monroy, *Rebirth*, 57.

27. For an overview of this topic, see Steven A. Reiss, "Introduction: Sport and the American Jew" and "A Fighting Chance: The Jewish American Boxing Experience, 1890–1940," both in *American Jewish History* 74(3) (March 1985): 211–221 and 223–54, respectively.

28. Monroy, *Rebirth*, 59, 60.

29. Donovan López, *Practice! Practice! Practice!: The History of the King Ranch Cowboys Baseball Team* (Kingsville: privately published by Donovan López, 1998), 31.

30. Jorge Prieto, *The Quarterback Who Almost Wasn't* (Houston: Arte Publico, 1994), and Mario (Mike) de la Fuente with Boye De Mente, *I Like You, Gringo—But!* (Phoenix: Phoenix Books, 1972). Prieto played college football in Mexico. For more information on U.S. football in Mexico see http://www.onefa.org/ and http://tackleo.com/. There is even now an arena football league in Mexico. More information on that can be found at http://limfa.com/. Also see Lee Treviño and Sam Blair, *They Call Me Super Mex* (New York: Random House, 1982), and Mario Longoria, *Athletes Remembered: Latino Professional Football Players, 1929–1970* (Houston: Arte Publico, 1997).

31. Arnoldo de León, *They Called Them Greasers: Anglo Attitudes toward Mexicans in Texas, 1836–1900* (Austin: University of Texas Press, 1983).

32. For an excellent overview of the conditions in South Texas during the twentieth century, see David Montejano, *Anglos and Mexicans in the Making of Texas, 1836–1986* (Austin: University of Texas Press, 1987).

33. Charlie Williams, "South Texas Football," *Texas Coach* (April 1979): 37, 60.

THE FOOT RUNNERS CONQUER MEXICO AND TEXAS
Endurance Racing, Indigenismo, *and Nationalism*
MARK DYRESON

In the deep darkness of early morning—3:05 A.M.—on November 7, 1926, three runners left the central Mexican town of Pachuca in the state of Hidalgo.[1] They were bound for Mexico City, one hundred kilometers away. A large crowd of state and local officials, including the governor of Hidalgo and the mayor of Pachuca, saw the runners off. The three ran down a highway illumined by the "white rays" of car and motorcycle headlights. A cacophony of crackling firecrackers broke the usual silence. A caravan of cars, motorcycles, and riders on horseback followed the runners out of Pachuca toward Mexico City. "Bitter cold winds" buffeted the men, one of whom ran bare legged "for the purpose of curing a back-ache." As they left the noisy pop of firecrackers behind, their bell-laden belts jingled in the night, marking a steady rhythm on their quest to race to Mexico's capital city.[2]

As they sprinted through the "thick veil of morning," astonished local *tlachiqueros* (day laborers) who worked the maguey cactus fields for the *pulque* (a fermented maguey beverage) industry gathered behind the stands of cacti that lined the roads, silently watching the runners lope down the highway. As the men reached the twenty-third kilometer of their journey, dawn broke in the east, bathing their course in a beautiful "roseate hue." The morning's first light revealed that they were clad in white sweaters adorned by ribbons of red, green, and white—tricolored symbols of the Republic of Mexico. By now they had left behind the motorcyclists and horse riders, who, exhausted by the pace, had all dropped out of the race by sunrise.[3]

As the villages along the highway to Mexico City awakened, curious crowds began to line the road to welcome the runners and urge them toward their destination. New bursts of firecrackers and loud shouts of encouragement joined the crunch of the runners' *guaraches* (sandals) on the gravel road, the jingling rhythms of their belts of bells, and the sputtering engines of the cars that noisily accompanied the racers. Near the midway point one of the runners, who had been battling a variety of ailments for many kilometers, dropped out. The remaining two continued their journey. Church bells tolled, bringing more spectators to the road as the men strode through the increasingly numerous villages near the outskirts of Mexico City. More and more cars clogged the road, carrying enthusiastic throngs who had heard about the runners' progress.[4]

By midmorning the runners glided through the village of Tulpetlac, birthplace of Juan Diego, the legendary figure who Mexican culture claims was the first and only man to behold *la Virgen de Guadalupe* (the Virgin of Guadalupe). At that ancient site onlookers exclaimed to the racers, "'Salud, oh gladiadores de las selvas mexicanas, sangre virgen en la hispana cruza! Salud!'" (Long life to you, gladiators of the Mexican woodlands, virgin blood of Hispanic mixture! Long life to you!) Half an hour later the runners reached the border of the Federal District of Mexico. As they coursed through the streets toward the stadium, which marked the finish line of the hundred-kilometer run, thousands of people turned out to cheer their feat. Their escort swelled to two hundred cars.[5] After entering the National Stadium, they ran three laps around the track, finally stopping at 12:42 P.M. to deliver a message from the governor of Hidalgo to the governor of the Distrito Federal (Federal District). A huge crowd hailed their performance. They had covered the entire distance in 9 hours and 37 minutes, setting a world's record for the distance.[6] The head of los Juegos Deportivos Centroamericanos (Central American Sporting Games), the event that showcased their exhausting expedition, certified their time.[7] Physicians checked their physical status and announced that they were unbelievably fresh after their long-distance jaunt.[8]

THE ORIGINAL GREAT TARAHUMARAN RACE

The new hundred-kilometer world record holders, who stood clad in white jerseys bearing the emblem of Mexico before an adoring crowd and Mexico City's political establishment at the National Stadium, were members of the Tarahumaran tribe from the Sierra Madre of northwestern Mexico.[9] According to the Mexican press, they ran *pro México* (for Mexico). The Mexican media, athletic officials, and political leaders hailed their hundred-kilometer record as "sin precedente en los anales deportivos del mundo" (without precedent in the sporting annals of the world).[10]

Tomás Zafíro and Leoncio San Miguel became Mexican national heroes when they crossed the finish line of their hundred-kilometer test, even though they spoke mainly their aboriginal language and knew very little Spanish. For their valiant performances the Mexican government rewarded them with two crimson silk bandana handkerchiefs, sixty yards of white cotton, and two "modern plows." The governor of Chihuahua insisted on the rewards since he had promised the Tarahumaran runners some remuneration to make up for the loss of their corn crops while they ran for Mexican pride during the late autumn harvest season. The press marveled that "the two modern plows were the first they [the Tarahumaras] had ever seen, as they have used primitive forked sticks."[11]

The organizers of *la carrera tarahumara,* or the "great Tarahumaran race," as the event came to be known in the English-speaking world, hoped that the long-distance spectacle would become a regular part of the "Universal Olympic Games."[12] They dreamed that their Tarahumaran countrymen would win honor for Mexico by thrilling the world with a repeat performance at Amsterdam, where the Games of the Ninth Olympiad would be held in 1928. They publicized the Tarahumaras' "feats of prowess because by so doing they not only will make known the extraordinary faculties of the Chihuahua Mountain Indians but will also oblige the public to drive away the black lies that foreigners as a rule tell of Mexico, through ignorance and calumny, by denying all national attainments to this country."[13]

Mexican sports officials and politicians wanted to use the Tarahumaras to discount "black legends" and herald a new Mexico rising from the violent destructions of the long (1910–1921) and bloody revolution. Zafíro and San Miguel symbolized postrevolutionary Mexico's commitment to *indigenismo,* a concerted effort to incorporate the nation's many indigenous peoples into the cultural and political mainstream of Mexican life. The Tarahumaran runners served as icons of Mexico's efforts to build a new postrevolutionary national culture. They seemed to have stepped from a Diego Rivera mural depicting Mexico's long-oppressed native masses as the heroic paragons of a new, stable, just, and integrated society.[14]

The mixture of folk and modern elements in the plan to employ Tarahumaran runners to win international notoriety epitomized Mexico's efforts to craft a new national identity. In running a modern version of their traditional tribal races in the center of Mexican urban life, the Tarahumarans signified the hope that Mexico's provincial proletariat could be rapidly assimilated into the modern mainstream of Mexican society and still preserve their essential folkways. In sprinting down a modern highway built for internal combustion engines, the Tarahumaras were acknowledging the new buses and cars that were transforming daily life even in some of the most isolated Mexican hinterlands.[15]

The fact that highways had yet to penetrate the remote Tarahumaran homeland made the feat all the more romantic. The racers offered the world a Mexican vision that rivaled the romantic sketches of Rivera and his fellow *muralistas*. The conclusion of the pamphlet that Mexican authorities produced to promote la carrera tarahumara, a brief essay by Jacobo Dalevuelta titled "El Indio, Redentor de la Patria" (the Indian, redeemer of the nation), captured the symbolic power of the Tarahumaras' exploit. "I used to think that the Indians were 'human beasts of burden,'" admitted Dalevuelta, "but I have seen the light." He wondered, "[W]hat will those people say now when two Indians, such as the Tarahumaras, whom we thought were only able to get drunk on 'tixhuino' or poison themselves with 'peyote,' have astonished the civilized world with that puissant physical demonstration of theirs such as the 'Tarahumara Race' actually was?" Dalevuelta insisted that the Tarahumaras' conquest of the one hundred kilometers between Pachuca and Mexico City represented the true fruits of the Mexican Revolution.[16]

GLOBAL REACTION

In spite of Mexico's efforts to publicize la carrera tarahumara, much of the world's media paid little attention to the event.[17] *The Times* of London made no mention of the new world's record. Other newspapers that covered sports extensively, from Shanghai's *North China News* to Cairo's *Egyptian Gazette* to Berlin's *Rote Fahne* to São Paulo's *O Estado de São Paulo,* failed to pick up the story. In los Estados Unidos del Norte, however, the press was fascinated by the hundred-kilometer race. An Associated Press (AP) wire service story on the event ran in many U.S. newspapers. On the front page of the *Dallas Morning News* of November 8, 1926, readers learned that "what is believed to be one of the most remarkable running performances in sporting history, if, indeed, the feat has a parallel in modern athletics, was witnessed today" in central Mexico. The AP account declared that the obscure Mexican tribe "reputedly produces the world's supreme runners." Indeed, reported the wire service scribe, the Tarahumaran tribe "derives its very name from words signifying foot racing."[18] News of the Tarahumaran foot racers also appeared on the front page of the *Los Angeles Times.*[19]

Outside of the American Southwest, the Tarahumaras did not make front pages but could be found among lead articles in the international news or sports sections of major dailies in New York, Washington, and Chicago.[20] The nation's most popular mass-circulation weekly compendium of news, the *Literary Digest,* and its new rival, *Time,* also ran features on the race.[21] In the United States the foot runners quickly became one of the many staples of the popular fascination during the 1920s and 1930s with Mexican folk culture and antiquities, joining Aztec artifacts, Rivera murals, and handblown glassware as symbols of the mass appetite for a particular version of Mexico that sold well in the United States.[22]

Whether the Tarahumaran runners were a Mexican publicity stunt or real threats to alter the global long-distance running landscape, they became the object of considerable debate in the United States. Some sports authorities believed their achievements made Mexico an athletic world power. A *New York Times* article proclaimed the Tarahumaras' hundred-kilometer run had "no parallel in sporting history." In a typical U.S. assessment of the antediluvian lifeways of the Tarahumaras, the New York correspondent revealed that they were "cave dwellers" who lived in lands so remote that "civilization has scarcely touched them; they are the unsentient children of the earth." The reporter predicted that "these two aboriginals," Zafíro and San Miguel, would be threats for gold medals at the Olympic marathon in Amsterdam in 1928. "They will certainly show greater stamina and the world will hear of the Tarahumares [*sic*], a tribe so little known that the name cannot be found in the standard dictionaries," concluded the feature story in nation's most prestigious newspaper.[23]

ARRANGING A TARAHUMARAN RACE IN THE UNITED STATES

The Tarahumaras' conquest of the hundred-kilometer distance between Pachuca and Mexico City ignited a fierce debate in the United States. Was the feat of the little-known tribe from the Chihuahuan hinterlands a mere curiosity that could be readily surpassed by "civilized" athletes, or were the Tarahumaras natural wonders who could radically reshuffle the national rankings of Olympic powers by lending their prodigious strengths to the Mexican team? Among the U.S. experts who offered their opinions, skepticism prevailed. It became clear that a single carrera tarahumara would not convince U.S. sports fans of Mexican prowess. To convince north-of-the-border critics, the Tarahumaras were going to have to repeat their achievement in the United States.

Mexican authorities realized that arranging a demonstration of Tarahumaran foot-running skill in the United States would further their designs to add an ultramarathon to the Olympic program and aid enormously in the battle to change Mexico's international image. Enrique C. Aguirre, Mexico's minister of physical education and the head of the Mexican YMCA, admitted as much in a January 1927 letter to Count Henri de Baillet-Latour, president of the International Olympic Committee (IOC). "We have received a number of requests from that country [the United States] to have our Indians appear in competitions there and though we do not wish to make them a subject for exploitation we do want to have them run in the United States for the sake of the impression they will have, which will be most favorable for Mexico," confided Aguirre to Baillet-Latour.[24]

Sensing an opportunity to take advantage of the media attention lavished on the Tarahumaran foot runners and Mexico's desires to promote their prodigies, athletic entrepreneurs at the University of Texas negotiated a deal with Mexican promoters of the Tarahumaras. To draw international attention to the third annual Texas Relays track-and-field carnival, university officials booked the Tarahumaras as the feature attraction. Determined to make the Texas Relays the equal of the older and more established national track-and-field meets such as the Penn Relays, the Drake Relays, and the Millrose Games, University of Texas athletic director L. Theo Bellmont secured a major public relations coup by arranging the first U.S. appearance of the much-ballyhooed Tarahumaras.[25] "Never has a race of this character been staged in the United States," declared the *San Antonio Express*. The Austin daily promised fans that the centerpiece of the Texas Relays would be the "grueling endurance race which will be staged by the Tarahumari [sic] Indians from the wilds of Chihuahua."[26]

Texas would provide the Tarahumaras' Mexican agents with a new venue in which to prove the doubters wrong and to continue their campaign to add a 100-kilometer event to the Olympic program. Scheduled for late March of 1927, just four months after their Mexico City triumph, the Tarahumaran runners planned to run even farther in their U.S. debut. Press releases promised that a Tarahumaran "trio of space eaters" would race along the highway from San Antonio to Austin, an unprecedented eighty-two-mile journey.[27] Word filtered out of Chihuahua in early March that Tomás Zafíro had run a 100-kilometer tune-up for the Texas Relays more than 2 hours faster than his Mexico City performance, finishing in an astounding 7 hours, 35 minutes. In the same venue a Tarahumaran woman ran 45 kilometers in 4 hours, 56 minutes, prompting Mexican officials to announce that they planned to bring a contingent of female ultradistance runners to Texas in an effort to spur the IOC to add a women's marathon as well as a men's 100-kilometer race as new Olympic events.[28] The promoters promised that the Tarahumaras would not run for money and thus keep their amateur standings and Olympic hopes alive. The foot runners' agents announced that any funds the Tarahumaran racers generated in Texas would be turned over to Mexican officials in order to build schools in the Tarahumaran homeland.[29]

The Mexican media anticipated that the Texas race would continue the Tarahumaras' ascent to the top of the distance-running world. Newspaper stories about the foot runners frequently referred to the Tarahumaras as future Olympic and world champions.[30] One of Mexico City's leading dailies, *Excélsior,* predicted that the Tarahumaras would garner an *estruendoso triunfo* (resounding triumph) in Texas that would make Mexico famous in every corner of the world.[31] Another story in the same newspaper confirmed their status as heroes of the revolutionary republic. The Tarahumaras, the reporter insisted, would run through Texas in order to make the name of Mexico *repercuta* (echo) around the globe.[32]

The Tarahumaras made the journey from their border crossing to Austin by Pullman railcar. The press claimed that they had never before seen a train. The *New York Times* reported that the technologically naive Tarahumaras had injured their feet—on which they routinely ran more than one hundred miles a week—by resting them on heating pipes in the Pullman car.[33] Emerging from the Katy train at the Austin station in the early evening of March 22 without any apparent foot trauma, clad once again in "native dress," and carting a huge store of supplies wrapped in "gaudy blankets," the Tarahumaran team met a throng of newspaper reporters and curious onlookers.[34]

Intrepid reporters quickly discovered that the Mexican government had spent fifteen hundred dollars to send the Tarahumaran team to Austin. The group included three female and three male athletes, two interpreters—since the runners spoke neither English nor Spanish—and a Mexican athletic official from Ciudad Chihuahua who served as the team's leader and spokesperson.[35] Tomás Rodríguez, the Ciudad Chihuahua YMCA manager who led the team, announced that the foot runners were thrilled to be in Texas. "'I have never seen them quite so delighted,'" declared Rodríguez.[36]

"PRIMITIVES" IN A "CIVILIZED" LANDSCAPE

The Tarahumaran team spent the next three days sightseeing in Austin, where their presence generated enormous excitement. Hyperbolic newspaper accounts depicted them as primitive noble savages who were having their first encounters with the "blandishments of civilization," although at least one of the men, Tomás Zafíro, had been in Mexico City for the original great Tarahumaran race.[37] Reporters portrayed them as complete primitives who had no previous contact with the modern world. A typical story described them as "nomads from the occidental mountain ranges of northwestern Mexico, who lives [sic] in caves and seek their food by running from place to place."[38] Railroads, cars, hotel elevators, and other modern devices allegedly astounded the Tarahumaras. After University of Texas athletic director Theo Bellmont introduced them to the radio and the phonograph, the Tarahumaras supposedly spent the rest of their trip in the United States demanding to hear music from the electronic wonders.[39]

Mexico City newspapers crafted the same sorts of narratives about "primitives" awed by the modern world. Mexican reporters contended that the urban landscapes of Austin and San Antonio astonished the normally taciturn Tarahumaras. Skyscrapers, yellow taxicabs, and *los servidores negros* (the African American porters at the train station) amazed the provincial Chihuahuans.[40]

The U.S. press took their interpretations even further. As the San Antonio-to-Austin race neared, popular ethnographies of the Tarahumaran way of life filled both the Texas and the national media. These pseudoanthropologies generally began by explaining that the name of the tribe itself could be translated as "foot runners" or "runners with balls" or a similar approximation. The stories described in grand, if not always accurate, detail the Indians' native running traditions. The press reported that they regularly ran hundreds of miles through the canyons and mountains of Chihuahua. They covered these enormous distances either barefoot or shod only in crude sandals. In Tarahumaran culture, women as well as men raced, a custom that Texas Relays officials planned to replicate by having the Tarahumaran women run 26 miles from Kyle to Austin while the men raced 82 miles from San Antonio to Austin. They kicked wooden balls to amuse themselves along the trails, implored tribal sorcerers to curse their opponents, and consumed strange foods to fortify their constitutions. They were rumored to ingest copious quantities of herbal potions and large doses of hallucinogens such as peyote while they ran.[41]

To promote the spectacle, many of the prerace stories indulged in vulgar stereotypes of Native Americans. H. B. Du Bose, a sports columnist for the *Austin Statesman,* alerted readers that the "redskins" would run from their "Alamo wigwam" to Austin. They "talk neither Espanol [sic], nor ENGLES [sic]," Du Bose smirked, and they were clearly dismayed when they realized that the car that would accompany them on their journey "would carry no firewater." Du Bose described the female Tarahumaran runners as "pretty—as an Indian sees beauty." He also noted that they were too young to "be properly called squaws."[42]

Nationally syndicated *New York Times* sports columnist John Kieran was a committed Tarahumaran skeptic. Kieran jested that "there were even some suspicious white men who suggested that the Indians ran short miles and timed themselves by the phases of the moon" in their Mexican runs. He observed that the U.S. venue for this new Tarahumaran feat would prevent the Mexicans from manufacturing any more legends about primeval prodigies. "This time they will run a distance measured in English miles and they will be timed by a split second watch, though, for that matter, in an eighty-two mile race, an alarm clock would do just as well," Kieran jabbed. Even if the Tarahumaras were to manage a respectable time on their San Antonio-to-Austin excursion, Kieran still insisted that "civilized" whites could easily best the Indians if they desired. "If there's any money in going after the record for eighty-two miles which the Indian braves expect to set . . . , there will be some white man hot on the trail before many moons," he asserted. Kieran was even more skeptical of the tales of female running prowess among the Tarahumaras. "There are plenty of conservative athletic observers who are willing to bet a grand piano to a flat note that the Tarahumaran squaws will be as far from the record as Portland, Me., is from Portland, Ore.," the *New York Times* expert maintained.[43]

The Tarahumaran runners found defenders in Austin among some of their fellow Mexicans who had ventured north to compete at the Texas Relays. The University of Mexico "Aztecs," under the leadership of Enrique Aguirre, a major proponent of adding a hundred-kilometer carrera tarahumara to the Olympic program, sent a twelve-person squad to the Austin track meet. Quarter-miler J. Nelson Furbeck, the son of German immigrants to Mexico City and a medical student at the University of Mexico, wrote a special column for the *Austin Statesman* defending Tarahumaran prowess and honor. Furbeck proclaimed that the Tarahumaras were the world's most athletic people, excelling not only in long-distance running but also in aboriginal lacrosse and in another stick-and-ball game that resembled golf. Furbeck argued that Tex Rickard, the sports promoter who ran Madison Square Garden, staged heavyweight champion Jack Dempsey's fights, and dabbled in professional football and a variety of other sporting industries during the 1920s, should begin to recruit in Tarahumaran country. "Tex Rickard, in his desire to be 'Emperor of All-American Sport,' from the cauliflower industry to marble shooting, would do well to make himself godfather of a village of Tarahumara," Furbeck contended. He defended their foot-racing tradition as one of the most remarkable demonstrations of physical prowess in human history.[44]

In Mexico, the press took up Furbeck's defense of the Tarahumaran athletes. *El Universal,* one of Mexico City's leading dailies, ran a series of stories proclaiming that the Tarahumaran foot runners were a sure bet to break another world's record in their 138-kilometer jaunt from San Antonio to Austin. The newspaper featured them in a series of photographs on the front page of the sports section and included a detailed map of Texas with the race route clearly marked. Even though the Tarahumaras were not competing directly against U.S. athletes, Mexican reporters depicted the Texas Relays as an event pitting the foot runners against U.S. track stars. Already famous for their endurance feats in los Estados Unidos del México, the Tarahumaras—Mexican journalists predicted—would win the hearts of fans in los Estados Unidos del Norte. The special correspondents for *El Universal* and *Excélsior* who accompanied the Mexican team to the Texas Relays reported that the Tarahumaras were the talk of Texas. Claims that they could outrun European and North American champions had generated enormous excitement about the impending ultramarathon.[45]

As the Friday, March 25, opening day of the Texas Relays approached, anticipation about the Tarahumaras' runs and the rest of the events grew. In addition to the University of Mexico, seventy-five other intercollegiate teams from the United States descended on Austin. Among them were delegations from Michigan, Michigan State, Kansas, Kansas State, Notre Dame, Drake, Illinois, Minnesota, Missouri, Oklahoma, and other major intercollegiate track powers. A host of Texas colleges, large and small, were also entered. More than a score of Texas high schools planned to run in the interscholastic division. The Tarahumaras were not the only Native American contingent entered in the relays. Haskell Indian School of Kansas entered "12 stalwart braves," led by "the Big Chief," all-American six-mile champion Philip Osif, a member of Arizona's Pima tribe.[46]

The press and University of Texas promoters pitched the Tarahumaran races as the central feature of the Texas Relays. An *Austin Statesman* correspondent blustered that "it is truly a landmark in athletic history in the world, as it is the first race of its kind ever to be staged in this nation."[47] On Thursday, March 24, the day before the men's race was scheduled to start, the Tarahumaras traveled the route in reverse, from Austin to San Antonio, in a motorcade. The cars were provided by the official automotive sponsor of the Texas Relays, Austin's Barker Motor Company. Reporter Bill Kleinman wryly observed that the Tarahumaran party headed to San Antonio in a Pontiac, "which was named for a famous Indian chief."[48]

Press observers traveling with the Tarahumaras noted that they looked dubiously at the great stretches of gravel-covered asphalt they would have to negotiate on the run back to Austin from San Antonio. The tough route would challenge their quest to break a forty-five-year-old record for an eighty-two-mile run of 13 hours, 31 minutes, and 5 seconds set by a New York City runner in 1882.[49] On their automobile journey to San Antonio they stopped among the Austin Road shops that sold Mexican curios to tourists. A shopkeeper gave black-and-white toy cows to the enthralled Tarahumaras. A *San Antonio Express* correspondent noted that "a Mexican water peddler, who watched the transaction, added to the good-will by emptying his pockets of the pennies which he had collected on his morning rounds, and presented them to the Indians."[50]

Arriving in San Antonio in the afternoon, the Tarahumaras learned that they would start from city hall rather than the Alamo. Following tribal traditions, they prepared for the run by drinking herbal tea, anointing their bodies with oil, and uttering "certain lucky phrases." They then retired to a private room to pray.[51] In a concession to modernity they prepared to run in "modern track suit[s]" rather than native "loin cloth[s]." They also planned to refrain from the Tarahumaran custom of kicking a wooden ball as they ran. San Antonio's mayor, John W. Tobin, gave them a message to carry to Gov. Dan Moody in Austin. "Since time immemorial runners have been recognized as messengers in both times of war and peace, and men with the endurance to bear such acts are indeed commendable in any race or tribe," read Tobin's memorandum. The Tarahumaras went to bed early that night, hoping to bring fresh commendations to their tribe and their nation on their impending odyssey.[52]

THE GREAT TEXAS TARAHUMARAN RACE

Repeating their tactics from the Pachuca-to-Mexico City race, the Tarahumaran men left city hall in San Antonio in the inky early morning darkness at 3:19 A.M. on Friday, March 25, 1927, bound for the Lone Star State's capital city of Austin. The "flashlight" of snapping photographers' bulbs lit their path as they headed from the center of San Antonio, down Commerce Street, to Houston, then to Broadway, turned onto Grayson, and then wound their way onto the Austin Road for the trip north. The silver bells on their belts jangled as they ran.[53]

With escorts trailing, the Tarahumaras ran in their bare feet along the asphalt highway through the cool spring morning. They donned sandals only for the "cruelest stretches" of the route, where thick gravel lay on top of the hard road surface. Breaking dawn revealed that the runners were clad in tracksuits emblazoned with the tricolored shield of Mexico.[54] As the daylight spread, an International Newsreel camera crew in the automobile escort began to film them.[55]

As the sun rose higher in the sky, crowds of curious Texans gathered in hamlets and towns along the route. Word of the racers' progress spread quickly through the Texas countryside. "Their reddish brown bodies glistened in the sun as they pattered along through curious throngs, especially in the towns," remarked the *San Antonio Express* correspondent covering the race.[56] The large congregations of fans surprised the runners. *Austin Statesman* observer H. B. Du Bose, misidentifying their homeland, noted that "in all their Andian [sic] hills never did they see such carrying on."[57] As the day grew warmer, the Tarahumaras "donned broad sombreros." They took water from dippers and ate "native food" while they ran.[58] A "stiff gale" hampered their northward journey, but the runners plowed through it.[59] Near San Marcos, the press reported that the Tarahumaras were running "with the rhythm and stamina of thoroughbred race horses."[60]

A little after noon, in their ninth hour of running, the racers cantered through Kyle, Texas, only twenty-seven miles from their finish line. At that juncture two of the runners, Tomás Zafíro and José Torres, were "breathing easily" and appeared in fine shape. The third runner, Augustín Salido, was suffering from cramps and considering quitting the ultramarathon. A few miles down the road the struggling Salido dropped out and was picked up by one of the trailing cars after covering a "mere" sixty-two miles (equaling the one hundred kilometers of the Pachuca-to-Mexico City race).[61]

At about the same time that Salido gave up his quest near Kyle, the three Tarahumaran women runners set off on their marathon run. To enhance press coverage, the starting location for their race had been moved from the original spot in Kyle to the offices of the *Austin Statesman*.[62] Several hundred curious onlookers saw them off. Newsreel crews filmed the "women in action." A motorcade accompanied sisters Lola Cuzarare and Juanita Cuzarare and their fellow tribeswoman, Juanita Paciencia, on their undertaking.[63] The women started in sandals but soon discarded them, as the men had, and ran in bare feet. Measurement problems in laying out the course meant that the women had to navigate 28⅝ miles rather than the standard 26 miles and 385 yards of a marathon. Just 2 miles from the finish, at the 26-mile mark, fifteen-year-old Juanita Paciencia dropped out. With the Memorial Stadium finish line in sight, sixteen-year-old Juanita Cuzarare quit running. Both complained that the paved streets they ran over made their feet too hot to continue. Only fourteen-year-old Lola Cuzarare finished the race, crossing the worsted in 4 hours, 49 minutes. A cheering crowd of more than ten thousand spectators gave her a standing ovation.[64]

As Lola Cuzarare finished, the two remaining Tarahumaran men were struggling through the outskirts of Austin. When they approached the capital city, the throngs of spectators arriving in cars to see them grew so great that the Tarahumaras had to run "through a barrage of carbon monoxide." The crowds swelled to the point where they even impeded the runners' progress. Horse-mounted police struggled to keep the course open. The curious masses slowed the Tarahumaras' pace to 4 miles per hour. They had averaged 7 miles per hour in the less-congested stretches over the first sixty-nine miles of the course.[65]

Finally reaching the heart of Austin about 5:00 P.M., they ran up Congress Avenue through fluttering decorative bunting of Mexican red, white, and green and American red, white, and blue. Crowds lined the streets along their path to Memorial Stadium. Anticipating their arrival, the university and the adjacent Guadalupe Avenue business district had closed at noon. Austin's public schools and most of the state government offices had also closed for the afternoon so that city dwellers could marvel at the foot runners. Mayor Tobin and other Texas luminaries waited at the finish line.[66]

The racers dashed through the city and arrived at Memorial Stadium. There the crowd rose to give them a thundering ovation. Large numbers of excited fans left their seats and rushed the finish line, delaying other events that had been going on as the Tarahumaras arrived. The two runners presented their message from the mayor of San Antonio to the governor of Texas. At the finish line, race organizers announced that the Tarahumaras had ended up running farther than originally projected: 89.5 miles instead of 82 miles. They had finished their remarkable feat in 14 hours, 46 minutes, despite walking for about an hour during the journey in the hopes that their cramping teammate Salido would be able to continue.[67]

After clearing the rowdy crowds that had rushed from their seats as the Tarahumaran men finished, the Texas Relays wound to a close. Runners set thirteen records in the third annual occurrence of the track meet. The University of Texas Longhorns won several upsets against some of the nation's best intercollegiate athletes. In addition, Haskell Indian School also turned in an excellent performance.[68] Austin High School dominated the interscholastic division. But all of the press accounts concurred that the Tarahumaras' races had been the highlight of the games—in spite of confusion over whether they had achieved a new world's record on their San Antonio-to-Austin junket.[69] "When it comes to distance running the Tarahumaran Indians from the mountains of Mexico hold the world at bay," marveled the *Austin Statesman*.[70]

INTERPRETING THE TARAHUMARAS' FEATS IN TEXAS

Once again, Tomás Zafíro had performed a startling feat of endurance. He finished in tandem with José Torres, running twenty-seven miles farther than he had in his Mexican debut.[71] In addition, the Tarahumaran women added a new wrinkle to the script for Tarahumaran races originally written on the highway from Pachuca to Mexico City. Once again, the Tarahumaras ran for Mexico as part of the Mexican plan to persuade the International Olympic Committee to place an ultradistance race on the program of the "universal" games.

Once more, Mexico celebrated their accomplishment. Mexico City's *El Universal* lauded the men's conquest of the highway from San Antonio to Austin and the women's 28-mile run with banner headlines on the first page of the sports section. "Los tarahumaras realizaron la gran hazaña" (The Tarahumaras accomplish their great feat), blared the typescript while pictures of the aboriginal champions dominated the page. The correspondent for *El Universal* reporting from Texas made it clear that Zafíro and Torres had failed in their quest to set a new world's record, falling 8 minutes and 55 seconds short of the existing 89-mile mark. However, the sportswriter insisted that the Tarahumaras would easily have beaten the record had they not been hampered by huge numbers of fans in cars and on foot who dramatically slowed their pace for the last 16 miles—from the Hill Country hamlet of Buda all the way to Memorial Stadium. In spite of their failure to break the world's record, "los Tarahumaras asombró del mundo deportivo" (the Tarahumaras astonished the sports world), declared the Mexican reporter. The "monumental carrera tarahumara" had passed into history, and the foot runners had dazzled the U.S. audience with their "estupenda proeza" (stupendous feat). Exhibiting the characteristic calm of "la raza bronce" (the bronze race), proclaimed *El Universal,* the Tarahumaran champions stood calmly in the center of Memorial Stadium while the thunderous cheers of thousands of Americans washed over them.[72]

Excélsior matched *El Universal*'s enthusiasm for the foot runners' Texas triumphs. Its headline proclaimed, "Singular triunfo de los Tarahumaras" (singular triumph of the Tarahumaras). J. Fernando Rojas, the *Excélsior*'s reporter at the race, marveled that the Tarahumaras ran to glory through a clamor of hosannas. In a nationalistic twist, Rojas wryly observed that the *incansable* (tireless) foot runners from the arid prairies of Chihuahua won their race in a land that had once been a part of the Republic of Mexico. They had run mile after mile, noted Rojas, past elegantly dressed white women and cheering white men. At the finish line they were lauded like gladiators *en los tiempos del imperio de los Césares* (in the times of the empire of the Caesars), Rojas wrote.

He lauded Zafíro and Torres for the quiet humility with which they received the adulation of the stadium masses.[73]

Other stories in *Excélsior* added interpretive layers of stoic resistance to pain, stunned *norteamericanos* (North Americans), visits from ancient relatives, and passionate kisses from American women to the Mexican versions of the Tarahumaras' triumph in Texas. One report revealed that the asphalt roads had cut Zafíro's and Torres's feet to ribbons. Other than sore-covered soles, the reporter noted, they finished in perfect condition. The story described Texans turning out in droves in every village and town along the route to greet the runners with unconcealed admiration. Caravans of fans in cars followed the runners, while burly norteamericanos on foot tried to keep pace with the Tarahumaras but quickly gave up their chase after a few hundred yards, exhausted by the amazing gait of the foot runners. In the tiny village of Buda, near the outskirts of Austin, an *anciano mexicano* (ancient Mexican) who had descended from Tarahumaran stock and had lived in Texas for many years brought a basket of fresh oranges to his kinsmen. The foot runners devoured the fruit, momentarily quenching their intense thirst.[74]

After their runs from Pachuca to Mexico City and from San Antonio to Austin, the foot runners reigned in Mexicans' imaginations as the heroes of a new nation rising from the ashes of more than a decade of civil war. In spite of the fact that the Tarahumaras had failed to better the world record for the distance, fans from Mexico City to Michoacán celebrated their triumphs.[75] Zafíro became an iconic figure in a Mexican comic strip. In the first panel of the cartoon, some Mexican yokels fawn over the sandal-shod Zafíro, who appears in Mexico City clad in his Mexican national jersey. "Look," they cry, "it's the Tarahumara Zafíro, who ran here from Pachuca without even breathing hard." As the comic unfolds, Zafíro stoically consents to run from Mexico City to Pachuca (reversing his actual route) in a high-stakes competition against a braggart local *mosca* (pain in the neck). The scoundrel cheats by riding a freight train for most of the race.[76] On the sports pages, Mexican journalists predicted that Zafíro or another Tarahumara would, in the very near future, break the Olympic record in the marathon. Speculation about their prospects for winning gold medals for Mexico in the upcoming 1928 Olympic Games in Amsterdam ran rampant.[77]

The monumental carrera tarahumara in Texas also revealed that the foot racers were being used for a variety of other purposes in addition to inspiring Mexican patriotism. For example, athletic marketers in the United States had designs for the Tarahumaran stars that differed from those held by the Mexican promoters. "Everybody knows now the story of the Tarahumara Indians and their wonderful feat of endurance," observed the editors of the *Austin Statesman*. "Not only have Austin people read of these Indians, but people who read newspapers, throughout the nation and all over Mexico and in Europe, also have heard of the Tara boys *and girls,*" the Texas daily noted. "And incidentally, they have heard of Austin through these runners," the *Austin Sunday American-Statesman* shrewdly concluded, in an effort to steal the publicity generated by the aborigines away from the campaign to promote Mexican nationalism and transform it into a promotion of this growing city in the Sunbelt.[78]

In the Texas press and the national media, tales of Tarahumaran endurance were accompanied by hyperboles. The nationally syndicated AP story on the race ran a lead that claimed the Tarahumaras had accomplished "a feat that would have killed an ordinary horse."[79] The *Austin Statesman* heralded their performance as "the greatest record ever, and [it] will likely stand until these Tarahumarans break it themselves." Exhibiting the endurance of "Arabian horses," the Tarahumaras had overcome heat, wind, and car exhaust to conquer the greatest distance ever attempted in a modern race, proclaimed the Austin daily. "Besides that, the bronze heroes of the wilds of Mexico shot the annual Texas Relays into the spotlight of the athletic world, which was anxiously waiting for results of their grueling long-distance run," cheered the hometown newspaper.[80] The editors also bestowed a special "laurel wreath for the living" on University of Texas athletic director Theo Bellmont for booking the Tarahumaras at the Texas Relays. "Bellmont has just placed Austin on the map," applauded the *Austin Sunday American-Statesman*.[81]

In the United States, interpretations of the Tarahumaras' prowess focused on the contrast between modernity and simplicity that the foot runners supposedly revealed. Commentators alternately lauded the Tarahumaras for their pristine lifestyle and satirized them for their uncivilized customs. They were both applauded for their rejection of modern excesses and lampooned for their embrace of primitiveness. Two stories in the *Austin Sunday American-Statesman* highlight this dialectic. Cheering the triumph of the Tarahumaras, one story heralded the tribe as the world's endurance champions. The extreme primitivism of Tarahumaran life, which protected them from all modern vices, accounted for their remarkable abilities. "No other man living under the environment of modern civilization possesses such qualities as the red men displayed to thousands who attended the third annual Texas Relay games," concluded the account.[82] In another report in the same newspaper, correspondent Kathleen Houston suggested that Augustín Salido, who had dropped out of the men's race after sixty-two miles, would no doubt blame his misfortune on the black cat that the driver of a support car had shown him or the "majestic birds"—the airplanes—that had scared him when they buzzed overhead.[83]

The day following the race, the Tarahumaras departed from Austin for their Chihuahuan home. Reports indicated that they might stop in El Paso for a week on the way back to run "some exhibition stunts."[84] In a story with a title including the phrase "Runners Heroes in Home Caves," team manager Tomás Rodríguez remarked that the Tarahumaran foot racers would be heralded as the greatest champions in the history of their tribe. "'A man is not great in his own country until he has gone away and made a name for himself, then he will be the lion of the hour,'" maintained Rodríguez. "'It is the same in the Sierras,'" confirmed the Ciudad Chihuahua YMCA leader.[85]

Austin Statesman sports columnist H. B. Du Bose reported that Rodríguez had been besieged by offers to capitalize on the Tarahumaras' prowess. Hoping that Rodríguez would sign the Tarahumaras to star in "romantic Indian stories," movie companies dangled large contracts in front of him. Vaudeville agents wanted to take the Tarahumaras on a national tour in which they would be exhibited in artificial huts placed in front of dramatic scenery that would supposedly replicate their lifestyle in the Sierra Madre. Sports agents sought the Tarahumaras for foot races to repeat their San Antonio-to-Austin exploits. Du Bose asserted that the offers were serious bids to cash in on the now world-famous Tarahumaras. "And, what's more, they were, in true American style, talking in term [sic] of money—the language that sounds best the world over—the golden eagle was the basis on which they hoped to win their argument," Du Bose revealed.[86]

The Austin writer insisted that Rodríguez had rejected all of the offers, however. "We are not out to capitalize in dollars and cents on the Tarahumaras' running ability," Rodríguez contended. "But it is the wish of many of us Mexicans to build up a better relationship between our country and yours," he professed. The Chihuahuan insisted that improved international relations between Mexico and the United States could come through sport. He asserted that the Tarahumaras had taught the U.S. public that "a great race of men lives in those mountains across the Rio Grande." Rodríguez hoped that the Tarahumaras had convinced the U.S. public and press that Mexicans lived clean and wholesome lives. He promised to bring the foot runners back to continue the international accord that had been created in Texas. "People who play together understand one another," he innocently concluded.[87]

Indeed, the Tarahumaras would be coming back in the very near future. As they departed from Texas, word spread in the media that University of Kansas athletic director Forrest "Phog" Allen had secured the Tarahumaras' services for the Kansas Relays, scheduled to be held a month later, at the end of April.[88] Austin journalist H. B. Du Bose confirmed that Rodríguez had agreed to have the "red men do their act" in another venue in the United States. Du Bose took pleasure in the news that the Tarahumaras would run only 45–50 miles from Kansas City to Lawrence in their second U.S. race, a trifling distance compared to their Texas excursion.[89] In Kansas, the Tarahumaras would face Apache and Navajo runners from the Southwest, tribes acclaimed for endurance running. Promoters and the press framed this new race as a showdown between Native Americans from both Mexico and the United States to see which nation was home to the world's hardiest aboriginals.[90]

In Mexico, the Tarahumaras were the heroes of revolutionary society and the living embodiments of new policies toward native peoples. Their feats were heralded as proof that a new Mexico was emerging and that the world would have to reckon with its indigenous champions. Over the next few years, athletic officials would send Tarahumaran foot racers to the Olympic Games and other international competitions in an effort to win gold and glory for Mexico. In April of 1927 a group of Tarahumaran men ran down the highway from Kansas City to the University of Kansas in Lawrence to promote the Kansas Relays. José Torres, who had finished alongside Tomás Zafíro in Austin a month earlier, won the Kansas ultradistance race. He set a blistering pace on the way to breaking the world's record for fifty-one miles. At the same time a squad of Tarahumaran women ran thirty miles from Topeka to Lawrence. Once again, only Lola (now referred to in the press as Lolita) Cuzarare finished the race, setting what was apparently a new world's record for that distance, given the lack of known records for women's endurance racing in the 1920s.[91]

In spite of the foot runners' feats in Texas and Kansas, the International Olympic Committee did not acquiesce to Mexico's requests to add a 100-kilometer race to the Olympic program. Nor did the IOC entertain Mexico's demands for a women's marathon. Indeed, following the 1928 Olympic

Games, the IOC, in reaction to a controversial women's 800-meter race at the first-ever Olympic track and field competitions for women, agreed to limit female athletes to distances of no greater than 100 meters.[92] Mexico did send Tarahumaran men to the marathon starting line at the 1928 games in Amsterdam, however. José Torres, a veteran of the Texas and Kansas supermarathons, finished a disappointing twenty-first among the seventy-five entrants.[93]

At the end of the 1920s, the Tarahumaran runners disappeared from "modern" competitions for decades. In the 1960s and 1970s feature stories in *National Geographic, Natural History,* and *Sports Illustrated* reanimated their legendary status as endurance athletes.[94] In the last decade of the twentieth century, the Tarahumaras reappeared in international races, winning several ultramarathons along rugged trails in the mountains of the western United States. Their victories on the new extreme racing circuit stirred a renewed interest in their running, which once again mixed liberal doses of admiration and romantic primitivism with large jiggers of intense nationalism and controversy.[95]

During the 1920s the foot racers starred in Mexico's plan to prove—through victories in international sporting arenas—that the postrevolutionary republic ranked with the world's leading modern nations.[96] Despite, or perhaps because of, their uneven performances in modern competitions, the foot runners continued to serve as icons of Mexican indigenismo. Mexican poet Alfonso Reyes celebrated their contributions to national identity in a famous 1935 verse that revels in their superhuman ability:

> The finest Marathon runners in the world,
> nourished on the bitter flesh of deer,
> they will be the first with the triumphant news
> the day we leap the wall
> of the five senses.[97]

In the United States the athletes served different purposes. In the 1920s the Tarahumaras became characters in the burgeoning sports entertainment industry. Like Native American football teams from Carlisle and Haskell Indian schools during the same period, the Tarahumaras were used to generate excitement in sporting events and to add an exotic flavor to the U.S. diet of leisure-time consumables.[98] The native runners evoked an old American history in a safely nostalgic fashion. Audiences could pretend they were immersed in the Wild West while remaining in the comfort of modern times. The contrast of modern and primitive could be used to thrill and amuse as well as to confirm the ultimate superiority of the civilized over the savage.

The Tarahumaras also signified the potential for amazing prowess that modern folk hoped was still alive somewhere in the human species. During the 1920s the foot racers played a crucial role in the growing global fascination with endurance records of all sorts, from airplane and automobile conquests of oceans and continents to the dance marathon craze. In a decade in which machines were obliterating traditional notions of time and distance, the appeal of the Tarahumaras involved modern anxieties and expectations. Would the car and the airplane render the human body obsolete? Would technology make human abilities insignificant? Running down roads designed for motor vehicles, the Tarahumaras sparked a series of new tests of the limits of the human machine.

The connection between modern roads and ancient running traditions was significant, at least to the modern minds that interpreted the ultramarathons. Inspired by the Tarahumaras, a year after the San Antonio-to-Austin run, promoters staged an amazing race along the new transcontinental highway from Los Angeles through the vast landscapes of the American West to the distant metropolis of New York City. Indeed, early reports claimed that the Tarahumaras would headline the transcontinental marathon, an opportunity they ultimately declined.[99] More ultramarathons would follow, with foot power challenging asphalt on the new highways of North America. Inspired once again by the legendary Tarahumaras, officials of the Pan American Exposition of 1937 planned a race from Mexico City to Dallas along the new pavement of the Pan American highway.[100] A half century later, legends about the Tarahumaras served as one source of inspiration for the emergence of ultradistance races through the landscapes of the American Southwest. Indeed, the Tarahumaras returned to modern racing at those events.

As historian Stephen Hardy has counseled, close attention to the commodification of sporting traditions is one of the crucial tasks in making sense of the past.[101] In transferring the Tarahumaras' foot-racing ability from the traditional folkways of the Sierra Madre Occidental to the national sporting cultures of the United States and Mexico, entrepreneurs transformed ancient practices into modern commodities that served political and commercial purposes. What did the Tarahumaran foot racers think of their sudden introduction to the marketplace, modern racing, and modern society? "The key to endurance, as all distance runners know, is not just a matter of sweat glands," writes Bernd Heinrich in *Racing the Antelope,* one of the best modern meditations on the science and philosophy of human running. "It's vision," Heinrich argues. "To endure is to have a clear goal and the ability to extrapolate to it with the mind—the ability to keep in mind what is not before the eye," he maintains. "Vision allows us to reach into the future, whether it's to kill an antelope or to achieve a record time in a race," concludes the evolutionary biologist whom *Ultrarunning* magazine selected as runner of the year in 1981, after Heinrich set a new world record for one hundred kilometers.[102]

What idea did the original hundred-kilometer foot racers, the Tarahumaras, have of their famous runs? Of their vision, no one can be certain since they appear in the historical records of the 1920s—and later decades—as ciphers for primitivism, the ethnographic constructions of modern interpreters who fashioned them into mirrors for what modern peoples were not. They spoke only in the stereotyped dialects of primitives, such as in *Time* magazine's allegedly authentic account of the Tarahumaras' brief speech after their original Pachuca-to-Mexico City run. "'We are, strong,' they replied, 'because we live in the open air. . . . Reverence lends wings to the legs. Only thus can a man be happy.'"[103] Visions in Mexico and the United States of what ends the Tarahumaras could serve by running were clear. The Tarahumaras' own visions remained obscure.

NOTES

1. I would like to thank the William P. Clements Center for Southwest Studies at Southern Methodist University for providing fellowship support and access to rare sources that were invaluable in this study. Thanks also go to César Torres, professor at SUNY–Brockport, for checking my translations of sources.

2. Miguel Gil, "El desarrollo e la sensación al carrera tarahumara" [the development of the sensational Tarahumaran race], in *Pro México: la carrera tarahumara* (Mexico, D.F., 1927), 10–15, 36–41, pamphlet found in Special Collections, DeGolyer Library, Southern Methodist University, Dallas, Texas. As a traveling correspondent for *El Universal* (Mexico City), Gil covered the race for the newspaper. *Pro México* is a forty-eight-page pamphlet produced to tout la carrera tarahumara. It was published in Spanish with English translations at the end. Where cited, titles are given in the original Spanish with English translations, as the publishers gave them, in brackets. Page numbers have been cited in both the Spanish and the

English versions. The Spanish version proved the most useful since the original English translation contains some very interesting usage errors.

3. Ibid.
4. Ibid.
5. Ibid. Quotation from pages 14 and 40.
6. Pablo Buendía Aguirre, "Como organizamos la carrera de cien kilómetros" [how we organized the hundred-kilometer race], in *Pro México*, 5–7, 28–31.
7. On the Juegos Deportivos Centroamericanos, see Richard V. McGehee, "The Origins of Olympism in Mexico: The Central American Games of 1926," *International Journal of the History of Sport* 10 (1993): 313–32. McGehee chronicles Mexican plans during the 1920s to use sports to promote Mexico as Latin America's leading nation. On the Tarahumaran runners and the promotion of Mexican nationalism, see Richard V. McGehee, "*Carreras, patrias, y caudillos:* Sport/Spectacle in Mexico and Guatemala, 1926–1943," *Southeastern Latin Americanist* 41 (1998): 19–32.
8. Francisco R. Serrano, "Certificado dando fe del suceso deportivo, expedido por el gobernador del Distrito Federal" [certification of the sporting success, issued by the governor of the Federal District] in *Pro México*, 35, 47–48.
9. Since the 1960s, anthropologists have referred to the tribe as the Rarámuri. "In the historical literature these Indians are invariably referred to as Tarahumaras, an obvious corruption of Rarámuri, the term used by the Indians in referring to themselves," wrote ethnographer Campbell W. Pennington in 1963. "Rarámuri is undoubtedly derived from rárá [foot], júma [to run] and ri [a particle]," concluded Pennington's etymology. Campbell W. Pennington, *The Tarahumar of México: Their Environment and Material Culture* (Salt Lake City: University of Utah Press, 1963), 1. Other ethnographers concur, including the best work, William L. Merrill's *Rarámuri Souls: Knowledge and Social Process in Northern Mexico* (Washington, D.C.: Smithsonian Institution, 1988). However, since the Rarámuris were invariably labeled Tarahumaras in the time period that this chapter covers, I refer to them as Tarahumaras to avoid confusion and provide consistency. Recent works on the tribe still use the term "Tarahumara," as well as "Rarámuri." See Bernard L. Fontana, with photographs by John P. Schaefer, *Tarahumara: Where Night Is the Day of the Moon*, 2d ed. (Tucson: University of Arizona Press, 1997); John G. Kennedy, *Tarahumara of the Sierra Madre: Survivors on the Canyon's Edge*, 2d ed. (Pacific Grove, Calif.: Asilomar Press, 1996).
10. That claim appears on the cover of *Pro México*.
11. "Mexican Indians Get Plows for Record 100-Kilometer Run," *New York Times*, Nov. 9, 1926, 29.
12. Allen Guttmann has argued persuasively that the modern Olympic move-

ment has historically been more "Western" than "universal." Allen Guttmann, *Games and Empires: Modern Sports and Cultural Imperialism* (New York: Columbia University Press, 1994), 120–38.

13. *Pro México*, 3.

14. Jean Charlot, *The Mexican Mural Renaissance, 1920–1925* (New Haven, Conn.: Yale University Press, 1967); Leonard Folgarait, *Mural Painting and Social Revolution in Mexico, 1920–1940: Art of the New Order* (New York: Cambridge University Press, 1998); Patrick Marnham, *Dreaming with His Eyes Open: A Life of Diego Rivera* (Berkeley: University of California Press, 2000); Diego Rivera with Gladys March, *My Art, My Life: An Autobiography* (New York: Dover, 1991).

15. The Tarahumaran homelands in Chihuahua were exempt from the postrevolutionary road-building boom. The railroad did not reach the interior of the formidable Barranca del Cobre of the Sierra Madre until 1961. Highways reached the Tarahumaras only in the last two decades of the twentieth century. Michael Jenkinson, "The Glory of the Long-distance Runner," *Natural History* 81 (1972): 54–65; Bernard L. Fontana, with photographs by John P. Schaefer, *Tarahumara: Where Night Is the Day of the Moon* (Flagstaff, Ariz.: Northland Press, 1979); W. Dirk Raat and George R. Janecek, *Mexico's Sierra Tarahumara: A Photohistory of the People of the Edge* (Norman: University of Oklahoma Press, 1996).

16. Jacobo Dalevuelta, "El Indio, Redentor de la Patria" (the Indian, redeemer of the nation), in *Pro México,* 24.

17. Noted Latin American sport historian Joseph Arbena argues that the race was designed to help in "reestablishing Mexican credibility in the international community." The failure to garner more international coverage no doubt disappointed Mexican officials. Joseph Arbena, "Sport, Development, and Mexican Nationalism, 1920–1970," *Journal of Sport History* 18 (1991): 352–54, 352 (quotation).

18. "Two Tarahumare Indians Run 62½ Miles in 9 Hours and 37 Minutes on Mexican Road," *Dallas Morning News,* Nov. 8, 1926, 1–2.

19. "Indian Runners Set World's Record," *Los Angeles Times,* Nov. 8, 1926, sec. 1, 1.

20. "Two Mexican Indians Run 62½ Miles in 9 Hours, 37 Minutes," *New York Times,* Nov. 8, 1926, 16; "Indians Run 62 Miles in 9 Hours, 37 Minutes," *Washington Post,* Nov. 8, 1926, 2; "Indians Run 62½ Miles in 9½ Hours," *Chicago Tribune,* Nov. 8, 1926, 23.

21. "The Nurmis of Mexico," *Literary Digest,* Jan. 1, 1927, 41; "Those Mexican Indian Runners: How They Get That Way," *Literary Digest,* July 9, 1927, 51–52; "In Mexico," *Time,* Nov. 22, 1926, 33.

22. Colin M. MacLachlan and William H. Beezley, *El Gran Pueblo: A History of Greater Mexico,* 2d ed. (Upper Saddle River, N.J.: Prentice Hall, 1999), 292–94.

23. "Indian Runners Can Tire Horses," *New York Times,* Jan. 16, 1927, sec. 8, 8.

24. Enrique C. Aguirre to Count Henri de Baillet-Latour, Jan. 27, 1927, "Jeux de l'Amérique Centrale" file, International Olympic Committee Archives, Lausanne, Switzerland. The author wishes to thank César R. Torres, professor at SUNY–Brockport, for discovering and sharing this document.

25. "Many Famous Track and Field Stars Entered in Texas Relays Friday," *Austin Sunday American-Statesman,* Mar. 20, 1927, 8; "Track Records Due to Fall at Texas Relays," *San Antonio Express,* Mar. 20, 1927, 1; "Texas Relay Program," *Austin Sunday American-Statesman,* Mar. 20, 1927, 9; "More than 850 Athletes Will Compete in Texas Relay Games," *Dallas Morning News,* Mar. 23, 1927, sec. 1, 11; "History of Texas Relay Games Shows Swift Progress," *Austin Statesman,* Mar. 25, 1927, 7.

26. "Track Records Due to Fall at Texas Relays," 1.

27. Roger M. Busfield, "Eyes of Sporting World Fastened on Indian Runners at Relay Games," *Austin Sunday American-Statesman,* Mar. 20, 1927, 9.

28. "Mexican Indian Breaks 100-Kilometer Mark: Women's Olympic Race at Distance Sought," *New York Times,* Mar. 2, 1927, 21.

29. Bill Kleinman, "Tarahumaras Prepare for Acts of Super Endurance," *Austin Statesman,* Mar. 24, 1927, 7.

30. "Los corredores tarahumaras arribarón ayer tarde a la ciudad de San Antonio," *Excélsior,* Mar. 23, 1927, sec. 1, 3; "Los indios tarahumaras van a realizar hoy una notable hazaña en el etdo. de Texas," *Excélsior,* Mar. 25, 1927, sec. 1, 1, 9; "Los tarahumaras a la Olímpiada de Amsterdam," *El Universal,* Apr. 12, 1927, sec. 2, 1.

31. "México enviara sus mejores corredores universitarios a los torneos de Texas," *Excélsior,* Mar. 16, 1927, sec. 1, 1.

32. "Los corredores tarahumaras arribarón," 3.

33. "Heated Pullmans Give Indians Swollen Feet, as Men and Women Runners Ride to Austin," *New York Times,* Mar. 23, 1927, 21.

34. "Texas Relay Games Take On Kaleidoscopic Aspect with Arrivals," *Austin Statesman,* Mar. 23, 1927, 6.

35. "850 Athletes Already Entered for Texas Relay Games," *Austin Statesman,* Mar. 22, 1927, 7; "Indians Reach Austin for 82-Mile Endurance Run," *San Antonio Express,* Mar. 23, 1927, 14.

36. "Indian Girls Start Record Marathon from *Statesman,*" *Austin Statesman,* Mar. 23, 1927, 1.

37. The "blandishments of civilization" line was the work of the Associated Press reporter covering the story. "Indians Arrive Thursday; Will Start from Alamo on Friday," *San Antonio Express,* Mar. 24, 1927, 13; "5 Miles a Sprint for Indian Runners," *New York Times,* Mar. 24, 1927, sec. 1, 30.

38. "Indian Girls Start Record Marathon from *Statesman,*" 1.

39. "Texas Relay Games Take On Kaleidoscopic Aspect with Arrivals," 6; "Indians Arrive Thursday," 13; "5 Miles a Sprint for Indian Runners," 30.

40. "Los corredores Tarahumaras arribaron," 3; "Cordial recibimiento en Austin, Tex., a los atletas y deportistas mexicanos," *El Universal,* Mar. 23, 1927, sec. 1, 7; "Tarahumaras to Race 80 Miles," *Excélsior,* Mar. 24, 1927, sec. 2, 2 (English page); "Tarahumaras Acclimatize for Marathon in the U. States," *El Universal,* Mar. 24, 1927, sec. 1, 2 (English page).

41. Frederick Tisdale, "The Greatest Long-distance Runners in the World," *Mentor* 16 (1928): 19–20; John A. White, "Tarahumaris Indians of Mexico Are Champion Runners," *American Indian,* Aug. 1929, 2; "Indian Runners Can Tire Horses," 8; Busfield, "Eyes of Sporting World Fastened on Indian Runners at Relay Games," 9; Kleinman, "Tarahumaras Prepare for Acts of Super Endurance," 7; "The Nurmis of Mexico," 41; "Those Mexican Indian Runners," 51–52; "In Mexico," 33.

42. H. B. Du Bose, "Duby's Sportorial," *Austin Statesman,* Mar. 24, 1927, 6.

43. John Kieran, "Sport of the Times," *New York Times,* Mar. 25, 1927, 19.

44. H. B. Du Bose, "Duby's Sportorial," *Austin Statesman,* Mar. 26, 1927, 5. Texas papers gave extensive coverage to the University of Mexico's team. "Mexican Relay Team Starts," *Austin Statesman,* Mar. 19, 1927, 1; "Mexicans Here," *Austin Statesman,* Mar. 22, 1927, 2; "Mexican Crew Unfurls Flag," *San Antonio Express,* Mar. 24, 1927, 13; "Among the Notables at the Relay Games We Find," *Austin Statesman,* Mar. 24, 1927, 7; J. Nelson Furbeck, "Tarahumaras, a Sporting Tribe of the Mountains," *Austin Statesman,* Mar. 23, 1927, 6.

45. "Mañana sale el equipo universitario para Texas," *El Universal,* Mar. 18, 1927, sec. 1, 5; "México enviara sus mejores corredores universitarios a los torneos de Texas," 1; *El Corresponsal,* "El la carrera de 138 kmts. en E. E. Unidos, tomarán parte los tarahumaras," *El Universal,* Mar. 20, 1927, sec. 2, 1; "Los tarahumaras contra los atletas americanos," *El Universal,* Mar. 21, 1927, sec. 2, 1; "Los corredores tarahumaras arribarón," 3; "Cordial recibimiento en Austin," 7; "Tarahumaras Acclimatize for Marathon in the U. States," 2; El Enviado Especial, "Los tarahumaras harán hoy la gran carrera S. Antonio–Austin, 86 millas en 13 horas," *El Universal,* Mar. 24, 1927, sec. 1, 1, 10; "Tarahumaras to Race 80 Miles," 2; "Tarahumara Indians Confident Will Break Eighty-mile Record," *El Universal,* Mar. 25, 1927, sec. 1, 2 (English page); "Los tarahumaras, listos para la prueba," *El Universal,* Mar. 25, 1927, sec. 2, 1; "Los indios tarahumaras van a realizar hoy una notable hazaña," 1, 9; "Herb Tea Given Indian Runners on Eve of Race," *Excélsior,* Mar. 25, 1927, sec. 2, 2 (English page).

46. "Track Records Due to Fall at Texas Relays," 1; "Many Famous Track and Field Stars Entered in Texas Relays Friday," 8. The student newspaper of Haskell Institute (Lawrence, Kans.) covered its team's performances in Texas as well. "Haskell Run-

ners to Texas Relays," *Indian Leader,* Mar. 25, 1927, 4. For a brief biography of Osif see Joseph B. Oxendine, *American Indian Sports Heritage,* rev. ed. (Lincoln: University of Nebraska Press, 1995), 250.

47. "History of Texas Relay Games Shows Swift Progress," 7.
48. Kleinman, "Tarahumaras Prepare for Acts of Super Endurance," 7.
49. "Indian Runners Set for 82-Mile Run Today; Three Sisters, Youngest 15, to Run 26 Miles," *New York Times,* Mar. 25, 1927, 16; "Indians Arrive Thursday," 13; "Six Indian Runners Hold Spotlight on Eve of Texas U. Relay," *Dallas Morning News,* Mar. 24, 1927, sec. 2, 16; "UT Classes to Suspend for Texas Relays," *Austin Statesman,* Mar. 24, 1927, 1.
50. "Indians Get Early Start for Austin," *San Antonio Express,* Mar. 25, 1927, 12; "Three Tarahumara Indians Leave San Antonio Early Friday Morning on 82-Mile Foot Race; Expect to Make Distance in 12 to 14 Hours," *Dallas Morning News,* Mar. 25, 1927, sec. 2, 15.
51. "Indians Triumph in 82-Mile Race; Texas Relays Begin," *Austin Statesman,* Mar. 25, 1927, 1, 7.
52. "Los indios tarahumaras van a realizar hoy una notable hazaña," 9; "Herb Tea Given Indian Runners on Eve of Race," 2; "Los tarahumaras harán hoy la gran carrera S. Antonio–Austin, 86 millas en 13 horas," *El Universal,* Mar. 24, 1927, sec. 1, 1, 10; "Tarahumara Indians Confident Will Break Eighty-mile Record," *El Universal,* Mar. 25, 1927, sec. 1, 2 (English page); "Indians Get Early Start for Austin," 12; "Three Tarahumara Indians Leave San Antonio Early Friday Morning on 82-Mile Foot Race," 15; "Indians Triumph in 82-Mile Race," 1, 7.
53. "Indians Get Early Start for Austin," 12; Bill Kleinman, "Tarahumara Red Skins Beating Path toward Memorial Stadium," *Austin Statesman,* Mar. 25, 1927, 6; "Three Tarahumara Indians Leave San Antonio Early Friday Morning on 82-Mile Foot Race," 15; "Endurance Is Best in World," *Austin Statesman,* Mar. 26, 1927, 5; "Indian Race Pilot Is at Wheel for 15 Hours," *Austin Statesman,* Mar. 26, 1927, 1.
54. "Indians Get Early Start for Austin," 12; "Three Tarahumara Indians Leave San Antonio Early Friday Morning on 82-Mile Foot Race," 15.
55. "Indian Race Pilot Is at Wheel for 15 Hours," 1.
56. "Indian Runners Cover 89 Miles within 15 Hours," *San Antonio Express,* Mar. 26, 1927, 10.
57. H. B. Du Bose, "Duby's Sportorial," *Austin Statesman,* Mar. 25, 1927, 6.
58. "Indian Runners Cover 89 Miles within 15 Hours," 10.
59. "Indians Triumph in 82-Mile Race," 1, 7; "Indian Runners Cover 89 Miles within 15 Hours," 10; "Two Indians Finish 89-Mile Race as Girl Matches Their Endurance in Going 28 Miles," *Dallas Morning News,* Mar. 27, 1927, sec. 2, 4.
60. "Indians Triumph in 82-Mile Race," 1, 7.

61. Ibid.; "Indian Runners Cover 89 Miles within 15 Hours," 10; "Two Indians Finish 89-Mile Race," sec. 2, 4.

62. "Indian Girls Start Record Marathon from *Statesman*," 1.

63. "Hundreds Watch as Indian Girls Start Long-distance Footrace," *Austin Statesman*, Mar. 25, 1927, 1.

64. The *Austin Statesman* pegged the distance of the women's race at 28⅝ miles. The other sources reported 28½ miles. "Relay Games Pass into History amid Blaze of Glory; Tarahumara Indians Bring Spotlight of World to Texas Relays," *Austin Statesman*, Mar. 26, 1927, 5; "Indian Runners Cover 89 Miles within 15 Hours," 10; "Two Indians Finish 89-Mile Race as Girl Matches Their Endurance in Going 28 Miles," 4; "Indians Run 83 Miles and Girls Race 26," *New York Times*, Mar. 26, 1927, 19.

65. "Indians Triumph in 82-Mile Race," 1, 7; "Indian Runners Cover 89 Miles," 10; "Two Indians Finish 89-Mile Race," sec. 2, 4; "Indians Run 83 Miles and Girls Race 26," 19.

66. "Indians Triumph in 82-Mile Race," 7.

67. "Relay Games Pass into History amid Blaze of Glory," 5; "Endurance Is Best in World," 5.

68. "Haskell Takes Seconds at Texas," *Indian Leader*, Apr. 1, 1927, 4.

69. "Relay Games Pass into History amid Blaze of Glory," 5; "Thirteen Texas Relay Records Broken Friday," *Austin Statesman*, Mar. 26, 1927, 5. The confusion over whether the Tarahumaran athletes had set a record stemmed from the change in distance. Organizers knew that the only recognized Amateur Athletic Union (AAU) record for 82 miles had been set in 1882 by a runner who left New York City and ran 120 miles before collapsing. The runner, who had been timed at various points along the way, reached the 82-mile mark in 13 hours, 31 minutes, 5 seconds. He fell victim to fatigue after running 120 miles in 22 hours. The AAU claimed he held all records beyond 35 miles. It was not clear to organizers of the Texas race what the old 89-mile standard had been, hence the puzzlement over whether the Tarahumaras had beaten his time. "Indians Get Early Start for Austin," 12.

70. "Endurance Is Best in World," 5.

71. Ibid.

72. "Los tarahumaras realizaron la gran hazaña," *El Universal*, Mar. 26, 1927, sec. 2, 1; "Por 8 minutos, 55 segundos, no rompieron un record mundial," *El Universal*, Mar. 26, 1927, sec. 2, 1; "Quiénes forman el equipo mexicano," *El Universal*, Mar. 26, 1927, sec. 2, 1; "Los indios llegaron a la meta aclamados," *El Universal*, Mar. 26, 1927, sec. 2, 1; El Enviado Especial, "Los universitarios conquistaron el cuarto lugar en los revelos," *El Universal*, Mar. 26, 1927, sec. 2, 1; "Tarahumaras in Great Race," *El Universal*, Mar. 26, 1927, sec. 1, 2.

73. J. Fernando Rojas, "Singular triunfo de los tarahumaras," *Excélsior*, Mar. 26,

1927, sec. 2, 1; "Tarahumara Feat Astounds World," *Excélsior,* Mar. 26, 1927, sec. 2, 2 (English page).

74. "Encontraron a un anciano de la raza," *Excélsior,* Mar. 26, 1927, sec. 2, 1.
75. "Causó alegría el triunfo de los indios tarahumaras," *Excélsior,* Mar. 29, 1927, sec. 2, 3.
76. "Los tarahumaras," *El Universal,* Mar. 31, 1927, sec. 2, 2.
77. "Los tarahumaras a la Olímpiada de Amsterdam," 1.
78. "Laurel Wreaths for the Living," editorial, *Austin Sunday American-Statesman,* Mar. 27, 1927, 8.
79. "Astounding Run Made," *Los Angeles Times,* Mar. 26, 1927, 1-2; "Girl, 14, Runs 28 Miles; 2 Men Cover 89 Miles," *Washington Post,* Mar. 26, 1927, 1-2; "Two Mexican Indians Run 89 Miles in 15 Hours," *Chicago Tribune,* Mar. 26, 1927, 21.
80. "Endurance Is Best in World," 5.
81. "Laurel Wreaths for the Living," 8.
82. "Endurance Is Best in World," 5.
83. Kathleen E. Houston, "Augustín Blames Plane, Black Cat; Runners Heroes in Home Caves," *Austin Sunday American-Statesman,* Mar. 27, 1927, 8.
84. "Indian Runners Off for Home," *Dallas Morning News,* Mar. 27, 1927, sec. 2, 4; "Indians Start Homeward," *Austin Sunday American-Statesman,* Mar. 27, 1927, 8.
85. Houston, "Augustín Blames Plane, Black Cat," 8.
86. H. B. Du Bose, "Duby's Sportorial," *Austin Statesman,* Mar. 28. 1927, 9.
87. Ibid.
88. "Tarahumara Indians to Run in Kansas," *San Antonio Express,* Mar. 28, 1927, 8; "Tarahumara: Indian Runners to Stage Exhibition at Kansas Relay Games," *Austin Statesman,* Mar. 29, 1927, 9; "Mexican Indians to Race," *New York Times,* Apr. 6, 1927, 32.
89. H. B. Du Bose, "Duby's Sportorial," *Austin Statesman,* Mar. 30, 1927, 11.
90. "Three Mexicans Finish Marathon Run," *Indian Leader,* Apr. 29, 1927, 3; "Haskell Entries in Distance Race," *Lawrence* (Kans.) *Daily Journal-World,* Apr. 22, 1927, 1; "Lawrence Run 6¾ Hours," *Kansas City Star,* Apr. 23, 1927, 1; "Indians Set Time Record," *Austin Statesman,* Apr. 24, 1927, 10; "Indian Runner Sets a World's Record," *New York Times,* Apr. 24, 1927, sec. S, 5.
91. "An Apache on His Heels," *Kansas City Star,* Apr. 24, 1927, 1; "Girl Runs 30.6 Miles," *Kansas City Star,* Apr. 24, 1927, 1; "Torres Wins Run from Kansas City," *Lawrence Daily Journal-World,* Apr. 23, 1927, 1; "Lolita Is Only Woman to Finish Race from Topeka," *Lawrence Daily Journal-World,* Apr. 23, 1927, 1; "New Racing Mark," *Topeka State Journal,* Apr. 23, 1927, 1; "Girl Ends Race," *Topeka State Journal,* Apr. 23, 1927, 1; "Torres Breaks World's Record for 51 Miles," *Topeka Daily Capital,* Apr. 14, 1927, sec. B, 9; "Notre Dame Ties World Record in University Quarter-mile Relay

at Fifth Annual Kansas Games," *University Daily Kansan,* Apr. 24, 1927, 1; "Indian Runner Sets a World's Record," 5; "Indians Set Time Record," 10.

92. The 100-meter limit lasted until the 1948 Olympics, and the 800-meter race returned to the 1960 Olympics. A women's marathon finally debuted in 1984 at the Los Angeles games. Allen Guttmann, *The Olympics: A History of the Modern Games* (Urbana: University of Illinois Press, 1994), 49–50; Alfred E. Senn, *Power, Politics, and the Olympic Games* (Champaign, Ill.: Human Kinetics, 1999), 43.

93. McGehee, "*Carreras, patrias, y caudillos,*" 23; Peter Nabokov, *Indian Running: Native American History and Tradition* (Santa Fe: Ancient City Press, 1981), 184–85. Nabokov repeats some of the standard explanations for the failure of the Tarahumaras to live up to expectations, including that they thought the race was going to be much longer than twenty-six miles and failed to pace themselves accordingly, that the "white man's" races gave them bad dreams, that exposure to modern diets sapped their prowess, that the large crowds scared them, and that putting shoes on their feet hampered their strides. Those claims are common in long-after-the-fact tales such as those by Edwin ("Bud") Shrake, "A Lonely Tribe of Long-distance Runners," *Sports Illustrated,* Jan. 9, 1967, 56–67; Jenkinson, "The Glory of Long-distance Running," 54–65; James Norman, "The Tarahumaras: Mexico's Long-distance Runners," *National Geographic* 149 (1976): 702–18.

94. Shrake, "A Lonely Tribe of Long-distance Runners," 56–67; Jenkinson, "The Glory of Long-distance Running," 54–65; Norman, "The Tarahumaras," 702–18.

95. Brad Smith, "Tarahumara Indians' Feats Inspire Awe," *Denver Post,* Aug. 26, 1993, sec. E, 1; "The Legend of the Tarahumara," *Runner's World* 28 (1993): 74–81; Alan Weisman, "Drug Lords vs. the Tarahumara," *Los Angeles Times Magazine,* Jan. 9, 1994, 10–15; Alex Markels, "A Run to Moonlight for Food and More," *New York Times,* Aug. 24, 1994, sec. S, 11; Alex Shoumatoff, "Trouble in the Land of *Muy Verde,*" *Outside* 20 (1995): 57–63, 149–54; John Tayman, "Let My People Burn Rubber," *Outside* 20 (1995): 27–28; Ron Arias and Betty Cortina, "Going the Distance," *People,* Oct. 30, 1995, 124–28; George Ramos, "6 Racers Are Running for Their Lives," *Los Angeles Times,* Sept. 25, 1996, sec. A, 1; John Weyler, "They're Sole Survivors in the Race for Life," *Los Angeles Times,* Oct. 16, 1997, sec. C, 1; Sonia Nazario, "100-Mile Run to Agony and Ecstasy," *Los Angeles Times,* Sept. 30, 1996, sec. B, 3; David Roberts, "In the Land of the Long-distance Runners," *Smithsonian* 29 (1998): 42–52; Alan Zarembo, "Running on Empty," *Newsweek* (international edition), Aug. 5, 2002, 52.

96. Antonio Laviín Ugalde, *México en los Juegos Olímpicos,* Mexico, 1968, 18–25.

97. Alfonso Reyes, "Yerbas del tarahumara," in *Twentieth-century Mexico,* edited by W. Dirk Raat and William H. Beezley (Lincoln: University of Nebraska Press, 1986), 196.

98. Michael Oriard, *King Football: Sport and Spectacle in the Golden Age of Radio and Newsreels, Movies and Magazines, the Weekly and the Daily Press* (Chapel Hill: University of North Carolina Press, 2001).

99. See "$25,000 from Pyle for 3,000-Mile Run," *New York Times,* Apr. 28, 1927, 20.

100. Sen. Morris Sheppard of Texas to Pres. Franklin Roosevelt, Mar. 9, 1937, State Department Records Division, Record Group 59, Box 5025, National Archives and Record Administration II, College Park, Md.

101. Stephen H. Hardy, "Entrepreneurs, Organizations, and the Sports Marketplace: Subjects in Search of Historians," *Journal of Sport History* 13 (1986): 16–18.

102. Bernd Heinrich, *Racing with the Antelope: What Animals Can Teach Us about Running and Life* (New York: Cliff Street Books, 2001), 164.

103. "In Mexico," 33.

PELOTEROS IN PARADISE
Mexican American Baseball and Oppositional Politics in Southern California, 1930–1950
JOSÉ M. ALAMILLO

"I've been in baseball since I was thirteen years old. I've been playing all sports and the only problem that kept me from making the majors was my color," bitterly complained Jess Guerrero. Before 1947, the deeply entrenched color line in U.S. baseball kept African Americans, black Latinos, and dark-skinned Mexican Americans like Guerrero from playing in the major leagues. Despite racial segregation in baseball, Mexican American *peloteros* (ballplayers) took to the diamonds every weekend afternoon to play independent sandlot and semiprofessional baseball. Community-based baseball clubs sprang up during the interwar years in Southern California's barrios and *colonias* (communities), introducing immigrant children to America's national pastime at a time when Mexican sport heroes were few and far between. In the context of economic exploitation, racial discrimination, and resurgent nativist attacks aimed at the Mexican population, second-generation Mexican Americans used baseball to proclaim their equality through athletic competition, without fear of reprisal, and to publicly demonstrate community solidarity and strength.[1]

This chapter examines the multiple meanings and uses of baseball clubs among Mexican Americans in Southern California during the 1930s and 1940s. First, it analyzes the way in which employers and social reformers sought to use them to Americanize and socially control the Mexican immigrant population. Second, to examine the attitudes and motivations of Mexican American ballplayers toward the game, this chapter focuses on community-based semipro baseball clubs throughout Southern California. One of these was the Corona Athletics Baseball Club, which boasted a lineup of male Mexican American ballplayers that claimed several championship pennants and earned a reputation for producing major league players. In the face of racial discrimination and limited economic opportunities that afflicted the Mexican population in this agricultural-industrial town, baseball took on both a symbolic and a real social significance.

Drawing upon C. L. R. James's idea of the political significance of cricket contests, this chapter describes the way in which Mexican Americans viewed baseball games as mirroring larger racial and class struggles that transcended the playing field.[2] Mexican Americans used baseball clubs to promote ethnic consciousness, build community solidarity, display masculine behavior, and sharpen their organizing and leadership skills. In this regard, they transformed the clubs into a political base from which to launch wider forms of collective action. To view them as sites of resistance, however, one must consider the way in which sporting venues reinforced gender hierarchies. In their sports clubs, baseball players re-created a masculine culture that extended into labor unions, effectively reproducing male domination and the exclusion of women from leadership positions in the labor movement.

Baseball arrived in Latin America during the mid-nineteenth century. U.S. sailors and returning Cuban émigrés first introduced baseball in Cuba, and the game then spread throughout the Caribbean region. In Mexico, Cuban workers introduced the game to the remote southeastern Yucatán peninsula in the 1860s, but it was not until the Porfirian era (1876–1910) that baseball's popularity extended to northern Mexico. With the influx of U.S. capital into remote areas of central and western Mexico, railroad and mining company personnel treated workers to their first baseball game. U.S. investors and Porfirian liberals recognized the game's potential to introduce modern industrial values such as teamwork and self-discipline to the lower classes in Mexico. Wallace Thompson, mining journal editor and author of five books on Mexico, observed the growing popularity of baseball with paternalistic approval: "A magnificent beginning has thus been made in the training of Mexican boys both in teamwork and in athletic development. . . . It seems that these features are being developed by baseball, which there, as elsewhere, has stimulated the sense of play and is certainly as near a 'national sport' as Mexico has so far attained."³

North of the Rio Grande, U.S. businesses subsidized sport teams to increase worker productivity and foster company loyalty. As militant labor unions made inroads among immigrant workers during World War I, industrial and agricultural companies stepped up efforts to counter labor unions by offering recreational programs. One of the leading producers of agricultural fruit in the country, the California Fruit Growers Exchange (CFGE; the exchange is also known by its trademark, Sunkist), organized a sophisticated corporate welfare system that included Americanization classes, a housing program, recreational facilities, and sport clubs. Sunkist officials encouraged growers to organize baseball clubs to improve workers' physical health and mental preparedness for the backbreaking fieldwork. Sunkist's industrial relations department director, G. B. Hodgkin, advised growers on how to best "handle" Mexicans: "In order to produce the desired workers, they have to become a member of a local society or baseball team . . . to increase their physical and mental capacity for doing more work."⁴

Sunkist's proposal persuaded citrus growers to form baseball clubs and build ballparks on ranch property. For example, Keith Spalding, son of sporting giant A. G. Spalding (of Spalding Sporting Goods) and author of *America's National Game,* owned and operated Rancho Sespe, a four-thousand-acre citrus ranch near Fillmore, in eastern Ventura County. Spalding transformed this old California rancho into a "model scientific farm" complete with modern packinghouses, office buildings, worker housing, recreation facilities, a musical group, and a baseball field. In northern Orange County, the La Habra Citrus Association sponsored "Los Juveniles," a baseball club composed of Mexican citrus workers. The association formed this group to replace the popular sport of cockfighting, which was conducted surreptitiously inside citrus orchards.

"The entire [Mexican] colony has become baseball conscious in a short time," observed one researcher, "and the interest exhibited in this great American sport has seemingly supplanted the former Sunday diversion of cock-fighting, which is common to many Mexican colonies in Southern California." To become "baseball conscious," however, according to the association, required compliance with manly codes of conduct. The team's "good sportsman" rules consisted of being "dependable, truthful, trustworthy, and never late for baseball practice." According to Jessie Hayden, the players were "never heard to use bad language at work or at play [and] never display[ed] [their] temper[s]." La Habra's baseball program linked baseball with modernity, manliness, and progress in opposition to the uncivilized, culturally backward, and supposedly unmanly character of cockfighting.[5]

Apart from the efforts of these employers, social reformers also sought to redirect immigrants from their own ethnic amusements and into Americanized forms of recreation and sports. Play reformers targeted immigrant children in schools, playgrounds, churches, and settlement houses in an attempt to mold them into a submissive working class with Anglo Protestant and middle-class values. Cary Goodman has shown how the play reform movement transformed autonomous street play into more controlled and organized play to counteract the perceived moral decay of street life in the cities, which reformers believed caused juvenile delinquency. The head of the Los Angeles Department of Playgrounds and Recreation encouraged mass participation in sports in the belief that it would "instill ideals of good sportsmanship, fair play, team work, clean living, and plant loyalty . . . bringing about a happy spirit of cooperation between employer and employee." Emory Bogardus and his sociology students at the University of Southern California researched the significance of sports and recreational activities in Los Angeles Mexican communities. Bogardus prescribed the use of baseball clubs to counter gambling, bullfighting, and cockfighting. "The Mexican 'takes' well to the national pastime of the United States, namely, baseball. More significant, through games such as baseball, he acquires a new meaning for teamwork."[6]

Employer and progressive efforts to reform workers' cultural lives were not limited to young men. Women were also introduced to recreation programs and sport teams in schools, churches, YWCAs, playgrounds, and settlement houses. For example, during the early thirties the San Diego Neighborhood House built a baseball diamond to "give girls an opportunity for recreation away from their numerous home responsibilities [and to] instill cooperation among the girls." The Neighborhood House formed an all-Mexican women's baseball team that occasionally played against all-male teams. As members of leagues that were sponsored by companies, schools, and settlement houses, Mexican American women also took up softball, organizing and participating in tournaments throughout Southern California. Examples of team names were "Los Tomboys" (Orange, Calif.), "Las Debs" (Corona, Calif.), "México Libre," "Kats" (Placentia, Calif.), and "Four-star

Eagles" (Los Angeles). Despite the sport's popularity, women's softball was considered a novelty attraction for male spectators and was usually scheduled as an exhibition game before men's baseball. The meaning softball had for women, however, differed from its significance to male spectators and team promoters; it allowed women to form female friendships and gain public visibility outside the home and workplace. As one former softball ballplayer remembered, "We use[d] to love playing softball, [and] even though some [of] us [players] were already married, we still never missed practice."[7]

The appeal of baseball was not limited to Mexican immigrants; the sport attracted people from all segments of the U.S. working classes. Early commentators hailed it as the nation's "melting pot" sport with the greatest potential for Americanizing foreign-born youngsters and children of immigrants, but the game's strict racial and gender system shattered this myth. While sport journalists celebrated the substantial influx of players of eastern and southern European descent into the major leagues during the midthirties, they overlooked more than fifty Latin American and U.S. Latino players that joined the major leagues before 1947, the year Jackie Robinson broke the color line. Those players originating from Mexico included Baldomero ("Melo") Almada, Jose Luís ("Chile") Gomez, and Jesse Flores. The East Coast bias, major-league focus, and white-black binary framework of much of baseball history has virtually ignored the sporting experiences of Mexican Americans, Asian Pacific Americans, and Native Americans in amateur and semi-professional baseball leagues throughout the American West.[8]

By its proximity to the U.S.-Mexico border and interior Mexico, Mexican American baseball was uniquely different. Unlike for other racial minority groups that adopted baseball as their favorite sport, Mexican baseball was a transnational phenomenon from its inception, straddling both sides of the border to entertain spectators who filled the stands to cheer for their favorite team. Baseball teams from Mexico routinely crossed the border to participate in southwestern tournaments. For example, Mexico's championship team, San Luís "México," was invited to participate in several Los Angeles area tournaments during the 1930 season. For these international games the Mexican consul was customarily invited to throw the first pitch.[9]

Along with boxing, baseball constituted the most popular sport in Southern California's Mexican communities. Mexican baseball teams often sprang up from within the community as a part of sport clubs, mutual-aid organizations, churches, and small businesses. A chief promoter of baseball sports was the Asociación Deportiva Hispano Americana, organized in 1927 by the leading Spanish-language newspaper of Los Angeles, *La Opinión,* and a board of directors composed of Mexican consuls, middle-class professionals, and small business owners. Another big promoter was La Asociación Atlética Mexicana del Sur de California, which was formed on the eve of the 1932 Los Angeles Olympics with the assistance of the city's recreation department. Persuaded by the rising popularity of baseball among second-generation Mexican American youth, La Asociación formed a separate baseball league, Asociación Mexicana de Baseball del Sur de California (Southern California Mexican Baseball Association), which consisted of more than fifteen amateur and semiprofessional teams. Some of the 1933 teams included the El Paso Shoe Store "Zapateros," Oxnard "Aces," La Habra "Juveniles," Carta Blanca "Cerveceros," Hermosa Mexican Club "Pescadores," Santa Paula "Limoneros," Placentia "Merchants," and Corona "Athletics."[10]

The original Corona Athletics Baseball Club was first organized in 1931 by Mexican American youth who worked in Corona's citrus industry. Many of the original members were introduced to baseball through a network of company-sponsored teams, including the Corona Foothill Lemon Company "Lemoneers" and the American Fruit Growers "Blue Goose." However, when companies failed to meet the players' demands for equipment and a diamond field, the athletes decided to form their own team. Although freed from strict company control, the Corona Athletics were still dependent on Corona's business community for financial backing and moral support.[11]

Of the fifteen Mexican American ballplayers that composed the Corona Athletics Baseball Club, some resided in the city's northside barrio, and several others in outlying citrus ranch communities. Within the city's circular shape, Sixth Street was considered the racial borderline that divided the Mexican northside and the white southside. The only time white residents crossed Sixth Street into the Mexican barrio was to catch a glimpse of the Corona Athletics. Although the ballplayers lived in separate communities, they all attended Washington School, designated as a "Mexican school." In many parts of the Southwest, Mexican children were segregated into such "Mexican schools," which offered little academic preparation and stressed vocational training and physical education. Because they needed to contribute to the family income, very few of these students continued on to high school, so they followed in their parents' footsteps—picking and packing citrus fruit.

Facing a bleak future in agricultural work, Mexican American boys turned to baseball. For example, Zeke Mejía decided early on to dedicate himself to school and sports. "I did not want to pick lemons like my father and needed an incentive to stay in school so I started playing sports, especially baseball. It taught me something about myself. I hated to lose then and still hate to lose now." Those who could not escape agricultural work had to learn to endure backbreaking labor. Former Athletics ballplayer Tito Cortez explained how agricultural work helped his athletic performance: "Working inside the [citrus] groves, carrying a heavy sack, climbing up and down the ladder, using a quick eye to pick lemons helped with my pitching and [baseball] training." Cortez related that working six days a week (ten hours per day) did not interfere with his baseball performance: "Everyone used to comment how we would work like a dog all week picking lemons, then [play] baseball all day on Sundays. But you see that was the only thing to do since there was no television." Cortez's experience supports Steven Gelber's contention that baseball culture reinforced workplace values such as appreciation of rationality, personal accountability, teamwork, and competitiveness among groups.[12]

Compared to their lower-rung position on the agricultural ladder, Mexican athletes could potentially move up as coaches and managers and thus gain valuable leadership and organizational skills. For example, three Mexican American community leaders, Marcelino Barba, Gilbert Enríquez, and Marcus Uribe, began their careers through participation in baseball teams and sport clubs. From 1931 to 1939 Barba worked in the packinghouses as a fruit crate assembler and machine operator while also managing the Athletics Baseball Club. As manager, Barba spent many hours scheduling ball games, soliciting sponsors, and organizing tournaments. Gilbert Enríquez worked in a shoe store while he coached the Athletics team and children from Washington School after class. Enríquez became the first Mexican American on the city's recreation commission and was founding editor of the Spanish-language newspaper *El Imparcial*. Marcus Uribe worked as a citrus picker until he lost his right arm in a work-related accident; he then became known as "El Mocho" (nickname meaning "the armless"). Despite his handicap, he replaced Barba as the Athletics' manager (1940–1948) and, because of his leadership experience and winning record, became an effective labor organizer.[13]

Apart from acquiring leadership skills, baseball players were able to travel and make new friends outside their immediate surroundings. During the summer months, when the lemon harvest ebbed, the Athletics traveled northward to Santa Barbara, to Coachella Valley in the eastern desert, and to the border towns of Mexicali and Tijuana. To offset the transportation expenses, the manager sometimes borrowed a hauling truck from a local packinghouse. Former Corona baseball player Zeke Mejía fondly remembered these experiences: "I liked to travel to new places because I liked meeting new friends. I remember traveling to Lake Elsinore, which was a long way in those days. But the only ride we could get was from a friend who hauled fertilizer in his truck. So all the guys crawled inside the truck and tried not to breathe during the ride. By the time we arrived to play we all smelled like fertilized fields. We did it because we loved the game." These sporting networks established during away games and tournaments later became important for community organizing and labor solidarity.[14]

In addition to helping to weld informal social networks and alliances, the baseball tours also provided masculinized forms of sociability. Apart from the game's competitive machismo, postgame drinking parties became a popular pastime among the athletes. Following each victory, the team manager would purchase food and beer for the players. Former Athletics pitcher Natividad ("Tito") Cortez remembered, "After the game, the managers would buy us *cerveza* (beer) and tacos. Sometimes we had a barbeque out there, roasted goat and made tacos." These postgame celebrations, however, were contingent on how much money they collected during the game. When they were short of funds, they visited their main sponsor, the Jalisco Bar, where they received free drinks. This popular male drinking establishment was jokingly referred to as "El Resbalador" (slippery place) because of the numerous inebriated ballplayers who accidentally slid into imaginary bases.[15]

Baseball's masculine culture both on and off the playing field often excluded women from participation and even spectatorship. Nevertheless, Mexican women attended Corona baseball games and helped fundraise by selling Mexican food at the events. Some Mexican American women also played in all-women softball teams that became popular during World War II. Following his tenure as Athletics manager, Marcus Uribe helped organize an all-Mexican American women's softball team called "Las Debs de Corona." The team was sponsored by the American Dry Cleaners and coached by two Anglo Americans; the players dressed in blue and gold uniforms with the sponsor's name emblazoned on their backs.[16]

Before World War II, Mexicans had to look elsewhere for recreational resources because of racial segregation in city parks and other leisure facilities. Like other southwestern cities, Corona maintained a segregationist policy that barred Mexicans from using the city park's field and swimming pool. In 1926, for example, the Corona City Council passed the following resolution: "It was moved that students, except foreigners, of the city have the freedom of the city [pool] on Tuesdays of each week until further notice." One resident defended the city's racist practices by claiming "So little can a Mexican appreciate a park." Mexican ballplayers thus gravitated toward empty lots or agricultural fields, which became makeshift diamonds. The Athletics team transformed an empty railroad yard, located in the northside Mexican barrio, into a diamond with bleachers and a concession stand. Because the managers of the Santa Fe Railroad were baseball fans, they allowed the Athletics to lease the land for a dollar per month. Additionally, by using the railroad yard, the team was able to bypass city regulations on alcohol consumption and food sales.[17]

For Corona's Mexican working-class community, the Athletics' baseball field represented an important cultural space. The ballpark's free admission policy was appealing to families, children, youth, and elders with limited discretionary incomes. Apart from watching their favorite team, these spaces offered families an opportunity to reunite with extended relatives and friends. This Sunday afternoon ritual fostered cultural pride among the Mexican residents regardless of class, gender, generation, and citizenship status. Following the ball games, Mexicanist-oriented organizations, aimed at preserving a Mexican national identity, occasionally staged patriotic celebrations complete with mariachi music, food, and speeches. Baseball historian Samuel Regalado has suggested that "[b]aseball in the barrios did more than help to preserve a strong sense of Mexican heritage within these communities, it wielded a sense of unity amongst the people—especially for those who had been in the United States only a few years." The children of Mexican immigrants, either born or reared in the United States, also gravitated toward America's national sport.[18]

During the thirties, second-generation Mexican American youngsters filled the stands every Sunday afternoon, hoping to realize their own "field of dreams." One recreation director interviewed Mexican American youth in Los Angeles and Phoenix about their favorite American sports and found that baseball was tops, followed by softball, boxing, basketball, and football. Mexican American organizations frequently attended Athletics ball games to support their friends and peers. For the ballplayers, emphasizing both their Mexican heritage and their American citizenship, however, was neither contradictory nor mutually exclusive; as historian George Sánchez has suggested, it involved a complex and ambiguous process contingent on historical circumstances. The ballplayers' bilingual and bicultural skills were necessary to solicit sponsors, negotiate contracts, and organize tournaments with sport promoters.[19]

To cover the team's expenses, managers passed a baseball hat around the bleachers for those who could contribute. They also sought financial backing from local Mexican and Anglo businesses. Former Athletics coach Jess Uribe explained the fundraising process: "From all the people that came to watch us, we would pass around a basket to collect money to support the team, but it was never enough. Only coins you would see because people were so poor. But still many people helped us cover the costs. For fifteen expensive uniforms we had to find support from the local businesses." He added, "We used to get sponsors from the Mexican businesses, especially bars. Each business would buy a baseball uniform and placed their name on the back." The Athletics club also held fundraising dances at the American Legion Hall to help offset transportation costs. These dances, announced in *El Imparcial* and the local Spanish-language radio station, featured traditional Mexican ballads by Al López's band and swing music performed by the Mexican American band. According to one newspaper announcement, "[t]he purpose of the dance [was] to raise money to cover necessary expenses, since passing the hat at each game [was] not enough." Apart from these efforts, baseball managers also enlisted the assistance of Anglo business establishments such as Corona Hardware, American Dry Cleaners, and Western Auto Supply.[20]

While some parents encouraged their children to participate in sporting activities, others were suspicious of the national sport because it competed with family obligations. Former Detroit Tigers pitcher and San Gabriel Valley native Hank Aguirre, nicknamed the "Tall Mexican," disclosed to his biographer his father's disapproval. Because the Aguirre family owned and operated a family grocery store, Aguirre's father wanted Hank to work in it and therefore had little patience with his son's budding baseball career. However, when Hank received his first bonus for signing with the Detroit Tigers in 1951, his father "put behind forever his lack of interest in baseball and his scathing views of the game as a waste of time." Major league pitcher Jesse Flores, nicknamed "El Guero" (Blondy), also encountered family resistance. Born in Guadalajara, Mexico, Jesse Flores migrated to La Habra with his family and later dropped out of school to work in the citrus orchards with his father. When

Flores joined the Chicago Cubs in 1942, his mother was not pleased. "She didn't really like the idea. She used to go to church and pray for me when I was pitching. She thought I was going to get hit in the head with the ball." Unlike Jesse's mother, Flores's father and brothers attended all of his games and supported his career choice. Flores played for seven seasons on three different teams, and after retirement in 1950 he became a successful scout for the Minnesota Twins. Reflecting on his major league pitching career, Flores concluded, "I think without baseball I would have been just another worker."[21]

Even with family obligations to fulfill, Mexican American ballplayers still took a chance at making it big in the major leagues. The Corona Athletics played in semipro leagues, which were not associated with the professional leagues and their minor league appendages. After achieving a winning average of .700 during the 1936 season, they were invited to participate in the California State Championship Semipro Tournament at Wrigley Field in Los Angeles. Although they lost, the Athletics demonstrated they had the potential to play in the major leagues. Not until Jackie Robinson broke the color line in 1947, however, did scouts begin to pay attention to the Athletics. Between 1947 and 1949, major league teams recruited three Athletics players: Tito Cortez, Ray Delgadillo, and Remi Chagnon. Later, in the early 1950s, Bobby Pérez and Louis Uribe signed contracts with the Brooklyn Dodgers. Although no Athletics player achieved major league star status, simply belonging to one of the most fiercely competitive baseball teams in the region was enough for some. Several of the players showed off their athletic prowess in photographs taken by a local studio. These photos were occasionally distributed at tournament games like baseball cards.

Before 1947, major league scouts recruited two semipro players of Mexican descent from Southern California. In 1933 Melo Almada became the first Mexican American to play in the major leagues for seven seasons—first playing for the Boston Red Sox, then with the Washington Senators, and finally with the 1939 Brooklyn Dodgers. Born in Huatabampo, Sonora, Mexico, to a wealthy landowning family, Almada moved to Los Angeles and played sports in the city's public school system during the twenties. As the star pitcher for the Los Angeles High School and the El Paso Shoe teams, Almada became an instant celebrity in the English- and Spanish-language print media. The former constructed an image of Almada as an assimilated "American" athlete, often referred to as "Mel" and occasionally mistaken for an Italian American. One sport journalist's account read, "Although proud of his Mexican lineage and completely loyal to it, he doesn't even look like a Mexican, being taller, broader and considerably fairer than most of the citizens of our sister republic." In contrast, *La Opinión* and the Mexico City newspaper *El Excélsior* proclaimed Almada a "Mexican national hero." Although lighter-skinned Latin American and Latino major league players, including Almada and Flores, partially benefited from "whiteness," they still faced ethnic stereotypes and subtle forms of discrimination.[22]

When Jackie Robinson crossed the color line, Mexican American semipro players became optimistic about their major league prospects. Tito Cortez was one of those who had major league dreams. Between 1937 and 1947 Cortez pitched five no-hitters for the Athletics. In 1947 the Cleveland Indians recruited him to play for their farm team in Tucson, Arizona. As a starting pitcher for the Tucson Cowboys, he helped the team reach the minor league playoffs. Cortez described his Tucson experience: "I received $125 a month plus $20 a month for rent. I stayed in a dormitory. When they signed me up, I began as a relief pitcher, then a starter pitcher. I was the only Mexican American in the team." Cortez's promising career, however, was cut short when a hit on the left eye by a ball left him partially blind. Cortez remembered breaking the news to the Tucson Cowboys. "When I told them I had an accident, they did not believe me. They sent me a contract and then another one. Finally I just tore it up." After ignoring their letters, he later discovered that he was blacklisted from playing in the major league farm teams. The Cowboys suspected that Cortez was one of a dozen American ballplayers who were recruited by the Mexican League, who offered higher salaries and bonuses. In response, baseball commissioner A. B. Chandler blacklisted all those who joined the Mexican League for five years. Although Cortez and other Mexican American ballplayers did not achieve major league status, they demonstrated athletic ability, leadership, and organizational capabilities that extended far beyond the realm of sports.[23]

In the racially charged climate of the thirties and forties, which was characterized by segregation, discrimination, and nativism, baseball took on a broad social significance within Mexican communities. A University of Chicago sociologist long ago observed, "The whole [Mexican] colony is always keenly interested in the baseball games especially when they play against outsiders. It is as though the honor and status of the colony were at stake." This observation underscores the fact that Mexican Americans' struggles to gain acceptance on the playing field involved both symbolic and actual racial contestation. The Corona Athletics' victories against all-white baseball teams challenged notions of white superiority and stereotypical ideas of Mexicans as "peons," "docile," and culturally inferior. Semipro player Frank Ruiz explained the wider racial significance of Mexican-Anglo matches: "They all wanted to beat us. If they couldn't beat us with the runs, they would try to beat us with the umpire, because we were a little better than they were. I guess they didn't want the Mexican kids to beat them, you know, the Anglos over there. We had a little rough time sometimes, but then we'd score more runs. There's no way they could say they won without enough runs." Mexican American ball players like Frank Ruiz also demanded respect and equal opportunity beyond the playing field. His bitter memories of "No Mexicans Allowed" signs posted at the local swimming pool and city park made him question whether equality really existed in America's national pastime. Ruiz said, "Being a Mexican, well, you might say you had two strikes against you," he added, "and we had good players. They could have made the big leagues."[24]

Racial and class differences were visible on the baseball diamond, especially when the all-Mexican American Corona Athletics played their main rival, an all-white company team sponsored by the Exchange Lemon By-Products company. The Exchange Lemon By-Product plant employed predominantly white workers and did not hire Mexican workers until after World War II. During one of their highly competitive matches, the *Corona Independent* reported that "The Exchange Lemon Products team evidently felt they could make a better showing and win more games if they altered their appearance. They appeared on the diamond Friday night with a brand new outfit consisting of flashy yellow and black jerseys, black caps and white trousers, and did they look snappy!" Their loud clothes and pretentiousness, however, did nothing to improve their game. The Corona Athletics beat them by a score of eleven to two.[25]

For male players, identification with the game's highly charged hit-and-run plays, aggressive batting, and brawls became part of the appeal and served to publicly demonstrate their masculinity. The competition between Mexican and white men represented a struggle over racial, class, and masculine pride. As Michael Messner has suggested, "subordinated groups of men often used sport to resist racist, colonial, and class domination, and their resistance most often took the form of a claim to 'manhood.'" In the highly masculinized world of baseball, Mexican American men attempted to reassert their racial and masculine identity. In this sense, players became heavily invested in winning because this was one way they could challenge racism and class oppression and, at the same time, maintain their masculine pride, honor, and respectability.

In some cases, verbal and physical threats to ballplayers' masculinity and racial pride led to fights on and off the playing field. Tito Cortez remembered one particular incident during a game between the Athletics and the Los Angeles Colored Giants: "One time the Athletics was [sic] playing a black team from Los Angeles, and one of the guys playing shortstop was batting and made a 'sissy' remark to the pitcher. Something about pitching like a girl, but the catcher heard what he said. He got up and took off his mask [and] chest protector and ran after him. You could only see his spikes kicking dirt behind."

Altercations between black and Mexican American players sometimes bristled with racial tension, but at other times both groups developed friendly relations. Former semipro Jess Guerrero was a member of the Los Angeles Colored Giants and fondly remembered being a teammate of the Giants' famous Negro league pitcher: "I couldn't play with no white team, but I played with the colored teams, I played with Satchel Paige." In culturally diverse Southern California, the Corona Athletics played against other ethnic teams such as the Los Angeles Nippons (Japanese American), Sherman Institute (Native American), Torrance Blues (white American), and the Colored Giants (African American).[26]

The Athletics club served as a gendered space in which Mexican American ballplayers created a collective masculine culture and identity. Displays of manly behavior revolved around excessive drinking, gambling away their hard-earned money, abusive language, competitiveness, and physical skill. In some cases these destructive activities led to domestic violence. Irene Contreras, former sister-in-law of an Athletics ballplayer, complained about the players' excessive drinking, which interfered with their family obligations and domestic relations. The disruptive, exuberant, and wildly aggressive working-class behavior of Athletics players overlapped with a more middle-class masculine attitude that stressed self-discipline, obedience, and acceptance of hierarchy. Athletes displayed both sorts of conduct on and off the playing field. Combative, hard-hitting behavior contributed to winning a game, but it could also undermine efforts to build a disciplined team. These competing outlooks, however, still maintained a rigid gender hierarchy.[27]

Baseball helped establish strong bonds of male solidarity and companionship that provided a basis for teamwork both on and off the field, but rebellious behavior could lead to divisions within the team. For example, when one Athletics player missed several practices and behaved "aggressively rowdy" during a game, the team manager benched him for several games. After his father protested to the manager, an argument ensued. After several attempts at reconciliation, the disgruntled player left the team altogether and convinced several others to join him in forming a rival baseball club, the Corona Cubs. Organized in 1946, the Cubs played at the city park diamond wearing uniforms donated by Pancho's Garage. A bitter rivalry grew up between the two teams in the late forties, especially over who was the best "Mexican" team in the city.[28]

Despite divisions in the group, the Athletics club supported the community's struggles against the established order. In the early 1940s the Athletics transcended their sporting function and became politically involved in the labor movement. Ballplayers who had learned about fundraising, organizational work, and collective action in the Athletics club became dedicated organizers for the United Cannery Agricultural Packing and Allied Workers of America (UCAPAWA), an affiliate of the Congress of Industrial Organizations (CIO).

In the agricultural-industrial town of Corona, citrus companies exercised excessive influence in government, schools, churches, and community clubs, making the residents politically and economically dependent upon the citrus industry. For example, the city's largest citrus companies, Jameson and Corona Foothill Lemon, maintained a foothold on city and county politics and used their influence to keep labor unions out of Corona. In spite of the citrus industry's dominance in this racially segregated city, Mexican residents created their own leisure spaces and formed their own sport clubs, which assumed a heightened political role during times of labor-management conflict.[29]

From 1937 to 1940 the UCAPAWA made great inroads among agricultural workers by establishing thirty-nine locals and securing wage increases and improvements in working and living conditions. Although a majority of farmworker locals were centered in the San Joaquín valley, the UCAPAWA also gained some support among Mexican citrus workers in Southern California. As part of their organizing strategy, the UCAPAWA formed baseball teams throughout Southern California. In Orange, for example, UCAPAWA Local 120 formed a baseball team that toured Southern California, winning semi-pro tournaments and discussing with others the values of unionization.

According to the *UCAPAWA News*, "This local has [distinguished] itself in continuous struggle, without fear of any sort, raising high its banner against the winds."[30]

Upon arriving in Corona in the summer of 1940, UCAPAWA organizers turned to the Athletics club for assistance. Led by CIO organizer Alfonso Ortiz, the union distributed flyers printed in English and Spanish, announcing several meetings with employees of the Jameson Company and the Corona Foothill Company. Not only did Athletics ballplayers help with these efforts, they also offered their playing field as a meeting site for the new local. During one of these gatherings, workers formulated a list of demands to present to their employers, including a wage increase, full union recognition, an eight-hour workday (with double pay on Sundays and holidays), free equipment, and transportation to the groves. Union organizers argued that Sundays and holidays were reserved for workers to attend baseball games and other leisure activities.

Because spaces for union organizing were limited in this citrus-dominated town, the Athletics baseball diamond became an important gathering spot for the newly formed UCAPAWA union. "The CIO came into Corona to organize the workers and, of course, the ranchers did not want us to organize," explained former union member Rudy Ramos. However, according to Ramos, "We used to meet on Sheridan and Grand Boulevard. There used to be a baseball field where the famous Athletics played. On this ballpark is where we used to meet because it was hidden from view and away from the police."[31]

Within months of forming the Corona union, the workers decided to go on strike in the early morning of February 27, 1941. More than eight hundred employees congregated at the ballpark to coordinate plans for picket-line duty and discuss their next move. Once the picketing began around the packinghouses and citrus ranches, the citrus growers launched a public campaign to discredit the CIO organizers as "communist agitators" and called upon law enforcement officials to intervene and patrol the ballpark. The *Riverside Daily Press* reported that several fights broke out after a mass meeting: "The meeting began at the ballpark, but the crowd gathered [at] another open field due to interference by police and stool pigeons." To prevent union gatherings at the ballpark, the city council passed a resolution to give more power to the police so they could designate the ball field's surrounding area as a "no parking zone."

In response, labor organizer and Athletics manager Marcus Uribe led a group of workers to city hall to protest the council's actions. Uribe presented a petition to the commission: "We petition the council to reconsider their undemocratic action of Tuesday last in order to prevent the office of chief of police from becoming that of a virtual dictator. . . . We ask this in order to allow the citizens of Corona, as a free people, the opportunity and the unabridged right of liberty." Although they failed to convince the city council to rescind their action, the baseball players and union supporters joined together to publicly challenge the undue influence of the citrus companies and city government on community life.[32]

After the union moved its meeting site to the outskirts of town, organizer Heliodoro Medina visited the headquarters of *La Opinión* to urge readers to prevent Mexican strikebreakers from undermining Corona's labor movement. After several strikebreakers from the Casa Blanca barrio were spotted, Medina recruited some of the Athletics players to contact Casa Blanca's baseball team managers to warn their players not to interfere. A few days later, Casa Blanca's workers walked out in solidarity with the Corona workers. In addition, Athletics ballplayers Tony Balderas and Charles Uribe visited ballparks in Placentia, Ontario, Santa Ana, Oxnard, and San Fernando to solicit support from their baseball teams. These social networks, which were established during baseball tournaments, helped spread last-minute information about the strike and cultivate working-class solidarity.[33]

The Corona Athletics' sporting networks helped gain support from other union-sponsored baseball teams. For example, UCAPAWA Local 120 in Orange, California, sent several members from their CIO baseball team to assist the Corona organizers. While established regional networks were activated during the two-month Corona strike, they were not enough to counter the police repression and the company's divide-and-conquer tactics. In an effort to break the strike, the citrus companies provided recreational activities for workers who were living in outlying ranches to prevent them from joining the picket lines. Former ranch resident Manuel Cruz remembered this tactic: "The company did not want us to come downtown because they were afraid that the [strikers] might gang up on us, so they bought us some ping pong tables, checkers, cards, and entertainment because we could not go to the show." Afraid of losing their homes and jobs, the ranch residents opted to stay out of the labor conflict, thus exacerbating divisions within the Mexican community.[34]

During the strike, Mexican American women walked in the picket lines, cooked food for strikers, raised money for the strike fund, and solicited support from local businesses. According to the *Corona Independent,* "[t]hree women representing the CIO were circulating [around] city business establishments to learn whether or not they were employing union labor." Even a beauty parlor was asked whether it was serving scabs. Despite the fact that they occupied the majority packinghouse positions (graders, packers, sorters), Mexican American women were denied leadership positions within the union structure, and some were discouraged by boyfriends and husbands from joining the picket lines. Alice Rodríguez remarked, "My husband did not want me to join the [picket] line, so I stayed home, so when the foreman came to the house to convince me to go back to work, I told him that I did not want to go against my friends." In spite of her husband's reluctance, Alice Rodríguez supported the strikers by printing flyers at home, babysitting, and providing moral support.[35]

In front of the Jameson packinghouse, during the afternoon of March 21, 1941, a barrage of rocks was thrown at passing police cars. The rocks broke a car window and hit a police officer on the head. Police responded by throwing gas canisters into the picket line and arresting the suspected offenders. Rudy Ramos, who was standing on the sidelines, recalled the chaotic scene: "The police threw tear gas at the strikers, but they picked it up and threw it back until [the police] decided to use their stick[s] against them. . . . Then the people dispersed, and others got arrested." The police escorted forty-nine Mexican male strikers to jail and booked them on charges of disturbing the peace, inciting a riot, unlawful assembly, and aggravated assault with a deadly weapon. Those arrested included a few former Athletics baseball players. Following the arrests, the strike ended, and of the several court trials, one resulted in a prison sentence. By the end of 1941, the union movement had suffered a crushing defeat.[36]

Despite their participation in the labor movement, the Mexican American women were excluded from leadership positions in the union. In effect, the union's marginalization of women reinforced the male domination of the labor movement that contributed to the failure of the strike. Although intense police suppression and worker divisions orchestrated by the citrus companies played an important role, the union organizers failed to incorporate women as integral leaders and seemed insensitive to their issues. Part of the difficulty in mounting a sustained challenge to racial and class oppression was the male player-workers' uncritical adoption of the central precepts of the company's definition of masculinity, which stressed acceptance of hierarchy in the home, at work, and on the playing field. Baseball clubs created a collective masculine identity that played a contradictory role in the militant labor movement.[37]

Despite the increased popularity of baseball among second-generation Mexican Americans, employers and social reformers were rarely successful in their efforts. From the perspective of employers and reformers, baseball offered an alternative to the perilous thrills of cheap amusements such as gambling, drinking, cockfighting, and other perceived antisocial activities. In their view, immigrant workers could potentially become "baseball conscious" and adopt American middle-class values of sobriety, thrift, and discipline both on and off the playing field. While some of them accepted certain aspects of Americanism, bicultural Mexican Americans imposed multiple meanings on this national pastime and transformed baseball clubs into masculine, cultural, and political spaces. Like the Cuban baseball players in Louis Pérez's trailblazing essay, Mexican American peloteros became "conscious of new meanings and mindful of [the] new possibilities" of baseball and began "to reinvent themselves self-consciously as agents of change."[38]

At a time when companies and play reformers sought to organize and control the community's sporting life, baseball brought the Mexican community together on Sunday afternoons.[39] In the early decades of the twentieth century, U.S. companies organized baseball clubs to increase the discipline, obedience, and productivity of its immigrant workforce. Social reformers also believed that baseball would ensure the ultimate assimilation and Americanization of immigrant populations. Even as some ballplayers accommodated baseball's promotion of capitalist values and middle-class notions of masculinity that stressed discipline, aggressive independence, and acceptance of hierarchy, others resisted and imposed their own meanings on these games.

For Mexican American peloteros, baseball games represented more than mere athletic competitions; within the context of unequal Mexican-white relations, they provided a venue for symbolic and real confrontations between the races. Apart from competitive sporting events, Mexican Americans politicized baseball clubs into social entities that provided a basis for wider forms of collective action. As the case of the Corona Athletics Baseball Club demonstrates, members learned valuable leadership, networking, and organizational skills that transcended the playing field and moved into the political arena. Thus, when labor relations in Corona's citrus industry deteriorated in

1941, Corona Athletics team members-turned-labor-organizers activated their sporting networks and honed their organizing and leadership skills in an attempt to challenge the power of the agricultural companies. Although the ballplayers' competitive masculine behavior and leadership capabilities displayed on the playing fields and picket lines helped mount a militant challenge, they also reinforced male domination by excluding women from management positions, thus highlighting the limits of working-class resistance both on and off the playing field.

NOTES

Thanks go to Gilbert González, Vicki Ruiz, and Samuel Regalado. This chapter is dedicated to the memory of Jeff Garcilazo and Lionel Cantú.

1. Jess Guerrero, interview by Pat Flores and Jerry Alexander, in *Personal Stories from Pico Rivera*, edited by Susan S. Obler (Whittier, Calif.: Rio Hondo Community College, 1976), 30 (hereafter Guerrero interview).

2. C. L. R. James, *Beyond a Boundary* (1963; reprint, Durham, N.C.: Duke University Press, 1993), 66.

3. Wallace Thompson, *The Mexican Mind: A Study of National Psychology* (Boston: Little, Brown, 1922), 97, 100. On the rise of baseball in Mexico, see William H. Beezley, *Judas at the Jockey Club and Other Episodes of Porfirian Mexico* (Lincoln: University of Nebraska Press, 1987); Gilbert M. Joseph, "Forging the Regional Pastime: Baseball and Class in Yucatán," in *Sport and Society in Latin America: Diffusion, Dependency, and the Rise of Mass Culture*, edited by Joseph Arbena (New York: Greenwood Press, 1988), 29–61.

4. *California Citrograph* (Los Angeles), Aug. 1921, 75. On the welfare programs of Southern California's citrus industry, see Gilbert G. González, *Labor and Community: Mexican Citrus Worker Villages in a Southern California County, 1900–1950* (Urbana: University of Illinois Press, 1994), 65–74; Matt García, *A World of Its Own: Race, Labor, and Citrus in the Making of Greater Los Angeles, 1900–1970* (Chapel Hill: University of North Carolina Press, 2001), 87–120.

5. *La Opinión* (Los Angeles), Sept. 16, 1934, 5; Jessie Hayden, "La Habra Experiment in Mexican Social Education," master's thesis, Claremont Colleges, Claremont, Calif., 1934, 20.

6. Cary Goodman, *Choosing Sides: Playgrounds and Street Life on the Lower East Side* (New York: Schocken Books, 1979), 33–58; annual report, Los Angeles Department of Playgrounds and Recreation (1926–1927), 20; Emory Bogardus, *The City Boy and His Problems: A Survey of Boy Life in Los Angeles* (Los Angeles: House of Ralston, 1926), 67–100; Emory Bogardus, *The Mexican in the United States* (Los Angeles:

University of Southern California Press, 1934), 60; David A. Bridge, "A Study of the Agencies Which Promote Americanization in the Los Angeles City Recreation Center District," master's thesis, University of Southern California, 1920, 106-108.

7. Cynthia J. Shelton, "The Neighborhood House of San Diego: Settlement Work in the Mexican Community, 1914-1940," master's thesis, San Diego State University, 1975, 105-109; *La Opinión,* May 1, 1932, 3; Alison M. Wrynn, "Women's Industrial and Recreation League Softball in Southern California, 1930-1950," master's thesis, California State University–Long Beach, Long Beach, Calif., 1989, 40, 66; Susan K. Cahn, *Coming On Strong: Gender and Sexuality in Twentieth-century Women's Sport* (New York: Free Press, 1994), 142.

8. Frederick Lieb, "Baseball—the Nation's Melting Pot," *Baseball Magazine* 31 (Aug. 1923), 391-93; Samuel O. Regalado, *Viva Baseball!: Latin Major Leaguers and Their Special Hunger* (Urbana: University of Illinois Press, 1998), 36, 50-51, 177.

9. Alan M. Klein, *Baseball on the Border: A Tale of Two Laredos* (Princeton, N.J.: Princeton University Press, 1997), 32-65; *La Opinión,* June 30, 1930, 6, and June 18, 1933, 5.

10. *La Opinión,* July 19, 1927, 1; July 4, 1932, 5; June 24, 1933, 3; Douglas Monroy, *Rebirth: Mexican Los Angeles from the Great Migration to the Great Depression* (Berkeley: University of California Press, 1999), 45-48; Albert Camarillo, *Chicanos in a Changing Society: From Mexican Pueblos to American Barrios in Santa Barbara and Southern California, 1848-1930* (Cambridge: Harvard University Press, 1979), 152.

11. José M. Alamillo, "Bitter-sweet Communities: Mexican Workers and Citrus Growers on the California Landscape, 1880-1941," Ph.D. diss., University of California–Irvine, 2000, 258-63.

12. Zeke Mejía is quoted in the *Riverside Press–Enterprise* (California), June 29, 1996, 2 (This newspaper can be found at the Riverside Public Library, Riverside, Calif.); Natividad ("Tito") Cortez, interview by author, Apr. 20, 1998, Corona, Calif. (hereafter Cortez interview); Steven Gelber, "Working at Playing: The Culture of the Workplace and the Rise of Baseball," *Journal of Social History* 5 (1979): 12-15.

13. Fred Eldridge and Stanley Reynolds, "Corona's Mexican Leaders," in *Corona, California: Commentaries* (Los Angeles: Sinclair, 1986), 44-48; Cynthia Alvitre, *Hispanic Centennial Review, 1886-1986* (Corona Public Library, Corona, Calif., 1986), 1-5; *Corona Independent,* Jan. 4, 1933, 3 (This newspaper can be found at the Corona Public Library, Corona, Calif.); *El Imparcial,* Aug. 13, 1949, 1 (This newspaper can be found at the Corona Public Library, Corona, Calif.).

14. *Riverside Press–Enterprise,* June 29, 1996, 3.

15. Cortez interview.

16. Margaret Zarate, interview by author, Jan. 7, 2000, Corona, Calif. (interview in author's possession). See also Joan Sangster, "The Softball Solution: Fe-

male Workers, Male Managers, and the Operation of Paternalism at Westclox, 1923–1960," *Labour/Le Travail* 32 (Fall 1993): 189–93.

17. Corona City Council minutes, June 1, 1926, Clerk's Office, Corona City Hall, Corona, Calif.; *Corona Independent*, Jan. 5, 1927, 4.

18. Samuel Regalado, "Baseball in the Barrios: The Scene in East Los Angeles since World War II," *Baseball History* 1 (Summer 1986): 57.

19. Ed Horner, "A Recreation Director in a Mexican-American Community," master's thesis, University of California–Los Angeles, 1945, 41–42; George J. Sánchez, *Becoming Mexican American: Ethnicity, Culture, and Identity in Chicano Los Angeles* (New York: Oxford University Press, 1993), 253–69.

20. Jess Uribe, interview by author, Feb. 20, 1998, Corona, Calif. (tape recording of interview located at the Corona Public Library, Corona, Calif.) (hereafter Uribe interview); *Corona Independent*, July 10, 1936, 1.

21. Robert E. Copley, *The Tall Mexican: The Life of Hank Aguirre, All-star Pitcher, Businessman, and Humanitarian* (Houston: Piñata Books, 1998), 11; Cynthia J. Wilber, *For the Love of the Game: Baseball Memories from the Men Who Were There* (New York: Morrow, 1992), 125–31; González, *Labor and Community*, 112–14.

22. Bill Cunningham, "Grandstand Grandee," *Colliers*, Aug. 24, 1935, 16, 30; *El Excélsior* (Mexico City), Nov. 25, 1933; *La Opinión*, July 4, 1933; Daniel Frío and Marc Onigman, "Good Field, No Hit: The Image of Latin American Baseball Players in the American Press, 1871–1946," *Revista/Review Interamericana* 2 (Summer 1977): 199–208; Regalado, *Viva Baseball*, 134–46.

23. Cortez interview. On the Mexican Baseball League, see Alan Klein, "Baseball Wars: The Mexican Baseball League and Nationalism in 1946," *Studies in Latin American Popular Culture* 13 (1994): 33–56.

24. Edward Jackson Baur, "Delinquency among Mexican Boys in South Chicago," master's thesis, University of Chicago, 1938, 131. Frank Ruiz, interview by Gilbert Rivera and Patti Berry, in *Personal Stories from El Monte Communities*, edited by Susan S. Obler (Whittier, Calif.: Rio Hondo Community College, 1976), 93.

25. *Corona Independent*, June 22, 1938, 5.

26. Michael A. Messner, *Power at Play: Sports and the Problem of Masculinity* (Boston: Beacon Press, 1992), 19; Cortez interview; Guerrero interview, 30. On Japanese American baseball in Los Angeles, see Yoichi Nagata, "The Pride of Li'l Tokyo: The Los Angeles Nippons Baseball Club, 1926–1941," in *More than a Game: Sport in the Japanese American Community*, edited by Brian Niiya (Los Angeles: Japanese American National Museum, 2000), 100–109.

27. Irene Contreras, interview by author, Dec. 4, 1999 (interview in author's possession).

28. Uribe interview; *Corona Independent*, Aug. 21, 1946.

29. Diann Marsh, *Corona: The Circle City* (Encinitas, Calif.: Heritage Media, 1998), 102; Alamillo, "Bitter-sweet Communities," 209–26.

30. Vicki Ruiz, *Cannery Women, Cannery Lives: Mexican Women, Unionization, and the California Food-processing Industry, 1930–1950* (Albuquerque: University of New Mexico Press, 1987), 41–57; *UCAPAWA News,* Sept. 1939, 10. (This newspaper can be found at the Bancroft Library, Berkeley.)

31. Rudy Ramos, interview by author, Feb. 5, 1998, Corona, Calif. (tape recording of interview at the Corona Public Library, Corona, Calif.; hereafter Ramos interview); *Citrus Worker News,* June 1940 (this newspaper can be found at the Corona Public Library, Corona, Calif.); *Corona Independent,* July 22, 1940, 5.

32. Corona City Council minutes, Feb. 25, 1941, City Clerk Department, Corona City Hall, Corona, Calif.; *Corona Independent,* Feb. 17, 1941, 6; *Riverside Daily Press,* Mar. 22, 1941, 10. (This newspaper can be found at the Riverside Public Library, Riverside, Calif.)

33. *La Opinión,* Mar. 13, 1941; *Arlington Times,* Mar. 14, 1941 (this newspaper can be found at the Riverside Public Library, Riverside, Calif.); Ramos interview.

34. *Corona Independent,* Mar. 1, 1941, 5; Manuel Cruz, interview by author, Jan. 14, 1998, Corona, Calif. (A tape recording of the interview is located at the Corona Public Library, Corona, Calif.)

35. *Corona Independent,* Feb. 27, 1941, 5; Alice Rodríguez, interview by author, Jan. 27, 1997, Corona, Calif. (tape recording of interview located at the Corona Public Library, Corona, Calif.); see also Vicki Ruiz, *Cannery Women, Cannery Lives,* 69–85.

36. *Corona Independent,* Mar. 21, 1941.

37. See Vicki Ruiz, *From out of the Shadows: Mexican Women in Twentieth-century America* (New York: Oxford University Press, 1998), 72–98.

38. Louis Pérez Jr., "Between Baseball and Bullfighting: The Quest for Nationality in Cuba, 1868–1898," *Journal of American History* 81 (Sept. 1994): 500.

39. Play reformers are social reformers who sought to reform immigrants and working-class youth toward more "wholesome" forms of recreation and sports and away from unregulated and "unwholesome" activities like gambling and drinking.

LOS HEROES DEL DOMINGO
Soccer, Borders, and Social Spaces in Great Lakes Mexican Communities, 1940–1970
JUAN JAVIER PESCADOR

This chapter analyzes the impact of organized sports on Mexican and Latino communities in Detroit and Chicago between 1940 and 1970.[1] I challenge the predominant assumptions that organized sports (primarily soccer) represent social forms that keep Mexican traditions alive in the United States, help Mexican immigrants escape from poverty, and reproduce traditional hierarchies from Mexico. Instead, I contend that organized sports in Mexican communities are forming strong roots within a U.S. working-class and leisure culture that emphasizes hard work, discipline, manhood, individuality, and competitiveness and reflects both shortcomings and aspirations of the Mexican and Latino experiences in the United States.

Subjected to urban segregation, social inequality, the influence of the Spanish-language media, and the Mexican government's policies for "communities abroad," Midwestern soccer clubs provide an ideal sphere in which to observe the different ways in which Mexican and Latino populations in the United States are shaping and enacting their understanding of diverse issues: community organization, Americanization, Mexicanization, Latinization, the migratory experience, citizenship, memory, and identity.

Moreover, mexicanos have envisioned soccer as a social space in which to initiate political participation, contest the dominant culture, defy urban segregation, disprove negative ethnic stereotypes, construct and display transnational ethnic loyalties, and celebrate a notion of Mexicanness based on the Mexican experience in the United States.

Few scholars have focused on the social significance of organized sports in Latino communities in the United States. The scant research available focuses exclusively on baseball, football, and boxing.[2] Current Chicano historiography on Midwestern communities, despite a remarkable development in recent years, has not incorporated sports and recreational culture in its approach and debate.[3] The new sports history, on the other hand, has just recently begun to explore the complex connections between race, ethnicity, immigration, nation, and sports in urban settlements.[4]

Using oral histories and archival and newspaper research, I closely follow the history of two different soccer associations in Chicago and Detroit from 1940 to 1970: Club Social y Deportivo México (CSD México; founded in 1958) and Club Deportivo Necaxa (active in the 1940s and 1950s). Soccer fields have emerged as crucial spaces in which issues of ethnic identity, social organization, community awareness, cultural transmission, and transnational networks are thought out, displayed, negotiated, and enacted.

This chapter illustrates the process by which Mexican soccer fields in Midwestern metropolises emerged as multidimensional border spaces where transnational and transborder social relationships were created, performed, and experienced. There the mexicanos adopted outdoor leisure activities and sport rituals prevalent in U.S. cities. At the same time, however, the soccer players, their families, and their friends, along with the food vendors, musicians, and spectators mexicanized the urban landscape and manifested their right to public facilities.

The soccer field emerges therefore as a border space between players and sponsors, between recent Mexican immigrants and middle-class Mexican Americans, between the city government and the barrio, between the Mexican national state and the Mexican *colonia* (community), between all-male players and female nonplayers, between urban segregation and recreational sports, and between private and public rituals centered around ethnic food.

In the 1940s Mexican communities in the Great Lakes region began to sponsor soccer teams in amateur leagues organized by European immigrants. Soccer, however, did not initially represent a challenge to baseball as the preferred collective sport for Mexican communities across the United States. Numerous factors explain the dominance of baseball and basketball in the

Mexican barrios. Basketball, football, and baseball had the full support of the school system and especially the social programs of the Catholic church. Deeply involved with Americanization drives, both schools and churches dismissed soccer as an activity of little social value and instead emphasized the practice of the mainstream sports in the United States.[5] Soccer was considered as too rooted in Mexico to have a future in her neighbor to the north.

The central issue, however, was the fact that, before World War II, the majority of mexicanos in both the United States and Mexico unquestionably preferred baseball to soccer and therefore opted to play the former. In Midwestern communities, as Richard Santillán has pointed out, Mexicans overwhelmingly preferred baseball to any other sport and consequently organized baseball games, clubs, and leagues of their own, beginning in the 1920s.[6]

In 1936 NBC began broadcasting professional baseball games to Latin America.[7] Since the 1880s Mexican ball players had sporadically joined major league baseball (MLB) franchises. In the 1930s players of Mexican descent such as Vernon ("Lefty") Gómez, Mel Almada, and José ("Chili") Gómez played for the New York Yankees, the Boston Red Sox, and the Philadelphia Phillies respectively.[8] Besides, the Mexican National Baseball League began in 1925, two decades before the creation of a truly professional soccer league in Mexico. In the 1940s Mexican baseball teams even attempted to lure professional players from the United States. MLB had produced high-quality athletes such as "Beto" Avila, the American League batting champion in 1954, of the Cleveland Indians.[9]

British workers introduced soccer to Mexico in the late nineteenth century. White-collar and skilled workers in the mining, textile, and other industries owned and managed by British companies inaugurated amateur leagues in Pachuca, Mexico City, Puebla, and Orizaba. At the dawn of the twentieth century a number of British sports clubs were dedicated to or included soccer teams and participated in amateur tournaments. In 1902 the Liga Mexicana de Football Amateur Association, which was organized by British clubs in Mexico, established the first regular competition. Originally conceived as a British tournament, the soccer championship was dominated by teams such as the Pachuca Athletic Club, British Club, Puebla Athletic Club, and Reforma Athletic Club; these groups included mostly English, Scottish, or Irish players in their lineups. By 1912 other European teams with French, German, and Spanish immigrants had joined the league, along with the Club México, the first composed of predominantly Mexican-born players.

Elite Mexicans with educational or traveling experience in Great Britain and Europe also decided to form soccer clubs in Mexico City and Guadalajara; Club Atlas in Guadalajara was one of these.[10] In the 1920s, with the sponsorship of recently formed unions and government agencies, Mexican teams increased their participation. The Compañía de Luz y Fuerza (Power and Electricity Company), the Secretary of War and Navy, and other agencies subsidized them.[11] In 1922 the first Mexican Soccer Federation was born.[12] In the 1920s and 1930s soccer clubs, such as the Asturias, España, and Aurrerá, which were organized by Spanish immigrants, dominated the league and outnumbered the British groups. In the first Mexican national team, in fact, only four Mexican-born players had been nominated for its first international game in 1923 against Guatemala. Only after protests and the intervention of the Mexico City authorities were the Spanish-born players—the majority in the first list of nominees—excluded.[13]

In the 1930s soccer increased in popularity in urban areas, especially Mexico City, Guadalajara, Puebla, and León. Although Spanish teams continued to dominate the league, Mexican teams sponsored by union workers, local factories, and state agencies began to challenge their supremacy. The arrival of considerable numbers of Spanish immigrants and refugees from the Spanish Civil War (1936–1939) gave a major boost to Spanish athletic clubs and accentuated the increasing sports rivalry between Mexicans and Spaniards.

In Mexico City, two Mexican-based clubs emerged as the most popular among the lower classes: Atlante, organized by union railroad workers and nicknamed "los morenitos" (the dark ones), and Necaxa, founded in 1922 and run by the union workers at the electric power company. The working classes, who traditionally disliked the professional Spanish-centered teams, adopted Atlante and Necaxa as their own and strongly identified with their cause. Necaxa's *electricistas* gained considerable renown by conquering the league's title on various occasions in the 1930s, always against the Spanish teams.[14] The symbolic victories achieved by Necaxa turned it into the most popular club in Mexico City, and governmental authorities in the nationalist regime of Lázaro Cárdenas backed it financially.

In the 1940s, with the increasing urbanization in central Mexico, Jalisco, and the Bajío area, soccer made significant advances but remained practically unfamiliar to the rest of the country. The Mexican government played a significant role in boosting Mexicans' participation by limiting the number of foreign players on each team. In 1943 the Federación Mexicana de Fútbol

(FeMexFut) was completely reorganized; the sport was professionalized, and very ambitious plans were made to expand it nationwide.

Thus, prior to the consolidation of the FeMexFut in the 1940s, semiprofessional soccer teams were made up of Spanish immigrants, refugees, college students, and some state union workers, all geographically concentrated in the urban areas of western and central Mexico.

In the 1960s soccer became a prosperous entertainment industry. It was directed at masses of viewers and listeners and competed directly with boxing and wrestling for prime time broadcasting. Under the auspices of radio and TV networks, Mexican teams based in Mexico City, Guadalajara, León, Toluca, Pachuca, Puebla, and other cities took part in national championships. In the 1950s and 1960s the old rivalries between Mexicans and Spaniards gave way to regional and class-oriented competitions and affiliations. In Mexico City, the Club América became the heir of former Spanish clubs, while the Club Guadalajara concentrated the support and endorsement of working-class nationalist fans. Replacing Necaxa as the most popular team, the Guadalajara Chivas Rayadas (Striped Goats) had ample support from the state of Jalisco and all other cities with soccer franchises, given its straightforward policy of admitting only Mexican players in its lineups. In the late fifties and early sixties Guadalajara had the best winning record and won the national championship on several occasions. Only after the celebration of the Olympic Games in Mexico City in 1968 and the Soccer World Cup in Mexico in 1970 did soccer displace baseball, wrestling, and boxing as Mexico's favorite sport.

In the 1940s soccer emerged in Mexican barrios in the Midwest only as a marginal sport. The regional origins of Mexicans who were living in Chicago and Detroit did not contribute to its expansion. Industrial centers in the Great Lakes attracted significant numbers of Mexican and Mexican American workers from several locations, especially western Mexico and South Texas. Mexicanos who were former residents of Texas or who had been born there certainly preferred baseball. This was also true of Mexican immigrants from the border states, where baseball had prevailed for decades. Immigrants from western Mexico (Jalisco, Michoacán, Guanajuato, and Zacatecas) came from rural communities, where soccer was barely known and rarely played. In fact, the best-known ethnographies of villages in Michoacán and Jalisco in that era fail to mention soccer at all.[15] These areas, vital to the establishment of Midwestern barrios, it seems, had been largely unaffected by soccer's professional development and expansion.

However, Mexican immigrants in the Great Lakes area were not unfamiliar with soccer. Although rural communities in the 1930s and 1940s did not practice the sport in significant numbers, many immigrants became acquainted with it in different urban environments, especially Guadalajara, León, and Mexico City, before traveling to the United States. Despite the fact that soccer was not popular in his native Ciudad Hidalgo, Manuel Correa, founder of the Club Taximaroa in Chicago, for instance, played soccer in the second division in Salvatierra, Guanajuato, in the early 1950s while working in a factory.[16] Juan R. Hernández, a pioneer player in Detroit's CSD México, was born in the United States but learned to play soccer in Guadalajara after joining the youth league sponsored by Club Atlas.[17]

Soccer was thus introduced to the Mexican barrios in the Great Lakes region probably by Mexicans who were from Mexico's central and western industrial cities. As George J. Sánchez has demonstrated for Los Angeles between 1900 and 1945, many Mexican immigrants were born in rural villages but had significant experience as urban workers in Mexico before settling in the United States.[18] This particular group, along with a few middle-class Mexican immigrants and immigrants born in urban areas, constituted the original nucleus of soccer for Mexicans in the Great Lakes region.

One of the first organized soccer associations in the area was the Club Necaxa in Chicago. Necaxa became active in the late 1930s and participated in the Chicago National Soccer League (CNSL; founded in 1919) in the 1940s. Created by European immigrants and with teams from several ethnic European communities, the CNSL is still one of the strongest amateur leagues in the United States. Necaxa's entry into this association certainly provided a robust symbol for the Mexican colonias to gather around.

The selection of the team's name, after the Necaxa from Mexico City, who battled the "foreign" teams in the Mexican League in the 1930s, indicates a wish to create an association attractive to all Mexicans in Chicago and especially those with previous industrial and urban experience in Mexico. In its Chicago version, the Necaxa would compete against the European teams, just as their prototype in Mexico had campaigned against the Spanish teams in the previous decade, and would gain support from industrial and urban workers of Mexican descent in the Windy City. Unlike baseball in the area, where Mexican teams were excluded by both formal and subtle mechanisms from joining the regular leagues, soccer in the CNSL provided an opportunity for mexicanos to play against teams composed of white players on equal grounds, to gain respect from their opponents, and to disprove anti-Mexican stereotypes.[19] Necaxa enabled a healthy competition to develop between Mexicans and ethnic Europeans, who had been at odds since the late 1910s.[20]

Created as a voluntary association, the Club Necaxa played a prominent role in shaping recreational and social activities for people of Mexican descent in Chicago. The local Spanish-language newspaper and a Catholic newspaper published by the Chicago parish of St. Francis (*ABC* and *St. Francis Crier*, respectively) soon began covering the Necaxa's games and the club's increasing number of nonathletic activities.[21] The club very soon evolved into a community center that hosted social and cultural activities. For instance, on Saturday, December 2, 1946, the Club Deportivo Necaxa celebrated its annual "grandioso baile," *amenizado* (livened up) by the Latin band Pancho Villa, who played regularly in a *lugar céntrico de la ciudad* and had been hired especially for the occasion.[22]

Dances that were organized to raise funds for the club were not the only social activities. On December 15, 1946, the Club Necaxa organized its first *posada*, a traditional Christmas celebration in Mexico. The posada is a religious festival carried out generally by laypeople. With popular chants, food, music, and piñatas, the posada commemorates Mary and Joseph's journey to Bethlehem. The 1946 posada combined these traditions with modern live music, dancing, raffles, prizes, and "pleasant surprises for everybody," including piñatas and candy for the children.[23] Necaxa celebrated the posadas at the Centro Social Mexicano on Sunday nights and did not appear to emphasize the Catholic or other religious elements of the traditional festival. Besides this holiday event, the Necaxa participated in traditional Mexican parades and festivities in Chicago with its "soccer queens."[24]

The Club Necaxa also held various activities on weekdays. One of the club's pamphlets, printed in the 1940s, shows the wide variety of social events that took place on a regular basis at the club's hall on Roosevelt Road. On Monday nights the group provided classes in English as a second language. On Thursday nights the club scheduled the screening of "interesting movies and dancing afterwards." On Sunday afternoons, after the soccer match, members gathered for dancing and conversation. Everything was advertised as free for the club members and their families.

The long list of sponsors and advertisers in the pamphlet illustrates the immediate recognition and financial support that the Necaxa received from the increasing number of Mexican-oriented businesses. Advertisers and sponsors included ten restaurants, grocery stores, and meat markets; eight bars and liquor stores; six record stores; Spanish-language radio programs; two tailor shops; two printing houses; one car repair business; one shoe repair store; one pharmacy; and a funeral home.[25]

These local businesses oriented toward Mexicans marketed themselves as offering a blend of authentic Mexican goods and hospitality and modernized American services. Casino Monte Carlo, for instance, advertised music by Jesse Martínez and his Romantic Troubadours, along with its banquet saloon, which offered "everything modern and at reasonable prices." Casino Monte Carlo's advertisement portrayed its establishment as "el lugar preferido para el esparcimiento del trabajador" (the preferred place for the worker's leisure time). Moreover, Cantina Casa Blanca's ad pictured a blonde dancer and touted the saloon as "la más favorita y concurrida de todos los mexicanos" (the favorite [place] and attended by all Mexicans), while mentioning its "refrigeradora directa para tener muy bien helada la cerveza tal y como le gusta a usted" (refrigeration to keep the beer well chilled, just the way you like it).

As the Necaxa program illustrates, Mexican soccer teams in Midwestern urban environments could become centers for social activities that extended beyond the boundaries of sports competition. Closely connected with the interests of a rising ethnic entertainment industry and the growing purchasing power of Mexican workers in Chicago, Mexican soccer teams provided a golden opportunity to establish ties among Mexicans as consumers, as clientele, and as a community. The Club Necaxa also supplied an outlet to Spanish-language radio programs to advertise schedules and musical shows. Through the radio programming in Spanish, Mexicans could have access to Mexican and Latin American music. For instance, every Saturday at 2 P.M., station WGES aired the "Hora Azteca" (Aztec Hour), while on Saturdays at 3:30 P.M. WEDC aired the "Hora Mexicana y Pan-Americana." Those new consumer tastes combined Mexican products and practices with modern, efficient U.S. standards.

No less important were the efforts of the Club Necaxa to teach English as a second language and to structure a recreational and social life for urban laborers. These activities were intended to familiarize Mexicans with a new industrial environment and to facilitate their assimilation into American standards of leisure and participation in voluntary associations. The club's activities clearly reflect a decision to articulate a social life for Mexicans in

Chicago on a permanent basis while cultivating Mexican cultural features more in accordance with the urban setting in the United States.

The Club Necaxa's range of social activities illustrates the ways in which Mexican workers in Chicago responded to various influences: a growing ethnic market that combined Mexican culture with American consumption patterns, an increasing need to create leisure and recreational spaces for an emerging working-class community, a growing desire to adjust to American standards of living, and a profound desire to find ways to represent the Mexican experience in Chicago as successful, prosperous, and harmonious with other immigrant groups, especially the Europeans.

Necaxa was thus a source of ethnic pride and a self-made image of the Mexican community that conveyed a message of athletic accomplishment, national identification, and personal diligence. Necaxa represented the Mexicans in Chicago's international arena as yet another immigrant group with a thriving culture and a positive contribution to make. As Mexicans in Chicago entered the urban and industrial labor force in large numbers in the 1940s, their discretionary time and budget expanded considerably, providing a social space for recreational activities. In her 1928 thesis on social conditions prevalent in Mexican neighborhoods in Chicago, Anita Jones described an increasing need for organized recreational activities.[26] Soccer teams provided not only a response to these new social expectations but also a chance to portray the Mexican community in positive terms, to re-create national symbols in a new country, and to foster a consumer culture oriented toward Mexican food, music, and entertainment.

In the closing statement of the club's pamphlet, the board of directors emphasized the identification of Necaxa with the Latin American community's hopes and aspirations:

> Necaxa Sports Club respectfully thanks the support provided by the Latin American community to its soccer foot-ball team and to its club in general in all the activities in the present year. Necaxa Sports Club hopes that [Latin Americans will] continue to help and motivate the team in the future, to always keep in high regard the name of our club and the pride of our race.
> Respectfully
> The Board of Directors[27]

In Detroit the colonia mexicana started to organize soccer clubs along the lines of the Necaxa Club team. The Detroit Soccer League, a predominantly European-immigrant organization, included several teams based on national origins (e.g., Lithuanians, Poles, Syrians, Greeks, Armenians, Russians). One team, named Hispanos Unidos (United Hispanics), was run by Spanish nationals but allowed players from Latin America to join. In the 1950s some of the Mexican players decided to branch out and create their own national team. In 1958 they created the Club Social y Deportivo México, under the management of Salvador Rojas and Román Pérez. The core of the group worked at the Ford Plant and the Great Lakes Steel Corporation. In 1948, when he was fourteen, Rojas had arrived from Jamay, Jalisco, to join relatives. In 1956 he was hired at the Ford Plant, where he worked until his retirement.[28]

Although CSD México did not have striking success in its first few seasons, it soon became an important social hub for the Mexican colonia in southwest Detroit. CSD México wore a uniform identical to that worn by the Club Guadalajara, the most popular soccer team in Mexico since the 1950s due to its winning record and its nationalist features. As with Chicago's Necaxa, the adoption of Guadalajara's uniform in Detroit represented an ethnic affirmation for Detroit Mexicans and, in particular, for those born in Jalisco. In its choices of name and uniform, the CSD México combined its desire to represent all Detroit Mexicans on the playing field and to emphasize the nationalism and regionalism displayed by the Chivas Rayadas in Mexico.[29]

Patton Park, where CSD México played, soon became a regular gathering place for Mexican families, who organized their Sunday activities around the games. Alex Rojas, Salvador's son, remembers that, every Sunday, players and their families first attended mass at Holy Trinity and then went together to Patton Park for the soccer match. While the game was on, the children played their own games, and families held picnics with Mexican products bought in La Colmena, the only Mexican grocery store.[30]

For Mexicans in the urban Midwest, the Sunday get-togethers became meaningful social events, of which the athletic competition was merely one of many activities. In Lansing, Michigan, for instance, the Cardinals, a Mexican American baseball team, began playing at Washington Park in 1963: "While the games were played, picnic tables were moved under shady trees and grills were used to cook traditional Mexican food like fajitas and chicharrones. The Latin American atmosphere also attracted migrant workers from nearby towns who were looking for a place to relax with their families on weekends.

The park had plenty of room for children to play and the events allowed them to interact with other Latin Americans in the Lansing area. 'Even people who didn't like baseball enjoyed picnics with family on a Sunday after church.'"[31] When the CSD México overcame consecutive losing seasons in the Detroit Soccer League (DSL), it became a serious contender as its player base widened in the Mexican community. The team had formal coaches, trained twice a week in summer, and used local gyms in winter as indoor facilities.

The association also registered as an official organization with formal elections, statutes, and regular membership. Envisioning a physical base, in 1960 the organizers of CSD México rented a hall on Michigan Avenue, near Tiger Stadium, to host social gatherings on weekdays. Diverse activities took place in the clubhouse: raffles, dances, domino games, and other *juegos de mesa* (tabletop games).[32] Following the Necaxa's path, Detroit's CSD México provided an opportunity to use recreational facilities, enter a voluntary association, structure a social life after work, reaffirm Mexican culture, and re-create Mexican traditions in combination with American values.

In the late 1970s the majority of pioneer players were no longer active in the fields and were in the process of retiring from their regular jobs. The CSD México remained a voluntary sport association until 1978, when the franchise was transferred to the owner of a local bar. The CSD México remained active until the discontinuation of the DSL in 1984 and 1985.

Through these voluntary ethnic sports associations, Mexicans and Mexican Americans in Chicago and Detroit created a social space in which they renewed their Mexican traditions and adjusted to life in the Great Lakes region. Interethnic competition in these communities provided an opportunity to disprove negative Mexican stereotypes and instead portray the Mexican presence in the Midwest as a success story. In that sense the Mexican soccer clubs mirror an experience in social organization similar to that of ethnic European sports clubs, their constant rivals and comrades. Moreover, soccer provided an arena in which they could compete with other immigrant and native players on equal ground. This enabled the players to achieve symbolic ethnic victories and foster an ethnic Mexican pride, much as the African American soccer teams and boxers did.[33] As participants in the ethnic European soccer leagues, the Mexican soccer clubs also gained visibility and respect from the outside community and secured access to otherwise limited outdoor recreational facilities.

The nonathletic achievements of the Mexican clubs in Chicago and Detroit are, however, considerably more important than the sport victories they won on the playing field. Both the CSD México and the Club Necaxa became authentic community centers for Mexican families in the urban landscape and responded to their desire to articulate a commitment to reside permanently in the United States.

Unlike other voluntary associations, however, these clubs did not have an explicit political agenda with regard to immigration, naturalization, class exclusivity, or other divisive issues among Mexicans in the United States. They also did not limit membership to particular subgroups within the Mexican colonia.[34] U.S.-born Mexicans, longtime and economically stable Mexican immigrants, and recent arrivals could participate in the clubs equally. This politically neutral and inclusive feature made the soccer clubs ideal voluntary organizations for people of Mexican descent.

In addition, these voluntary organizations functioned as social spaces within which to develop leadership skills. Salvador Rojas, for instance, president of CSD México in the 1960s, was later elected president of the Comité Patriótico Mexicano in Detroit for six years.

Centered partly on the athletic performance of its players but more importantly on the family and communal activities before, during, and after the soccer games, soccer clubs generated a sense of a place for men, women, and children, in which each subgroup could socialize in its own way. For those who attended these gatherings but did not actually play, the athletic performance and the game's outcome were practically irrelevant, compared with the opportunity to socialize and establish networks with other families. Far from undergoing a process of "aborted assimilation," as has been suggested, Mexican communities in Chicago and the Great Lakes area turned their baseball, soccer, and other voluntary sport associations into new venues to claim access to urban spaces and create social zones in which they could develop and consolidate a sense of community and shared experience.[35]

Richard Santillán has pointed out that, for Mexican baseball teams in the Midwest, sports events contained important elements of political empowerment, cultural unity, and community identity.[36] The history of the Necaxa and México clubs corroborates these findings.

As George Sánchez has demonstrated in his study of Mexican immigrants in Los Angeles, mexicanos reshaped their native traditions in a complex process of cultural adaptation and negotiation in response to the challenges posed by their new environment and their expectations of creating a permanent life in the United States.[37] Vicky Ruiz has analyzed the social interactions of Mexican women who participated in Americanization projects in El Paso. Her work elucidates the emergence of an intense process of cultural coalescence.[38] The mexicanas responded to their new environment by creating social spaces that addressed their particular needs and affirmed their ethnic culture: "They [Mexican American women] navigated across multiple terrains at home, at work and at play. They engaged in cultural coalescence. The Mexican-American generation selected, retained, borrowed, and created their own cultural forms."[39] The history of the Mexican soccer clubs in the Great Lakes region provides another example of such interactions and the creative ways the Mexican communities reshaped and generated their sports and recreational traditions to build a better life in the United States.

NOTES

1. This chapter is part of a broader research project on the impact of organized sports on urban Mexican communities in the Great Lakes area between 1940 and 2000. I would like to thank Manuel Correa, Luís Soto, Juan R. Hernández, Alex Rojas, and Franco Hernández Borja for their invaluable help and generosity. Preliminary versions of this chapter were presented at different conferences and seminars. I thank the following people for their comments and suggestions: Deborah Kanter, Theresa Meléndez, Lisa Fine, Leslie Moch, Anne Rubenstein, Antonia Castañeda, and Luz María Gordillo. I have received generous support for this research from the Great Lakes Culture Institute, the Race Initiative Project, and the Chicano/Latino Studies Program at Michigan State University.

2. See Samuel O. Regalado, "The Minor League Experience of Latin American Baseball Players in Western Communities, 1950–1970," *Journal of the West* 26 (1987): 65–70; Samuel O. Regalado, "Baseball in the Barrios: The Scene in East Los Angeles since World War II," *Baseball History* 1 (1996): 47–59; Samuel O. Regalado, *Viva Baseball!: Latin Major Leaguers and Their Special Hunger* (Chicago: University of Illinois Press, 1998); Adrián Burgos, "Playing America's Game: Latinos and the Performance and Policing of Race in North American Professional Baseball, 1869–1959," Ph.D. diss., University of Michigan, 2000; Richard Santillán, "Mexican Baseball Teams in the Midwest, 1916–1965: The Politics of Cultural Survival and Civil Rights," *Perspectives in Mexican American Studies* 7 (2000): 131–51; Gil Salazar and Noé Hernández, *Lansing's Latin American Leagues: History in the Making* (East

Lansing: Michigan State University, 2000); and Gregory Rodríguez, "Palaces of Pain, Arenas of Mexican American Dreams: Boxing and the Formation of Ethnic Mexican Identities in Twentieth-century Los Angeles," Ph.D. diss., University of California–San Diego, 1999.

3. For scholarly works on Mexicans in the Midwest, see Dionicio N. Valdés, *Barrios Norteños: St. Paul and Midwestern Mexican Communities in the Twentieth Century* (Austin: University of Texas Press, 2000); Juan R. García, *Mexicans in the Midwest, 1900–1932* (Tucson: University of Arizona Press, 1993); and Zaragosa Vargas, *Proletarians of the North: A History of Mexican Industrial Workers in Detroit and the Midwest, 1917–1933* (Berkeley: University of California Press, 1993). Only the research by Valdés includes historical developments for the second half of the twentieth century.

4. See Steven A. Riess, *City Games: The Evolution of American Urban Society and the Rise of Sports* (Chicago: University of Illinois Press, 1989); Steven A. Riess, *Major Problems in American Sport History* (Boston: Houghton Mifflin, 1997); S.W. Poppe, *Patriotic Games: Sporting Traditions in the American Imagination, 1876–1926* (New York: Oxford University Press, 1997); S.W. Pope, ed., *The New American Sport History: Recent Approaches and Perspectives* (Chicago: University of Illinois Press, 1997); and Alan Bairner, *Sport, Nationalism, and Globalization: European and North American Perspectives* (Albany: State University of New York Press, 2001).

5. Santillán, "Mexican Baseball Teams in the Midwest, 1916–1965," 132–34.

6. Ibid.

7. Regalado, *Viva Baseball!* 175–77.

8. See Burgos, "Playing America's Game," 176.

9. Regalado, *Viva Baseball!* 16, 55.

10. See http://www.atlas.naranya.com/index.php.

11. See Javier Bañuelos, *Balón a tierra: Colección crónica del fútbol mexicano, 1896–1932* (Mexico City: Editorial Clío, 1997).

12. See http://www.femexfut.org.mx/portal/index.php.

13. See http://www.femexfut.org.mx/portal/index.php; also Carlos Calderón Cardoso, *La selección nacional I: Con el orgullo a media cancha (1923–1970)* (Mexico City: Editorial Clío, 1997).

14. See http://www.rayos.org/; also Carlos Calderón Cardoso, *Por amor a la camiseta: Colección crónica del fútbol Mexicano, 1933–1950* (Mexico City: Editorial Clío, 1997).

15. See Ralph L. Beals, *Cherán: A Sierra Tarascan Village* (Washington, D.C.: U.S. Government Printing Office, 1946); Donald Brand, *Quiroga: A Mexican Municipio* (Washington, D.C.: U.S. Government Printing Office, 1951); George M. Foster, assisted by Gabriel Ospina, *Empire's Children: The People of Tzintzuntzán* (Washing-

ton, D.C.: Smithsonian Institution Publications in Social Anthropology no. 6, 1948); Paul S. Taylor, *A Spanish-Mexican Peasant Community: Arandas in Jalisco, Mexico* (Berkeley: University of California Press, 1933).

16. Manuel Correa, interview by author, Chicago, Nov. 2000.
17. Juan R. Hernández, interview by author, Detroit, Sept. 2001.
18. George J. Sánchez, *Becoming Mexican American: Ethnicity, Culture, and Identity in Chicano Los Angeles, 1900-1945* (New York: Oxford: Oxford University Press, 1993), 44-47.
19. See Salazar and Hernández, *Lansing's Latin American Leagues;* Santillán, "Mexican Baseball Teams in the Midwest, 1916-1965."
20. See David Stafford Weber, "Anglo Views of Mexican Immigrants: Popular Perceptions and Neighborhood Realities in Chicago, 1900-1940," Ph.D. diss., Ohio State University, Columbus, 1982, 134-61.
21. See Deborah Kanter, "We Are the Good Neighbors!: Parish and Neighborhood in Mexican Chicago, 1942-1965," paper presented at the annual meeting of the American Historical Association, San Francisco, Jan. 3-6, 2002, 10.
22. "Grandioso baile en el West End Women's Club . . . dedicado al equipo de Foot-Ball 'Necaxa.'" Chicago Area Project, Box 49, Chicago Historical Society. I would like to thank Deborah Kanter for bringing this document to my attention.
23. Poster, ABC, año X, epoca IX, número 870, Chicago, December 21, 1946.
24. Rita Arias Jirasek and Carlos Tortolero, *Mexican Chicago* (Chicago: Arcadia, 2001), 57.
25. "Grandioso baile en el West End Women's Club."
26. Anita Jones, "Conditions surrounding Mexicans in Chicago," master's thesis, University of Chicago, 1928, 66.
27. "Grandioso baile en el West End Women's Club."
28. Alex Rojas, interview by author, Detroit, Sept. 2001.
29. For a history of the Club Guadalajara in Mexico and its enormous popularity in Jalisco and central Mexico in the 1950s and 1960s, see Greco Sotelo Montaño, *Chivas: La construcción de un orgullo* (Mexico City: Editorial Clio, 1999).
30. Franco ("Borja") Hernández, interview by author, Detroit, Sept. 2001.
31. Salazar and Hernandez, *Lansing's Latin American Leagues,* 19.
32. Rojas interview.
33. For the role of ethnic sports clubs for European immigrants, see Riess, *City Games,* 256, 114-17.
34. See David G. Gutiérrez, *Walls and Mirrors: Mexican Americans, Mexican Immigrants, and the Politics of Ethnicity* (Berkeley: University of California Press, 1995); and David G. Gutiérrez, "Migration, Emergent Ethnicity, and the 'Third Space': The Shifting Politics of Nationalism in Greater Mexico," *Journal of American His-*

tory: Rethinking History and the Nation State: Mexico and the United States as a Case Study (Special Issue) 86(2) (Sept. 1999): 481–518.

35. Louise Año Nuevo Kerr, "The Chicano Experience in Chicago: 1920–1970," Ph.D. diss., University of Illinois–Chicago, 1976, 116–58.

36. Santillán, "Mexican Baseball Teams in the Midwest, 1916–1965," 146.

37. Sánchez, *Becoming Mexican American*, 271–74.

38. Vicki L. Ruiz, *From out of the Shadows: Mexican Women in Twentieth-century America* (New York: Oxford University Press, 1998), 50.

39. Ibid., 67.

WEARING THE RED, WHITE, AND BLUE TRUNKS OF AZTLÁN
Rodolfo "Corky" Gonzales and the Convergence of American and Chicano Nationalism
TOM I. ROMERO II

When Rodolfo ("Corky") Gonzales, chair of the Crusade for Justice, filed a $30 million libel suit against the *Rocky Mountain News* in February 1974, he was not merely suing a local newspaper for its inaccurate representation of those involved in his organization.[1] Gonzales was also using a revered U.S. institution—the courts—to challenge the terms and conditions upon which the local mainstream press, another venerated institution, portrayed the goals and objectives of the Chicano movement. A few years earlier, Gonzales had described his feelings about the nation's mainstream media: "The press is a powerful voice feeding ideas, conventional falsehoods, and biased opinions by their daily brainwashing bombardment that mesmerizes and hypnotizes our American public in a state of apathetical drowsiness and confused patriotism."[2] Despite such rhetoric, however, Gonzales's lawsuit against the *Rocky Mountain News* suggested that he understood how the press could effect social change.[3] In arguing that the press had the ability to plant "the seed of guilt, doubt or misunderstanding in other people's minds," Gonzales recognized the ability of a public representation to seriously undermine the ability of Chicanos and Chicanas to mobilize against inequity and injustice in the United States.[4]

More than twenty years earlier, however, Palmer Hoyt, the young publisher of the *Denver Post,* had described a much different role for the press in the cause of social change. According to Hoyt, "The only protection that American civil liberties have, and thus minority groups, is in the free press of America. In the free press, which includes newspaper[s], radio, magazines, and motion pictures, everybody gets a chance to present their side."[5] Although Hoyt believed that the unfettered presentation of ideas would uphold American values, he knew that such representations would not lead to radical or rapid change—and to him, this was a good thing. To a fellow publisher who had recently come into conflict with members of Colorado's Chicano community, Hoyt had this caustic reply: "We have to keep working with them, and one of the best ways to do a job is printing all of their demands. There are many reasons for this, but one of these is . . . the unreasonableness of their demands, due largely to the fact that they have no leaders to whom they listen. It makes it important that the rank and file of the Chicanos and the public generally know or just find out how preposterous their demands and requests are."[6]

Alluding to the "militant" stances taken by Colorado Chicano such as Gonzales and the Crusade for Justice, Hoyt implied that the civil liberty demands of Chicano nationalists were not legitimate in the minds of the American public. Rather than a reasonable claim to be part of multicultural and multiracial United States, Gonzales's rhetoric, which included an appeal for Chicano nationalism, represented to Hoyt—and to others in the Colorado press—a rejection of the nation they envisioned.

While Hoyt, along with his fellow editors and publishers, held a largely negative view of Chicano and Chicana activists, he ignored the ways in which the "free press" in the United States was a crucial component in shaping the public persona and political emergence of Gonzales in the formative years of the Chicano movement. Indeed, Hoyt failed to grasp the language and symbolism of America in the Chicano nationalism articulated by Corky Gonzales. For a majority of Chicanos and Chicanas, racial, gender, class, and ethnic biases have limited their ability to influence public representations of themselves.[7] Yet social justice activists like Gonzales have relied heavily upon the news media to advance their particular cause.[8] As Gonzales demanded concessions from U.S. society while positioning his place in the Chicano community, his public image in the media was critical to his ultimate failure or success.

The surfacing of Gonzales in the mainstream press and his subsequent political capital rested in part on his connection to the ideas, imagery, and symbols of the United States. As Gary Gerstle notes, nationalism has forced "virtually every group seriously interested in political power . . . to couch their program in the language of Americanism."[9] The press has been one of the most important agents in transmitting and, in many cases, shaping the language and perceptions of the nation.[10] Most importantly, Gonzales's public emergence occurred at the precise historical moment that American civic and racial nationalism came together to transform the meaning of "nation" in a multicultural, multiracial United States.[11]

Catalyzed by the threat that racial oppression posed to national and international perceptions of American values and ideals, the interests of whites and people of color came together in forums such as newspapers to challenge conventional understandings of inequality.[12] The convergence of interests, however, unleashed further alterations in the varied meanings of "race" and "nation." As one set of actors in this transformation, Chicano cultural nationalists self-consciously rejected a color-blind civic Americanism in favor of "a common anti-American language of Chicanismo to press their demands."[13] Ironically but not surprisingly, one of the most recognizable proponents of Chicano cultural nationalism rose to prominence as a result of his long-standing association with highly mutable American ideals.

This chapter explores the relationship between American and Chicano nationalism through the public representation of Rodolfo ("Corky") Gonzales in the mainstream newspapers of Denver, Colorado, his hometown. The story begins in 1947, when Gonzales became engaged in a complex and increasingly tumultuous relationship with Denver's mainstream press. Entering the public consciousness as a boxer in the late 1940s, Gonzales quickly rose to prominence in the scandal-ridden profession. As a skilled, honest, and hard-working Mexican American fighter, Gonzales represented the consummate American hero to sportswriters in Denver's two mass-circulation dailies, the *Rocky Mountain News* and the *Denver Post*.

Most importantly, his early public identity in Denver was inexorably intertwined with his value in resurrecting the fortunes of professional prizefighting in the city. As Gonzales retired from boxing and entered the political ring, the newspapers' portrayal of him as an "all-American" boxer was infused with racial and ethnic meaning. Such representations informed his well-publicized emergence as the nationalistic and militant leader of young Chicanos in the 1960s.[14] As Gonzales made the journey from boxer to Democratic operative to cultural nationalist, his all-American boxing image converged with the vision of Chicano self-determination that he would embrace.

BOXING'S ALL-AMERICAN SAVIOR

In 1951, Rodolfo ("Corky") Gonzales was on top of the world. It was August 21, and Gonzales had just won a grueling, ten-round decision over his opponent, Charley Riley, before 3,622 screaming fans in Denver's city auditorium.[15] This was not, however, just another win. By defeating Riley, who was ranked as the number three contender for the featherweight title in the nation, Gonzales served notice to the boxing world that he was one of the top fighters in the United States. Moreover, his victory was more than just a personal achievement. It was also a triumph for the boxing fans of Denver, a city that had endured years in which the drama, action, and excitement of professional prizefighting had become a faded memory. The crowd at the Gonzales-Riley bout appeared to herald the reemergence of Denver as a "main event" boxing venue.

The misfortunes that plagued Denver boxing were symptomatic of deeper and more serious ills infecting the sport. The ineptitude of the Colorado Boxing Commission and the absence of well-funded local fight promoters were minor nuisances compared to the widespread perception of professional boxing as virulently corrupt.[16] Perhaps the most dramatic and pivotal event that confirmed these suspicions occurred in 1947. Before a grand jury in New York City, Rocky Graziano, the "Golden Boy" of boxing, who, next to Joe Louis, was the biggest drawing card in the sport, admitted that he had been offered $100,000 to throw a fight against Denver fighter Reuben Shank.

The Gonzales-Riley bout and the overflow crowd that packed the auditorium marked the long comeback of respectability to Denver's professional rings. Central to this resurgence was Corky Gonzales. Having proved himself in the local amateur ranks by winning two Golden Gloves titles in 1946 and 1947, Gonzales became an immediate local sensation when he became the bantamweight champion of the national Amateur Athletic Union (AAU) in April 1947.[17] Not surprisingly, the Denver papers gave significant coverage to the new title holder. For instance, following Gonzales's coronation as the AAU national champion, the *Rocky Mountain News* described the manner in which he captured the city's—and the newspaper's—imagination: "Corky

Gonzales will lead the *News*-Elks team into action against the famed Cleveland Golden Gloves in the banner boxing show at City Auditorium next Wednesday night. The classy 18-year-old bantamweight from the East side will return home as the first national champion out of Denver since the early '20s, when Eddie Eagan, now chairman of the New York Boxing Commission, was crowned lightheavyweight king. . . . Gonzales' appearance on the card will highlight what promises to be the finest amateur boxing event ever held in this city."[18] In winning the title, Gonzales brought more than just a championship belt back from New York. For the *Rocky Mountain News* at least, he returned vintage pugilism to a disillusioned boxing city.

Gonzales's championship held implications beyond returning high-caliber boxing to the Mile High City. In the months following Rocky Graziano's dramatic testimony against a Denver fighter, Gonzales's rise through the amateur ranks accentuated crucial distinctions between the amateur and professional spheres. Unlike professional fighters, amateur pugilists usually boxed under the colors of local boxing clubs. With success at the local level, an amateur fighter could go on to fight for his city, his state, and even his country. Not fighting for money, with its corrupting influence, an amateur instead fought for the honorable reward of local, state, and national pride. Hence, Gonzales's amateur training signified all that was right with the sport.[19] This distinction was not lost on Denver's newspapers. For both dailies, it was a matter of great consequence that Gonzales had become the first national champion from Colorado since the early 1920s. In winning the AAU national bantamweight championship, Gonzales secured a measure of national respect that had not been given to a Colorado fighter in more than twenty years.

The Denver newspapers emphasized that Gonzales had not become champion by being soft, lazy, or susceptible to questionable influences. Instead, as Chet Nelson of the *Rocky Mountain News* pointed out, Gonzales became a boxer "the hard way," earning bumps and bruises in his rise through the amateur ranks.[20] For sportswriters like Nelson, amateur experience held immeasurable benefits for Denver's youth. In local Catholic high school programs, the YMCA, public schools, and recreation centers, boxing teachers were waging a "campaign against delinquency" in Denver and other urban areas. Amateur boxing provided lessons, skills, and virtues from "which [boys] returned better adjusted to modern life."[21] Yet boxing encompassed more than just character building. As the *Rocky Mountain News* made patently clear, the crucible of the ring forged "clean-cut, red-blooded American boys."[22]

To Denver's two major dailies, Gonzales, with his exemplary record as an amateur, represented all that was ideal.

In one memorable photograph in the *Rocky Mountain News,* a beaming Gonzales, clothed in an argyle sweater, playfully pulled the hair of his AAU teammate Ernest ("Red") Martínez. With a caption describing the action as "a bit of friendly hair pulling" to test the player's strength, the picture had meaning far beyond what the accompanying article could convey.[23] Reflecting precisely what could not be fully articulated in the text, the picture demonstrated how Corky and Red were ideal "clean-cut, red-blooded American boys." Moreover, they were not solely boxers. Taken outside of the ring, the photograph implied that these young men were also upstanding citizens. Hence, the meaning of the picture was clear: With his youthful purity, amateur training, and boxing skill, Gonzales represented the type of local fighter who could propel boxing back to respectability in the Mile High City.

Turning pro near the end of 1947, Gonzales carried his clean-cut amateur image into his professional career. Fittingly, both the *Rocky Mountain News* and the *Denver Post* gave strong support to Gonzales when he took on this new challenge. Yet the backing of both dailies did not stem only from a desire to cover a local boy who had made good. For Denver's sportswriters, Gonzales represented a remedy to the ills affecting professional boxing in the city. Particularly when Gonzales fought in Denver, both papers heralded his bouts as a major step forward for the city's boxing future. For instance, after Gonzales's first professional fight in Denver in 1948—in which he scored a unanimous decision over Howard Jackson—the *Denver Post* declared that professional boxing had "hit the comeback trail," thanks in large part to the "flashy straight punching" and popularity of the Denver fighter.[24]

Despite Gonzales's success, the comeback of boxing in Denver was not guaranteed. Knowing that payoffs there were not nearly as lucrative as in other major cities, Gonzales and other professional fighters largely avoided contests within the city. It was not until two years later, in August 1950, that Gonzales once again captured Denver's boxing imagination when he agreed to fight Cuban pugilist Luís Galvani in City Auditorium. Significantly, both newspapers emphasized that this fight would be an excellent meter to test the "weak pulse" of boxing in Denver.[25] As a result, the future of boxing there appeared to rest on the shoulders of two young Latino men. Although Gonzales was knocked out for the first time in his professional career, Denver's newspapers were mesmerized by the details of the fight. For the sportswriters, the Gonzales-Galvani fight represented the pure ideal and potential of professional prizefighting in Denver. In an editorial headlined "Two Little Guys Do Boxing a Big Deed," Marvin McCarthy of the *Denver Post* trumpeted the complete turnaround of professional boxing in the city: "Citizens who formerly had been furtive about it were walking Denver's main streets Saturday openly bragging they were boxing fans, the fighters themselves had discarded masks and smoked glasses, managers were giving their right names. . . . Boxing, you see, once again had become a respectable pursuit in Denver and had ceased to be some sort of dark doings practiced down the levees and up tenderloin alleys."[26]

Central to this change was Gonzales and the raw determination he displayed in the ring. Repeatedly knocked down by Galvani, Gonzales constantly returned to his feet. As McCarthy declared, "With his demonstration of pure courage that adventure authors write about, Gonzales probably made more friends in defeat . . . than he ever did in victory." Even though he was overwhelmed, Gonzales won the hearts of many who had become disillusioned with professional prizefighting.[27] For the sportswriters of Denver, the reemergence of boxing could not be discussed without speaking of the talent, determination, and pure courage of Corky Gonzales.

WHAT COLOR ARE THOSE TRUNKS ANYWAY?

While the Galvani fight established Gonzales's importance to boxing in Denver, it also highlighted the way in which Denver's two major dailies made explicit and implicit racial and ethnic distinctions between the hometown Gonzales and his non-Anglo opponents. Denver's mainstream press framed the Gonzales-Galvani fight in terms that stressed Galvani's foreignness and his inability to speak English. For example, when commenting about the prefight open house that was held the morning before the contest, McCarthy argued that "Galvani is mighty lucky. He doesn't speak English, nor does he read it. Therefore, he gets off light and cannot possibly be required to wade through the stuffy details herein."[28]

Even more overtly, Cahn drew clear national and ethnic distinctions between Galvani, the foreigner, and Gonzales, with his "native" hometown following. In an article Cahn pointed out that fight promoter Morris ("Lonesome Wolf") Salzer was calling for all "cigar makers" in Denver to come to the fight. Accordingly, Cahn explained that "Lonesome Wolf's predicament stems from the arrival of Luis [sic] Galvani and the discovery that the fistic champion of all Cuba does not understand the English language. Boxing protocol calls for Salzer to dig up a rooting section for Galvani when he tangles with Denver's Corky Gonzales. . . . Just imagine what will happen if the fans start yelling for Corky to 'sock him in the [sic] La Ponza' [sic] and there are no cigar makers around to warn Galvani in his native tongue that this means in the bread basket or downstairs."[29]

Remarkably, Leonard Cahn transformed the Spanish words *la panza* into a local expression that Denverites could easily understand. By juxtaposing the native Gonzales and his hometown fans to the foreign Galvani, Cahn articulated a multilingual America that embraced Gonzales's heritage. Although Galvani certainly understood the meaning of *la panza,* his Cuban citizenship prevented him from publicly participating in the discourse of Americanism taking place around the ring.

The Denver newspapers also highlighted Gonzales's distinct ethnic and racial background. To dramatize his fistic accomplishments, the *Rocky Mountain News* and the *Denver Post* would often refer to him as "Señor Corky Gonzales" from the east side of town.[30] The home of a large proportion of Denver's Mexican Americans and African Americans, the East Side was one of the most segregated and impoverished areas of the city.[31] For Gonzales, the references by sports journalists to this part of town did not carry ambiguous meanings. Instead, such allusions unequivocally defined his racial and ethnic identity as something other than white.

Underlying these suggestions of Gonzales's cultural background were important conceptions of what life in the ring represented to men of color in the United States. More than a career in which to make money, boxing offered a respectable way of life—one of a relative few—for people of color. In a revealing article, Jack Carberry, sports editor of the *Denver Post,* outlined the importance of boxing in racial uplift. Quoting William McGregor Keefe, "the brilliant sports editor of the *New Orleans Times-Picayune,*" Carberry related the following story: "Boxing is, and has always been a game which attracted what we are given to calling 'hungry youths.' By 'hunger' it is not necessarily meant that boys who engaged in boxing lacked sufficient actual food. Rather, the word has been used to indicate a group, or sections of our people. Here in the south that is why you see so many Negro fighters—why in some other sections the boxers are boys from the minority groups. These boys, for the most part, are lads who are willing to train, and to do so conscientiously, shunning the soft life and depriving themselves of pleasures and do[ing] a lot of road work."[32]

Although Denver was far from the South, Carberry pointed out that the same racial and ethnic attitudes were clearly at play. Even more important, the rough-and-tumble of the ring provided an important societal mission. As Carberry argued, "boxing provides for boys," especially "in minority group areas . . . an outlet for energies which otherwise might be directed toward delinquencies."[33] In the ring, Carberry believed, "minority boys" utilized their skills in productive and socially legitimate ways.

Correspondingly, when a young man of color like Gonzales became professional, it represented something altogether different from when a white boxer decided to make the same move. Importantly, white boxers served as a foil to the noble intentions of "minority" fighters. Again, Carberry—quoting William McGregor Keefe—outlined these distinctions: "The trouble is that the first thing the white fighter wants after he wins one or two bouts is an automobile. Boxers of the past knew that it was necessary to work out twenty rounds or so each day before engaging in a ten-round fight. They thought nothing of doing miles and miles of road work. The only road work the white fighter wants today is a dash in his convertible. There are white fighters who would not walk six blocks. Negro fighters in the south think nothing of doing five to ten miles of roadwork. When they get in the ring those phony legs of the white boys cave in on them."[34]

Reading between the lines, it is easy to perceive where much of the blame for the corruption of professional prizefighting lay. In their desire for immediate material compensation, white fighters had sullied the sport with poor preparation. Moreover, Keefe's attitude also implied fears concerning the sordid end to which such an approach to training could lead. Having neither the skill nor the stamina to stand in the ring, a white fighter might be tempted to throw a fight. This mindset shaped and refined the attitude of Denver's mainstream press toward Gonzales, whose association with Denver's East Side distinguished him as racially nonwhite and thus seemingly immune to corrupting influences. In an age of increasing racial and ethnic tensions in the United States, young men of color like Corky Gonzales represented the realization of the ideals of boxing.

Gonzales's actions as a professional boxer suggest that he worked to cultivate a positive image. In both newspapers he earned a reputation as an honest and hard-working pugilist. Conscious of corruption in the professional ranks, Gonzales signed contracts only with highly reputable and respected local promoters such as Morris ("Lonesome Wolf") Salzer, Jack Kanner, and K. S. Barnett whenever he fought in Denver. Additionally, Gonzales began to realize the importance of the mainstream press in bolstering his future success outside of the ring. In a turnabout in the days leading up to a rematch with Charley Riley in the spring of 1952, Gonzales redirected the ethnically and racially centered dialogue of the sports journalists into support for his own Chicano-oriented business.

During his training sessions, he began telling reporters of the grand opening of his new restaurant, Corky's Corner. Such a strategy provided widespread publicity. Postfight coverage in the *Rocky Mountain News* included the following: "Corky in business: Defeat before the dynamite fist of Charley Riley last night will not interfere with Corky Gonzales' grand opening of his new restaurant tonight. . . . The Denver featherweight will inaugurate 'Corky's Corner,' which will specialize in Mexican dishes."[35] The *Denver Post* ran a similar feature that praised Gonzales's entrepreneurial pursuits: "Corky has been . . . a pretty smart youngster. He saved enough out of his earnings to buy himself a little place he calls 'Corky's Corner' at Thirty-seventh and Walnut streets. He has cleaned it up real nice and has served notice in no uncertain language that it will be run the same way—clean as any tavern can be run. He is going to specialize in Mexican food—it will, he says, be good and hot."[36]

Although Gonzales lost to Riley, both Denver newspapers were still invested in his success. For the narrative that each paper created, the story needed an appropriate ending. With Riley's defeat of Gonzales, both papers realized that the end of Gonzales's boxing career was near. The *News* commented that "it's hard to believe that a youngster has reached the end of the fistic trail at 23 . . . but it was impossible to overlook the tell-tale signs the other night."[37] As a result, Denver's mainstream press strongly pulled for Gonzales's new restaurant to be a success. Carberry of the *Post* related a sentiment held by many: "We would like nothing better than to see Corky succeed financially—succeed to a point where he would never be tempted to take the gloves down off the peg again."[38] Importantly, Carberry's statement revealed the societal limitations of boxing as a professional career.

Ultimately, boxing was only a sport. It represented a means—of achieving success and respectability—rather than an end for men of color like Gonzales. Corky's Corner, on the other hand, was a symbol of everlasting achievement in U.S. society. In launching his restaurant, Gonzales was tapping into what one contemporary described as a sacred "American tradition," where "any ambitious youth with industry, average intelligence, and thrift [could] save enough to start a small business, and if he has real initiative and ability, can develop it into a profitable business of considerable size."[39] Gonzales's business venture allowed him to capture American ideals such as personal autonomy to a much greater degree than his boxing career enabled him to. No longer having to answer to managers, promoters, or the Colorado Boxing Commission, Gonzales was his own boss. Appropriately for Denver's two major dailies, Corky's Corner was the perfect reward for the bumps and bruises Gonzales had suffered in his attempt to achieve the American dream.

REENTERING "THE RING"

Retiring in 1953, Gonzales no longer graced Denver's sports pages. Instead, he turned his full-time attention toward making Corky's Corner a success. Rising out of Gonzales's restaurant venture was an increased awareness of the problems afflicting his East Side neighborhood.[40] As early as 1949, when Judge Phillip Gilliam of Denver's nationally renowned juvenile court made Gonzales an honorary probation officer, Gonzales began to understand the troubles of Denver's Chicano community, and he came to see that many of the problems centered on Mexican American youth and their high rates of criminal incarceration. As Judge Gilliam soberly stressed, Mexican American cases accounted for "more than 50 percent" of his daily docket.[41] Influenced by the judge, Gonzales became actively involved with Gilliam's Friday night club for boys. Upon retiring from the professional ranks, Gonzales opened a free boxing gymnasium for barrio youth and visited local schools, where he gave inspirational talks aimed at keeping teenagers off the streets and out of trouble.

An important development in Gonzales's relationship with Judge Gilliam was his introduction to the world of politics. Partly because of his success in the ring and partly because of his nascent community activism, local Democratic leaders courted Gonzales in hopes of bringing him into the party fold.[42] Also influenced by the progressive priest Rev. Neal Patrick Moynihan, Gonzales took his first political steps when he walked door to door in the East Side to help elect Quigg Newton to a second term as Denver's mayor. Subsequently, Gonzales became vigorously engaged in many different politically active organizations. Using his boxing reputation as a stepping-stone, he participated in the Denver and Colorado GI Forum, the Latin American Educational Foundation, and the Good Americans Organization. Moreover, he did not restrict himself to membership in exclusively Mexican American organizations. Understanding the need for political patronage to rise in the Democratic ranks, Gonzales also became an active member of Anglo-dominated political associations such as the Knights of Columbus, the Nuggets' Booster Club, and the Friday Luncheon Club.

Gonzales's heightened political consciousness was by no means unique among Chicanos during the early 1950s. Throughout the Southwest, Mexican Americans increasingly became politically active in order "to forge a movement that would help break the economic, political, and cultural isolation of Mexican-Americans in the United States."[43] Dubbed the "Mexican American generation" by historians, citizens of Mexican descent formed political working groups such as the GI Forum and the Community Service Organization to protect and expand their rights.[44] As did pre-1950s Mexican American organizations such as the League of United Latin American Citizens or the Mexican American Movement, these postwar groups emphasized the rights and privileges of Mexican Americans as citizens of the United States. Yet the Mexican American generation of the 1950s wanted to "synthesize their experience based on their relationship to their Mexican roots, their Mexican American reality, and their search for an American future."[45] The search for an "American future" was perhaps the most important aspect of the political synthesis they advocated.

For an emerging Mexican American community leader like Gonzales, boxing and business success provided a prominent example of the realization of an "American future." This fact gave Gonzales an asset that many political leaders of the Mexican American generation did not possess. In the early 1950s the Democratic Party courted him because his success had won respect in both the Mexican American and the Anglo communities. In bringing Gonzales into the party fold, Democrats hoped to use him to tap the potential strength of the Mexican American vote. Paradoxically, as Gonzales ascended through Denver's political rings based on his community involvement, his boxing past rather than his participation in mobilizing Mexican Americans became an integral part of defining and explaining his political presence in Denver's two major dailies.

As in his boxing career, Gonzales had to prove himself in the political ring, and it would take years before he could be considered a contender. After retiring from boxing, Gonzales rarely appeared in either the *Rocky Mountain News* or the *Denver Post,* perhaps a reflection of his low position in the local Democratic political machinery; Gonzales simply did not possess the political clout that warranted much press coverage. A more plausible explanation, however, had to do with the benign neglect with which Denver's two major dailies had treated local Mexican American political leaders generally. One study of the period noted that, in Denver's mainstream press, "the Spanish-Americans and the later arrivals[,] the Mexicans[,] . . . received much the same treatment the colored man has in the south . . . The Spanish-speaking citizen was looked upon as only fit for labor in the sugar beet fields, in railroad section gangs, and other poorly paid tasks."[46] Unable to conceive that Mexican Americans could move beyond these occupations, writers and editors in both dailies, not surprisingly, did not believe that Chicano and Chicana political leaders even existed.

These attitudes had begun to shift when two socially conscious editors, Jack Foster of the *Rocky Mountain News* and Palmer Hoyt of the *Denver Post,* joined their respective papers in 1940 and 1946. Although Denver's mainstream press continued to portray the Mexican American community in a largely negative light, in the 1950s these representations were designed to arouse the paternalist sympathy of Denver residents rather than to provoke racial and ethnic antagonism. Beginning in the late 1940s, Denver, like many communities in post–World War II United States, established commissions to quell racial tension in the metropolis.[47]

Denver politicians, in particular those in Mayor Quigg Newton's administration, became concerned with the city's burgeoning Mexican American population. These concerns were strengthened by a study finding that Denver's largest minority was one of the most impoverished and troubled groups in the city.[48] The cause of the downtrodden meshed easily with the emerging agendas of Denver's mainstream press.[49] In one speech, Palmer Hoyt emphasized that "the civil rights issue does not involve just the struggle of . . . minorities to overcome the restrictions of second-class citizenship. It involves much more. It involves the conscience of the nation."[50] After stereotyping people of color for so long, Denver's mainstream press developed a "conscience" in relation to the needs and concerns of the city's minority communities.

The clearest example of this emerging attitude was a series of articles in the *Rocky Mountain News* in 1954. Launching the series as a "Study of Critical

Denver Problems," the *News* revealed the ambiguity with which Denver's Mexican American population had been perceived.⁵¹ Appropriately, this ambivalence began with the nomenclature the newspapers used to refer to Mexican Americans. Stated the *News,* "The phrase 'Spanish-American' is used in its inclusive, popular sense. It includes the Spanish-speaking and those with Spanish surnames. Actually, of course, Denver's 'Spanish-Americans' are not hyphenated persons. Most of them are native born United States citizens—the aliens among them are less than one-fortieth of their total—and their heritage is more Mexican and Indian than Castilian." After identifying the largely nonwhite genealogy of the group, the paper went on to discuss Denver's "Spanish-American problem." Over the following six days, the *Rocky Mountain News* documented a plethora of ills that apparently plagued the community. Stressing that "Spanish-Americans" had the highest crime, infant mortality, and high school dropout rates as well as the lowest incomes and worst housing of any of Denver's ethnic and racial groups, the *Rocky Mountain News* drew a bleak and tragic picture of the entire community.⁵²

Moreover, it was not just discrimination that led to such a situation. According to the *News,* the combined heritage of "American Indian and colonial Spaniard" left Denver's Spanish Americans "not well-suited to the ways of modern American life." Indeed, the paper argued that the cultural traditions derived from racial intermixing left "a lack of leadership in their own ranks."⁵³ Although a year later the *News* indicated that "recent months have seen some progress . . . toward Spanish-American leadership," such examples were muted in the face of racial and ethnic stigmatization.⁵⁴ Despite the participation and emergence of Mexican Americans such as Corky Gonzales in civic life, writers and editors at both the *Rocky Mountain News* and the *Denver Post* failed to find stories of community leaders and political activists to consistently highlight in their pages.

Between 1955 and 1964, detailed coverage of Gonzales's role in the "Spanish American" community was the exception rather than the rule. Instead, the brief appearances that Gonzales did make reflected the enduring legacy of his boxing past. For example, in the sparse coverage of his unsuccessful bid for a city council seat in 1955, both papers consistently referred to him as the "former professional boxer."⁵⁵ By highlighting his boxing past, both papers underscored the personal relationship that Gonzales had with Denver's citizens. Not Rudolph, Rodolfo, or Gonzales, he was instead often referred to by the more congenial "Corky." In using this nickname, both mainstream newspapers explicitly and implicitly distanced Gonzales from the tragic condition of the "Spanish American" community. Throughout the 1950s, his racially and ethnically neutral boxer image was instead the dominant theme.

In 1958 and 1959 Gonzales inadvertently jeopardized his personal relationship with Denver's mainstream press after he was arrested for allegedly assaulting an off-duty policeman at a Denver nightspot.[56] Covering the assault and the subsequent trial, both the *News* and the *Post* attempted to reconceptualize their vision of Corky Gonzales. In a significant extension of his past public representations, both papers created an image that highlighted his political and physical prowess as both a Democratic ward captain and a former professional boxer. For instance, after reporting the accusations by patrolman Frank Michaelson that Gonzales had beaten him over the head with the patrolman's own nightstick, the *Rocky Mountain News* made sure to inform readers that "Gonzales, at one time a ranking featherweight boxer, is the Democratic captain in North Denver District No. 3."[57] This theme continued during Gonzales's trial as both the *Rocky Mountain News* and the *Denver Post* created overt parallels to his boxing past. For example, on the first day of the trial, the *Denver Post* headlined its coverage: "Gonzales in 'Ring' with Jury." Opening the narrative by describing how the "featherweight boxer sat confidently in his corner . . . as his Denver Municipal Court main event got under way before a crowded courtroom of fans," the *Post* created a drama that had the same atmosphere and many of the same ingredients as any of Gonzales's seventy-five professional fights.[58]

Perhaps most important, the trial and subsequent coverage completed the amalgamation of Gonzales's boxing past and political present. During the second day of the trial, Democrats such as former agriculture secretary Charles F. Brannan, Colorado Supreme Court justice-elect and future federal judge William E. Doyle, Denver County Democratic chair Lawrence Henry, and State House leader Robert Allen all testified on Gonzales's behalf. In covering this development, the *Rocky Mountain News* noted that "four political pugilists . . . entered a Municipal courtroom ring on behalf of another veteran fighter—Corky Gonzales, Denver boxer."[59]

Accompanying the article was a picture of Gonzales as a young boxer. Together, photo and text suggested that Gonzales was "boxing" in the courtroom ring, with Denver political heavyweights serving as his ringside managers. A familiar image of Gonzales thus emerged in Denver's print media.

Not just a former boxing hero, Gonzales was also a comer in Denver's political rings.[60] Although the trial ended with a hung jury in which five of the six members voted for acquittal, it was revealed shortly afterward that the one juror who believed Gonzales was guilty was Arden H. Mitchell, a GOP precinct committeeman.[61] Remanded to trial, the case was eventually dropped by the Denver district attorney's office. The whole affair ultimately became more a matter of politics than of right or wrong, and coverage of the court case made known Gonzales's new fistic clout in Denver politics.

Although Gonzales would not again receive significant press attention until 1964, his trial and subsequent press coverage after 1959 highlighted critical transformations in future representations. Most important, the boundaries of Gonzales's boxing past were expanded to embrace his political present. No longer just a "former professional boxer," Gonzales became a pugilist of a much different kind. His rise in the local Democratic Party provided rich opportunities for Denver's mainstream press to use such metaphors. The court case highlighted the manner in which Gonzales's boxing past proved to be a tremendous asset in press representations. Although he may have assaulted an officer, the *Rocky Mountain News* and the *Denver Post* turned his trial into a boxing spectacle similar to his most important amateur and professional fights. From this point forward, Gonzales, in the mainstream media, always engaged someone or some cause in the metaphorical political ring. As he became more politically active and outspoken, his boxing past explained and perhaps justified to the public the politically belligerent stances that he would take.

THE GREAT BROWN HOPE

Having received his share of bruises and knockdowns in the Democratic Party, Gonzales appeared poised to fight in the more lucrative venues of the Denver political ring. While his service as a Democratic district captain demonstrated his loyalty to the party, Gonzales's success in registering large numbers of "Spanish American" voters made him a potential heavyweight contender. In 1960 Gonzales established his place with the Democratic Party when he coordinated Colorado's ¡Viva Kennedy! campaign. In the process, Gonzales orchestrated an unprecedented turnout of Chicano voters in support of the Democratic presidential ticket.[62] Reflecting trends throughout the Southwest in which "Mexican American activists self-consciously concentrated on mobilizing voters as an ethnic bloc," almost exclusively within the Democratic Party, Gonzales's success in registering Mexican American voters earned him an esteemed spot in the local Democratic Party ranks.[63]

He did not, however, always follow the party line. Earning a reputation for his outspoken and independent comments, Gonzales was not afraid of criticizing Democratic politicians.[64] Although local party leaders were unsure of how to interpret his political independence, his success in mobilizing Mexican American voters was something Democratic leaders could not ignore. Party leaders also recognized Gonzales for his active service on bodies such as the steering committee of the Antipoverty Program for the Southwest, the national board of Jobs for Progress, and the community board of the Job Opportunity Center. As a result, Gonzales was sought for his knowledge and expertise concerning the urban poor of Denver and the Southwest.[65]

At the same time, the "War on Poverty" began to take shape across the nation, following Pres. Lyndon B. Johnson's call to arms in March 1964. The federal government committed itself to a broad range of community programs to combat poverty and impoverishment in the United States.[66] In order to wage its campaign, the federal government created the Office of Economic Opportunity (OEO) to coordinate local programs such as the Neighborhood Youth Corps and Head Start. Operating under the doctrine of "maximum feasible participation," the OEO encouraged the full involvement of poor people in the local programs that it administered. Although ambiguously conceived and never fully defined, this doctrine created an expectation among representatives of the poor (or poor people themselves) that they would actively take charge of the antipoverty funds.[67]

Moreover, Mexican American leaders assumed that their community would be one of the prime beneficiaries of the War on Poverty. As the Kennedy Administration began to conceive the program, Walter Heller, chair of the Council of Economic Advisors and "the most influential proponent of a poverty program in 1963," emphasized that, "having mounted a dramatic program for one disadvantaged group [civil rights for blacks], it was both equitable and politically attractive to launch one specifically designed to aid other disadvantaged groups."[68] While Kennedy did not fulfill the hopes of many Mexican American leaders, their spirits were raised when Lyndon B. Johnson became president. Remembering verbal commitments that Johnson had given the Mexican American community in exchange for their support both as a senator in Texas and as a presidential candidate in 1964, Mexican

American leaders strongly believed that Johnson's War on Poverty would finally address the problems the community faced.[69]

Hence, Chicano leaders hoped that Mexican Americans would be named to important and influential antipoverty posts.[70] In Denver, such hopes began to be fulfilled when Mayor Tom Currigan named Gonzales as director of the Neighborhood Youth Corps (NYC) in June 1965. Four months later, the board of Denver's War on Poverty—with Mayor Currigan's enthusiastic endorsement—elected Gonzales as chair.[71] In addition, Bernard Valdez and Mary Chávez, both Mexican Americans, respectively chaired the Denver Welfare Department and the Mobilization against Poverty. Believing that federal and local governments were committed to helping Mexican Americans, Chicano antipoverty leaders were prepared to disperse the funds into the community.[72]

In the public discourse of the War on Poverty, Denver's two major dailies focused on the Mexican American community as the city's most impoverished group. Accordingly, both newspapers sought Gonzales for his views concerning the needs of Denver's poor people. In the fall of 1965, Gonzales had his first significant opportunity since his prizefighting days to redefine his own public representation in Denver's mainstream press when the *Rocky Mountain News* prominently featured him in its analysis of the city's "poverty battle."[73] The former boxer reformulated the type of fighter he represented: "I'm an agitator and a trouble-maker. That's my reputation and that's what I'm going to be. They didn't buy me when they put me in this job." Recalling his reputation as a "clean-cut" boxer, Gonzales made it clear that he was not going to be tainted by corruption. The fluid and tactful skills he showed as a professional boxer, however, transformed into a more confrontational style. Because there was a "war" to win rather than a single boxing match to score points, it was the precise image that Gonzales wanted to convey.

By the mid-1960s, Gonzales had become increasingly frustrated at the pace of social change. Particularly concerned with violence between young Mexican Americans and the police, he questioned the ability of Denver's Democratic and Republican leaders to address the problem in a meaningful way.[74] As a result, he began to believe that more forceful and direct action would be needed to bring about reforms in the community. The explosive word "war," which had entered the official lexicon to describe the legislation against poverty, captured perfectly Gonzales's sense of the intensity of the struggle that was needed. As a result, the *News* interview with Gonzales created a narrative of a rightful war that was being fought by an unorthodox leader: "The typical occupant of such a position as Denver's War on Poverty shuns involvement in picketing and demonstrations like the plague. But Gonzales is unabashedly a man of the streets. That's where the people are, that's where the action is, that's where he'll make a good part of his battle."[75]

Moreover, the same interview shows that Gonzales also employed war imagery to establish his distinctiveness. "He pours vials of scorn on those he labels 'Coyotes'—the equivalent in the Spanish-named community, he explains, of 'Uncle Tom' in the Negro community. He lashes at these 'generals' of the 'banquet table,' these Spanish-named persons who have abandoned the mass of the people because of personal prosperity." The metaphors and imagery Gonzales used to describe the U.S. war on poverty suggested that its targets should also be elitism and racism. In this war, the *News* made it clear that it was people like Gonzales who promised to bring the hostilities to a rapid end.

The most dramatic shift of representation during the *Rocky Mountain News* interview had to do with the unambiguous emphasis on Gonzales's racial and ethnic identity. By 1966 the paper made it publicly clear whom Gonzales represented, quoting him as saying, "The Negro has done it in Denver. Now we have to do it too." In order to clarify his statement, the article specified that "The 'we' in that sentence, if there is any doubt, means the Spanish-named. Gonzales drives the point home." Completing a circle in which the mainstream press had implicitly embraced and explicitly ignored his background since 1947, Gonzales was finally addressed specifically in terms of his racial and ethnic distinctiveness. This change was precipitated by Gonzales himself. Whether decrying the depravity of the Spanish American "coyotes" or comparing Chicanos and Chicanas to African Americans, Gonzales actively worked to link himself directly with Denver's Mexican Americans: "The people identify with me. If someone—if a newspaper takes a crack at me, they take a crack at them. They know I am on their side. . . . I am their leader."[76] In covering Gonzales, Denver's two major dailies could no longer separate his Chicano identity from his career activities.

Significantly, Denver's mainstream press began to realize that Mexican American leaders did exist. Not just a local community figurehead, Gonzales seemingly had access to the upper echelons of power in the United States. The "clean-cut" Gonzales—champion of his barrio—typified the type of leadership that the *News* advocated for transforming the condition of Denver's Mexican American community.

FROM ALL-AMERICAN BOXER TO CHICANO MILITANT

Wars tend to follow incoherent and chaotic paths. From its inception, the poverty war was under bitter attack. Whether from liberals such as Saul Alinsky, blasting the antipoverty program for its ineffectiveness, or from conservatives like Sen. John Tower of Texas, decrying the rise of Democratic power, the War on Poverty faced extreme opposition.[77] In addition to the national concern over the feasibility of the program, many feared that "militants" and "radicals" were taking charge of local antipoverty funds. As a result, critics claimed that the War on Poverty had turned into a street fight between established politicians and the "militant" poor. Finally, both detractors and proponents complained that competing minority groups were undermining the program. One *Denver Post* editorial noted that Denver's minorities were indeed bitterly fighting over "quota[s] of well-paid jobs."[78] As a result of such accusations, many perceived that the true goals and intentions of the War on Poverty programs had been tainted. At the nexus of these concerns, Gonzales and Denver's mainstream press became embroiled in a controversy surrounding the direction of Denver's own poverty war.

In April 1966, the *Rocky Mountain News* published a series of articles alleging that Gonzales was no longer the proper man to orchestrate Denver's poverty program. The front-page coverage began with the following: "Antipoverty officials are keeping a wary eye on Rudolph [Corky] Gonzales, chief of Denver's War on Poverty, Inc. There is a feeling Gonzales might be placing too much emphasis on Spanish-American problems rather than the broad spectrum of the poor."[79] The *News* detailed an alleged investigation of Gonzales by the OEO. While questioning whether local NYC members had been paid in a timely manner, the article focused directly on Gonzales's responsibilities as the head of a multiconstituency government program. Accordingly, the *News* article pointed out that Gonzales's explicit public embrace of his Chicano identity created tension in Washington, D.C. It quoted an unnamed OEO source as saying that "when he [Gonzales] reaches the point of representing a group rather than a whole clientele, it will be up to the local organization to do something about it." In the following days, scrutiny of Gonzales became more intense; the *News* called him "quite a wild man" who had been conducting "militant activities on behalf of Spanish-Americans."[80]

Because he had so effectively linked himself to Mexican Americans, the controversy was not just about Gonzales. Instead, it also reflected concern in Denver about increasing racial tension.[81] These fears were not articulated solely by the *Rocky Mountain News*. In an editorial that appeared the same day as the allegations in the *News*, the *Denver Post* criticized unnamed minority groups for selfishly haggling over antipoverty funds.[82] Significantly, both papers feared open hostility between Denver's Chicanos, African Americans, and whites while also expressing uneasiness about increasing "militant" activity. Especially as it concerned Denver's Chicano community, each paper's coverage intimated that the community had gone out of control. Whether they were "Spanish Americans," "Mexican Americans," or the "Spanish surnamed"—all references in the *News* coverage—Denver's Chicanos no longer acted as a victimized, impoverished, and downtrodden group. For Denver's mainstream press, Corky Gonzales, as the "militant wild man," was emblematic of this change.[83]

Almost immediately, Gonzales worked to contest the negative images that the *Rocky Mountain News* conveyed. In a media blitz, he appeared on radio talk shows and local television newscasts denouncing the *News*'s journalistic integrity. Emphasizing that the allegations were not aimed solely at him, Gonzales emphatically stated that the *News* was attacking the entire Chicano community.[84] He also organized a large protest outside the *Rocky Mountain News* offices. In front of signs declaring "Corky All the Way" and "Viva la justicia!" he called for Denver's Mexican American community to begin an economic boycott of the newspaper: "We feel the *Rocky Mountain News* has taken it on themselves to discredit and destroy the War on Poverty. We are asking the Spanish-named people and all people of good conscience in this community to join us in canceling subscriptions."[85] While Gonzales wanted to be identified as the leader of Denver's Mexican American community, he also wanted the image to be on his own terms and conditions.

Poverty officials in Washington, D.C., bolstered Gonzales's case against the *News*. James Kelleher, the source for the *Rocky Mountain News* reports, issued a press release denouncing the paper and challenging its objectivity. The statement—carried solely in the *Denver Post*'s pages—was a strong endorsement of Gonzales and his actions as director of the NYC. According to Kelleher, "allegations, insinuations and special writing . . . have been limited to one Denver newspaper and one reporter."[86] In spite of Kelleher's message, Mayor Currigan dismissed Gonzales as director of the NYC for his forceful public criticism of the *Rocky Mountain News*. Most important in the dismissal, however, was Gonzales's increasing public identification with Denver's Chicano community.[87]

Giving full support to Mayor Currigan's action, in 1966 the *Denver Post* published an editorial headlined "Corky Was Asking for It." Although the *Post* said it agreed "with Gonzales when he says he was recently subjected to unfair public criticism, and we know it is his nature to respond directly and forcefully to what he considers injustices," the editorial nevertheless gave three reasons for supporting the dismissal. First, the *Post*'s editorial staff argued that "Gonzales recently had not conducted himself with very great dignity or propriety." As the head of two important antipoverty posts, Gonzales had apparently crossed the line of acceptable activity. Second, the editorial emphasized that Gonzales was not giving the poverty war the attention it deserved due to his many "outside activities." With his numerous trips throughout the Southwest in addition to grassroots community organizing, Gonzales, in the eyes of the paper, was stretched thin. Finally, the editorial argued that "Corky Gonzales was bound to run into trouble sooner or later because he was trying to hold down two jobs in the antipoverty war."

Ultimately, the *Post*'s editorial suggested that Gonzales had become too much of an activist on behalf of Denver's Mexican Americans. In the realm of "acceptable" and "unacceptable" behavior, this was something the *Post* could not endorse. In ending its editorial, however, the *Post* was faced with a paradox that mere condemnation of Gonzales's actions could not reconcile: "As we have said before, this setback does not mean the end of Corky Gonzales, as Tom Currigan may find out politically the next time around. Whatever his shortcomings, Gonzales genuinely represents a strong segment of Denver's Spanish-named community, the city's largest cultural minority." Not able to condone Gonzales's forceful activism, the *Post* nevertheless could not ignore his political importance among Denver's Mexican Americans.

In the wake of Currigan's dismissal of Gonzales, a significant backlash erupted. Protesting and picketing the mayor's office, a large contingent of Mexican Americans denounced Mayor Currigan and his administration. On April 27, 1966, the Friday following Gonzales's firing, Denver Chicanos and Chicanas staged a mass protest and rally directly across the street from the mayor's office in the City and County Building to voice criticism against the *Rocky Mountain News,* Mayor Currigan, the Democratic Party, and their collective treatment of Denver's Mexican Americans.[88] In the late afternoon of a cold April day, Mexican American leaders such as State Rep. Frank R. Anaya and the state chair of the GI Forum, Joseph Huerrera, gave rousing speeches to a large and vocal crowd from the bed of a large flatbed truck. Although he was invited, Mayor Currigan refused to attend. The central figure, however, was Corky Gonzales. With sporadic shouts of "¡Viva Corky!" and "Corky all the way!" the large crowd waited to hear Gonzales speak.

Both Denver dailies sent reporters to cover the rally.[89] In particular, coverage by the *Denver Post* revealed the extent to which Gonzales had begun to embrace Chicano nationalism. In his speech before the crowd, Gonzales declared the rally as "the beginning—the real beginning—of political action of Spanish-named people. . . . We're going to show people from all over the southwestern United States what the Chicano can do when he organizes. And it's all starting here today."[90] Though they were not aware of it at the time, the *Denver Post* and the *Rocky Mountain News* were witnessing the genesis of a Denver-based, cultural nationalist movement that would resonate with others throughout the Southwest. By placing Gonzales at the center of the action, however, both the *Post* and the *News* aided understanding of the larger civil rights claims of Mexican Americans. Through the persistent use of American symbols and imagery, each paper created a snapshot of the country. In the case of Gonzales, his journey from minority boxer to social agitator reflected the collective Chicano struggle that emerged in the fractured landscape of the United States.

Through the end of the 1960s, both the *Rocky Mountain News* and the *Denver Post* struggled to find and incorporate a new image of Corky Gonzales. Recognizing his increasing "militancy" and dissatisfaction with the system, both papers could no longer easily categorize him. One *Denver Post* article highlighted the uncertainty and complexity of Gonzales's public persona: "Street fighter, stoop laborer, professional boxer, bail bondsman, organizational politician, poet, political rebel, playwright, minority group member. And candidate for mayor. That's Rudolph Gonzales. Or Rodolfo Gonzales. Or Corky Gonzales. He's known by all three names. Known, and glared at or applauded, depending upon the company he's in."[91] In all of these roles listed by the *Post,* Gonzales personified the multifaceted dimensions, fissures, and continuities in American culture and life.

WHATEVER HAPPENED TO . . . ?

Over the next several years, Denver's mainstream press continued to present Gonzales in inconsistent and often conflicting ways. When in doubt, however, each paper would always come back to Gonzales's boxing career to explain his Chicano nationalism. Gonzales himself recognized that such a fusion made sense: "Boxing gave me confidence in myself. Now, I'm trying to teach self-confidence and self-reliance to other Chicanos and to provide an element of freedom for our youth."[92] With the election in 1983 of Federico Peña as the first Mexican American mayor of the city (and in the county), however, the vocal activism and bombastic rhetoric of Gonzales and the Crusade for Justice seemed vestiges from a bygone era. In describing a confrontation between Chicano youth and the police in the early 1980s, the *Denver Post* observed that "the tear-gassing incident belongs to an era that appears to be happily past, and appears unlikely to return in a city run by a Hispanic mayor who emphasizes open government, a new police chief and a reorganized Police Department."[93]

To be sure, Gonzales did not sit by passively to let a new generation of Chicano and Chicana leaders take his place. From appearing at community demonstrations to suing the Denver Police Department for police brutality, Gonzales still battled for Denver's Mexican Americans. Yet the closure of the Crusade for Justice in 1983 ensured that Gonzales would become an anachronism for Denver's major dailies. Without the leverage over Denver's papers that he had had during the 1960s and early 1970s, by 1985 Gonzales had been relegated to the "Whatever Happened To . . . ?" column that explored Denver's past.[94]

But Gonzales was not merely an aging relic of a long-gone era. In January 1988 he returned to public life when the Colorado Sports Hall of Fame inducted him as its first Latino member. The day after his induction, Tom Gavin, then editor of the *Denver Post,* commented on the dynamic resurrection of Gonzales's public image: "I smiled and laughed at the Corky Gonzales news. That smile was recognition of a fine athlete. Make no mistake, he was a fine athlete! The laugh was prompted by knowledge that Corky Gonzales is also Rodolfo Gonzales. That Rodolfo Gonzales. The social and racial justice agitator. The rock-the-establishment militant. The spit-it-out confrontationist. The founder of the Crusade for Justice, a battle-with-police, picket newspapers, educate the young, inculcate pride, preserve-Hispanic-heritage organization which, at its height, shook this town in a way the Black Panthers never did. Yeah, that Rodolfo Gonzales."[95] Gonzales was in Denver's sports pages once again. As in the past, his boxing and activist career could not easily be separated.

The public representation of political figures like Gonzales is subject to a competing and often conflicting agenda of editors, publishers, and news writers.[96] Yet employees "working within the complex news culture echo and reproduce culturally embedded ways of seeing the world, including stereotyping. They follow cultural codes to distinguish what is of consequence, what is legitimate, and who has the status to say what is true."[97] No different from the hundreds of mainstream newspapers throughout the United States, the *Rocky Mountain News* and the *Denver Post* reflected this reality. Most of all, the press attempted to speak for a diverse U.S. body politic through "narratives of nation and community."[98] By representing the "commonsense" symbols and terminology of U.S. culture, the press helped to provide "answers to questions of identity and connectedness in a fluid world."[99] For Gonzales, malleable images of Americanism connected him to Denver and its Chicano community.

Finding success as an amateur and professional boxer at a particularly critical moment in the city's boxing history, Gonzales became a natural subject of Denver's mainstream news. Jack Lule points out that newspapers tell "the great stories of humankind for humankind."[100] As mythic re-creations, "news stories too regularly celebrate the exploits of heroes. From sports stars to movie stars, astronauts to artists, presidents and prime ministers, the news tells stories of heroic men and women. The news produces and reproduces the timeless patterns: the humble birth, the early mark of greatness, the quest, the triumph, and the return. The news daily brings us stories of the Hero, stories that proclaim—but also help define—greatness."[101]

The boxing and subsequent political career of Corky Gonzales scaled mythic heights. He rose through the amateur and professional ranks in one of the darkest periods in Denver's and the nation's professional boxing history. He displayed honesty, courage, and valor. Moreover, racial markers further confirmed his uniqueness. Although he was never referred to as a "Spanish American" in coverage of his fights, there were important signifiers of this fact, not only in his surname but also in references to Denver's East Side. Such indirect allusions reinforced his popularity with Denver's mainstream press, especially in light of the criticism of corrupt white fighters. Thus, as a "minority boy" striving to rise in the United States, Gonzales the boxer symbolized the highest of American ideals.

The culmination of Gonzales's boxing career did not mean the end of his appearance in Denver's mainstream press. It was only the beginning of a much more complicated but no less mythic relationship. As a result, Denver's two dailies reconfigured the racial dynamics of his boxing past as he rose through the city's Democratic Party. In the 1960s and 1970s, Gonzales's fights were waged exclusively on behalf of Denver's Chicano community. As he became involved in politics and political action, his boxing persona was an important source of political capital in a racially fractured U.S. society.[102]

Even when Gonzales became embroiled in confrontations with the law, his legal conflict was recast as an epic bout paralleling his most significant fights. Hence, Gonzales's American boxing past resolved his Chicano political present. The "all-American" boxing hero meshed seamlessly into the Chicano cultural nationalist that he would become. Indeed, the seemingly belligerent political demands that Gonzales made did not seem out of character in relation to the "predominately male-dominated political language" of Chicano nationalists.[103] In these terms, Gonzales's early Chicanismo was an extension of his boxing past and fit together well with a desire by many Americans—including news journalists—to dismantle racism, poverty, and inequality in Colorado and the country as a whole.[104]

Forced to reconceptualize who Gonzales was and what he represented, Denver's mainstream press revealed the limits of the language of Americanism with regard to Chicano and Chicana nationalists. In the 1950s and early 1960s both the *Rocky Mountain News* and the *Denver Post* had used Gonzales's racial-ethnic characteristics as a foil to the corruption of boxing and as an essential element in his rise to political prominence; by 1966, however, those same attributes had become suspect. In the 1970s both papers refused to condone the relationship between Gonzales, the Crusade, and violence in Denver's streets. The lawsuit that Gonzales filed in 1974 suggests the ways in which he attempted to use U.S. institutions to contest his marginalization in Denver's mainstream press. As social conditions changed, however, he once again graced Denver's sports pages when he became the first Latino and Chicano inductee of the Colorado Sports Hall of Fame. As in his boxing and political career, Gonzales once more broke down barriers.

Sports, politics, and nationalist discourse were intricately connected in the public emergence of Rodolfo "Corky" Gonzales. Accordingly, his story tells us much about the individual and collective challenges facing a multicultural and postethnic America.[105] As a solitary minority boxer, Gonzales embodied so-called American values of individual hard work, thrift, and good fortune. But when he became the leader of an increasingly vocal and discontented group, his Chicano nationalism represented the deep fissures that existed in U.S. society. Negotiating these identities across time, both the *Rocky Mountain News* and the *Denver Post* attempted to redefine and reconceptualize Gonzales in the familiar American imagery and symbolism that both papers recognized. Ultimately, neither paper could compartmentalize his many public images. By wearing the red, white, and blue trunks of Aztlán, Gonzales demonstrated one way in which American and Chicano nationalism could be resolved in the cauldron of tensions that shaped and continues to produce the language of nation and community in the United States.

NOTES

I wish to acknowledge George J. Sánchez, María E. Montoya, Aimes McGuinness, Richard Delgado, Jean Stefancic, Laurie Blumberg-Romero, Carol Hoke, and the *Aztlán* peer reviewers for helpful comments and editorial suggestions that significantly enhanced the structure, presentation, and ideas in this chapter.

1. *Crusade for Justice, Escuela Tlatelolco, and Rodolfo Gonzales v. the Denver Publishing Company, the Rocky Mountain News,* U.S. District Court, District of Colorado. National Archives Branch Depository, Lakewood, Colo. RG 21, Civil Action no. C43168.

2. Rodolfo Gonzales, "Yellow Journalism and Yellow Bellies," *El gallo: la voz de la justicia,* July 28, 1967.

3. Jack Lule, *Daily News, Eternal Stories: The Mythological Role of Journalism* (New York: Guilford Press), 2001, 192; Bernadette Barker-Plummer, "News as a Political Resource: Media Strategies and Political Identity in the U.S. Women's Movement, 1966–1975," *Critical Studies in Mass Communication* 12 (1995): 307–23.

4. Peter Blake, "$30 Million Libel Suit Filed against *News* by Crusade," *Rocky Mountain News* (Feb. 26, 1974).

5. Palmer Hoyt, Transcription of American Town Hall Meeting at University of Denver, Feb. 18, 1949. Palmer Hoyt Papers, Box 42, FF 1. Western History Collection, Denver Public Library.

6. Palmer Hoyt, letter to Frank S. Hoag Jr., Mar. 29, 1971. Palmer Hoyt Papers, Box 13, FF 7, Western History Collection, Denver Public Library.

7. Marco Portales, *Crowding Out Latinos: Mexican Americans in the Public Consciousness* (Philadelphia: Temple University Press, 2000); Irene Ledesma, "Texas Newspapers and Chicana Workers' Activism, 1919–1974," *Western Historical Quarterly* 26 (1995): 309–31; Bradley S. Greenberg, Michael Burgoon, Judee K. Burgoon, and Felipe Korzenny, *Mexican Americans and the Mass Media* (Norwood, N.J.: Ablex, 1983); Francisco J. Lewels, *The Uses of the Media by the Chicano Movement: A Study in Minority Access* (New York: Praeger, 1974); Leo Anthony Sánchez, "Treat-

ment of Mexican Americans by Selected U.S. Newspapers, January-June 1970," master's thesis, Pennsylvania State University, State College, Penn., 1970.

8. Lule, *Daily News, Eternal Stories;* Barker-Plummer, "News as a Political Resource."

9. Gary Gerstle, *Working-class Americanism: The Politics of Labor in a Textile City, 1914-1960* (Cambridge: Cambridge University Press, 1989), 8.

10. Benedict Anderson, *Imagined Communities,* rev. ed. (London: Verso, 1991), 46.

11. Gary Gerstle, *American Crucible: Race and Nation in the Twentieth Century* (Princeton, N.J.: Princeton University Press, 2001), 8-11.

12. Mary L. Dudziak, *Cold War Civil Rights: Race and the Image of American Democracy* (Princeton, N.J.: Princeton University Press, 2000), 47-114; Derrick Bell, "*Brown v. Board of Education* and the Interest-convergence Dilemma," *Harvard Law Review* 93 (1980): 524-25.

13. Ernesto Chávez, "Imagining the Mexican Immigrant Worker: (Inter)Nationalism, Identity, and Insurgency in the Chicano Movement in Los Angeles," *Aztlán: A Journal of Chicano Studies* 25(2) (2000): 112; Ignacio M. García, *Chicanismo: The Forging of a Militant Ethos among Mexican Americans* (Tucson: University of Arizona Press, 1997).

14. Ernesto Vigil, *The Crusade for Justice: Chicano Militancy and the Government's War on Dissent* (Madison: University of Wisconsin Press, 1999); García, *Chicanismo;* Christine Marín, *A Spokesman of the Mexican-American Movement: Rodolfo "Corky" Gonzales and the Fight for Chicano Liberation* (San Francisco: R and E Research Associates, 1977).

15. Ralph Moore, "Corky Decisions Riley: Referee's Vote Decides Thriller before 3,622," *Denver Post,* Aug. 22, 1951.

16. Jeffrey T. Sammons, *Beyond the Ring: The Role of Boxing in American Society* (Urbana: University of Illinois Press, 1988), 156-66.

17. "Gonzales Wins National Title," *Rocky Mountain News,* Apr. 10, 1947.

18. "Gonzales to Fight Here against Cleveland," *Rocky Mountain News,* Apr. 11, 1947.

19. Steven A. Riess, *City Games: The Evolution of American Urban Society and the Rise of Sports* (Urbana: University of Illinois Press, 1989), 151-68, 172-81.

20. Chet Nelson, "Good Crop in Finals," *Rocky Mountain News,* Jan. 30, 1947.

21. Elliott J. Gorn, *The Manly Art: Bare-knuckle Prize Fighting in America* (Ithaca, N.Y.: Cornell University Press, 1986), 251.

22. Nelson, "Good Crop in Finals."

23. Stuart Hall, "The Determinations of News Photographs," in *The Manufacture of News: Social Problems, Deviance, and the Mass Media,* edited by Stanley Cohen and Jack Young (London: Constable, 1973), 176-90.

24. John Wix, "Danos Upset, Corky Grabs Judges' Nod," *Denver Post,* Feb. 28, 1948.

25. Leonard Cahn, "Pro and Cahn: Salzer Sends S.O.S.," *Rocky Mountain News,* Aug. 7, 1950; Marvin McCarthy, "Bad News, Galvani! You're Named 'It,'" *Denver Post,* Aug. 11, 1950.

26. Marvin McCarthy, "Two Little Guys Do Boxing a Big Deed," *Denver Post,* Aug. 13, 1950.

27. Ibid.; see also Leonard Cahn, "Galvani KO's Gonzales in Ninth," *Rocky Mountain News,* Aug. 12. 1950; and Leonard Cahn, "Pro and Cahn: Corky Still Chipper," *Rocky Mountain News,* Aug. 14, 1950.

28. McCarthy, "Bad News, Galvani!"

29. Cahn, "Pro and Cahn: Salzer Sends S.O.S."

30. See Chet Nelson, "Great Fight Show Promised," *Rocky Mountain News,* Apr. 15, 1947, and Chet Nelson, "Should Be Good Fight," *Rocky Mountain News,* Aug. 11, 1950; also "Gonzales to Fight Here against Cleveland."

31. Denver Area Welfare Council, "The Spanish-American Population of Denver: An Exploratory Survey," 1950; F. L. Carmichael, "Housing Trends in Denver, 1939–1949," University of Denver, Bureau of Business and Social Research, 1949.

32. Jack Carberry, "Second Guess: Paroke Boxing's Dead—and Ring Game Suffers," *Denver Post,* Feb. 29, 1952.

33. Ibid.

34. Ibid.

35. Leonard Cahn, "Riley Scores Knockout over Corky in 8th Round," *Rocky Mountain News,* Apr. 26, 1952.

36. Jack Carberry, "Second Guess: Friday Marked Finis to City's Ring Trail," *Denver Post,* Apr. 28, 1952.

37. Leonard Cahn, "Pro and Cahn: End of the Road for Corky?" *Rocky Mountain News,* Apr. 28, 1952.

38. Ibid.

39. Kurt Mayer, "Small Business as a Social Institution," *Social Research* 14 (1947): 338.

40. Vigil, *The Crusade for Justice,* 8.

41. Robert L. Perkin, "Poorest of Denver's Poor," *Rocky Mountain News,* Feb. 1, 1954.

42. Vigil, *The Crusade for Justice,* 8–9.

43. Mario T. García, *Mexican-Americans: Leadership, Ideology, and Identity, 1930–1960* (New Haven: Yale University Press, 1989), 25.

44. Ibid., 1–22; Juan Gómez-Quiñones, *Chicano Politics: Reality and Promise, 1940–1990* (Albuquerque: University of New Mexico Press, 1990), 34–66.

45. García, *Mexican-Americans*, 25.

46. Mortimer P. Stern, "Palmer Hoyt and the *Denver Post:* A Field Study of Organizational Change in the Mass Media of Communication," Ph.D. diss., University of Denver, 1969, 327.

47. Richard Delgado and Jean Stefancic, "Home-grown Racism: Colorado's Historic Embrace—and Denial—of Equal Opportunity in Higher Education," *University of Colorado Law Review* 70 (1999): 745.

48. Denver Area Welfare Council, "The Spanish-American Population of Denver."

49. William H. Hornby, *Voice of Empire: A Centennial Sketch of the* Denver Post (Denver: Colorado Historical Society, 1992), 33–40; Alan Swallow, letter to Palmer Hoyt, Oct. 11, 1963, Palmer Hoyt Papers, Box 9, FF 13, Western History Collection, Denver Public Library.

50. Palmer Hoyt, "The Three-legged Stool: Civil Liberties, Prosperity, and Defense," Apr. 21, 1960. Palmer Hoyt Papers, Box 43, FF 13, Western History Collection, Denver Public Library.

51. Robert L. Perkin, "Study of Critical Denver Problems," *Rocky Mountain News,* Jan. 31, 1954.

52. Robert L. Perkin, "Can We Blame the Poor after Half-century of This? Underpaid, Ill Fed, Badly Housed," *Rocky Mountain News,* Feb. 2, 1954; Robert L. Perkin, "Health Conditions in City Show Wide Variance: High Infant Death Rate Plagues Denver's Poor," *Rocky Mountain News,* Feb. 4, 1954; Robert L. Perkin, "No Running Water, No Heat," *Rocky Mountain News,* Feb. 3, 1954; Perkin, "Poorest of Denver's Poor"; Robert L. Perkin, "Schools Can Help If They Are Used: Denver's Problem Starts When the Kids Drop Out of Class," *Rocky Mountain News,* Feb. 5, 1954; Robert L. Perkin, "What Are the Solutions to This Denver Problem?" *Rocky Mountain News,* Feb. 6, 1954.

53. Perkin, "Schools Can Help If They Are Used."

54. Robert L. Perkin, "*News* Finds Indications of Progress: Denver's Spanish-Americans—a Year Later," *Rocky Mountain News,* Feb. 27, 1955.

55. See "'Corky' Takes Verbal Swing at Opponent," *Denver Post,* May 15, 1955; "Four Seek Downtown Area Council Seat," *Rocky Mountain News,* May 7, 1955.

56. "Democratic Captain Jailed following Brawl in Tavern," *Denver Post,* July 26, 1958.

57. "Gonzales Is Accused of Assault, Battery," *Rocky Mountain News,* July 29, 1958.

58. "Gonzales in 'Ring' with Jury," *Denver Post,* Jan. 8, 1959.

59. Barbara Browne, "Political Pugilists Cheer Corky's Cause," *Rocky Mountain News,* Jan. 9, 1959.

60. Zeke Scher, "Dem Leaders Defend Corky," *Denver Post,* Jan. 9, 1959.

61. "Jury's Split Decision Gives Corky Reprieve," *Rocky Mountain News,* Jan. 10, 1959.

62. Marín, *A Spokesman of the Mexican-American Movement,* 2.

63. David G. Gutiérrez, *Walls and Mirrors: Mexican Americans, Mexican Immigrants, and the Politics of Ethnicity* (Berkeley: University of California Press, 1995), 181.

64. Vigil, *The Crusade for Justice,* 24–25.

65. Julie Leininger Pycior, *LBJ and Mexican Americans: The Paradox of Power* (Austin: University of Texas Press, 1997), 155.

66. Thomas Jackson, "The State, the Movement, and the Urban Poor: The War on Poverty and Political Mobilization in the 1960s," in *The "Underclass" Debate: Views from History,* edited by Michael B. Katz (Princeton, N.J.: Princeton University Press, 1993), 403–39; James T. Patterson, *America's Struggle against Poverty, 1900–1980* (Cambridge: Harvard University Press, 1981), 136.

67. Patterson, *America's Struggle against Poverty, 1900–1980,* 146.

68. Ibid., 134–35.

69. Pycior, *LBJ and Mexican Americans,* 151–58; Mario T. García, *Memories of Chicano History: The Life and Narrative of Bert Corona* (Berkeley: University of California Press, 1994), 210–12.

70. Pycior, *LBJ and Mexican Americans,* 154.

71. Stephen J. Leonard and Thomas J. Noel, *Denver: Mining Camp to Metropolis* (Niwot: University Press of Colorado, 1990), 395.

72. Pycior, *LBJ and Mexican Americans,* 153–58.

73. Jack Gaske, "Our Poverty Battle: Gonzales Views His Poverty Role," *Rocky Mountain News,* Sept. 29, 1965.

74. Vigil, *The Crusade for Justice,* 20–21.

75. Gaske, "Our Poverty Battle."

76. Ibid.

77. Patterson, *America's Struggle against Poverty, 1900–1980,* 144, 146–48.

78. "Misunderstanding the Poverty War," *Denver Post,* Apr. 2, 1966.

79. Dan Thomasson, "Poverty Chief's Acts under Scrutiny," *Rocky Mountain. News,* Apr. 21, 1966.

80. Dan Thomasson, "Denver's Poverty War under Watch," *Rocky Mountain News,* Apr. 22, 1966.

81. Thomasson, "Poverty Chief's Acts under Scrutiny."

82. "Misunderstanding the Poverty War."

83. Thomasson, "Denver's Poverty War under Watch."

84. Vigil, *The Crusade for Justice,* 25–26.

85. John Toohey, "Gonzales at Issue: Sen. Allott Requests Shriver Probe Denver War on Poverty," *Denver Post,* Apr. 23, 1966.

86. "Here's Telegram Text Sent by OEO Official," *Denver Post,* Apr. 24, 1966.

87. Vigil, *The Crusade for Justice,* 25-26.

88. Ibid.

89. Fritz Lalendorf, "Gonzales Stages Protest Meeting," *Rocky Mountain News,* Apr. 30, 1966; Robert Kistler, "1,200 Cheer Gonzales at 'Vote Revolt Rally,'" *Denver Post,* Apr. 30, 1966.

90. "They Came to See—and to Hear Corky," *Denver Post,* Apr. 30, 1966.

91. Tom Gavin, "Civic Equality: Gonzales Seeks to Regain Lost Pride," *Denver Post,* May 11, 1967.

92. Harry Farrar, "Corky Pulls No Punches in Crusade: Seeks KO over Racism, Social Ills," *Denver Post,* June 6, 1973.

93. Karen Odom, "La Raza Park Incident May Fade into the Past," *Denver Post,* May 21, 1984.

94. Judith Brimberg, "'Corky' Still Won't Pull Punch at 57: Whatever Happened to Rodolfo 'Corky' Gonzales?" *Denver Post,* July 28, 1985.

95. Tom Gavin, "Gonzales Dons a Fitting Crown," *Denver Post,* Jan. 6, 1988.

96. Donna L. Dickerson, "Framing 'Political Correctness': The *New York Times*' Tale of Two Professors," in *Framing Public Life: Perspectives on Media and Our Understanding of the Social World,* edited by Stephen D. Reese, Oscar H. Gandy Jr., and August E. Grant (Mahwah, N.J.: Erlbaum, 2001), 163-74

97. Ibid., 173.

98. Martin Conboy, *The Press and Popular Culture* (London: Sage, 2002), 180.

99. Robert H. Wiebe, *Who We Are: A History of Popular Nationalism* (Princeton, N.J.: Princeton University Press, 2002), xv; Conboy, *The Press and Popular Culture,* 180.

100. Lule, *Daily News, Eternal Stories,* 15.

101. Ibid., 23.

102. Gerstle, *American Crucible,* 268-310.

103. Chávez, "Imagining the Mexican Immigrant Worker," 111-12; García, *Chicanismo,* 86-116.

104. Dudziak, *Cold War Civil Rights.*

105. Gerstle, *American Crucible,* 347-74; David A. Hollinger, *Postethnic America: Beyond Multiculturalism* (New York: Basic Books, 1995).

ON-FIELD FOES AND RACIAL MISCONCEPTIONS
The 1961 Donna Redskins and Their Drive to the Texas State Football Championship

JORGE IBER

Although some in academia and journalism may disagree with them, a preponderance of Texans would likely wholeheartedly endorse the words of former Houston Oilers coach "Bum" Phillips, who said, "There is something about high school football in Texas that captures the essence of what sport is all about. It's about pride; it's about entire communities coming together for a common cause."[1] From its humble beginnings in the late nineteenth century, football has become the most honored athletic endeavor for young men throughout the Lone Star State. In this regard, Texas joins the rest of the former Confederate states, for while football is popular everywhere in the United States, one author has noted that "the game has a specific and dominating grip on the South." Folklorist Charles R. Frederick Jr. has argued that the attraction of the sport in this region has partly to do with the "emotional satisfaction derived from playing football [that] is rooted in pride of place and the American ethos of determined, do-it-yourself individualism. To win a football game in the South is to establish year long bragging rights by proving superiority on the gridiron." Frederick further observes that Michael Novak, in his 1976 book, *The Joy of Sports: End Zones, Bases, Baskets, Balls, and the Consecration of the American Spirit,* detected the connection between this sport and another major social force of the South: religion. Novak argued that the ebullience felt by fans as a result of a football victory can be compared "with the ecstatically emotive experience of fundamentalist Protestantism."[2]

The passion for football runs deep in all of the former Confederate states, including Texas. As of 2003, the state had more than fifteen hundred high school teams playing the sport, and for many decades the state's secondary institutions have consistently produced some of the fastest, largest, and most heavily recruited players in the nation. Many communities have come to measure their success and importance by the number of gridiron championships their local high school eleven have earned. Given many Texans' obsession with the sport, there is something special about winning a state championship, and even more so when a team like the 1961 Donna High School Redskins overcomes great odds to triumph against not only on-field foes but racial misconceptions as well.[3]

For many Texans in metropolitan areas and isolated hamlets, the fact that individual stars once graced their local high school fields or that the hometown squad won a regional or state championship is a source of great satisfaction. In his 1999 work on the various levels (high school, collegiate, professional) of gridiron competition in the state, *Texas Football Trilogy: A Season in the Lone Star State,* Mitchell Krugel efficiently summarizes the passion for this sport embraced by many Texans: "All of the stories about God creating football in Texas might not be true, but deep in the heart of this state that spans more than 250,000 miles of real estate, they seem to believe as much. Football may have been born in some East Coast fraternity house, but it grew up in Longview and Big Springs and Galveston and Killeen and Pilot Point and New Braunfels and the other outposts of Texas that become ghost towns on any Friday night. For grandmothers and their grandsons, one kickoff leads to another."[4]

In his work *The Pigskin Pulpit: A Social History of Texas High School Football Coaches,* historian Ty Cashion has suggested that one explanation for football's importance in the state is that many people perceive gridiron competition as developing and engendering traditionally revered Texan characteristics such as "self-reliance, sacrifice, discipline, accountability and survival—in a word . . . manliness, in its most positive sense." The success of the locals could in many ways "even determine the self-perception of entire communities as well as how outsiders viewed those places." For some Texans, "battles" on the gridiron have come to replace the Civil War, the war for independence, and the tribulations with Native Americans. As one fan told Myron Cope, a

Saturday Evening Post reporter in 1966, "'We think we're still frontiersmen. There are no more wars down here, so we [use football] to make our own.'"⁵

Over the more than eighty-year history of the sport (as officially sanctioned by the University Interscholastic League, which is the official governing and sanctioning body of Texas high school athletic and academic competitions), teams from most areas of the state have had their moments in the championship sun. During the 1920s, Waco dominated and won three titles, and the 1950s saw both Lubbock and Wichita Falls win multiple championships. From the 1960s through the early 1980s Brownwood High School tallied seven crowns under the direction of Gordon Wood, until recently the coach with the most victories and state championships in Texas high school football history. Before the start of the 1990 season, forty-nine separate teams had enjoyed winning streaks of at least twenty-four games (with the eleven-man record being seventy-one consecutive victories by Carroll High School of the Fort Worth suburb of Southlake).⁶

Although gridiron success appears fairly well spread over Texas' vast and varied regions, one section of the state, the Rio Grande Valley (composed of Cameron, Hidalgo, Starr, and Willacy counties), has not often shared in this tradition. The Valley, populated primarily by Mexican Americans, has often been referred to as a football coach's "cemetery." When Charlie Williams arrived at Pharr–San Juan–Alamo High School (Hidalgo County) in 1962, colleagues assured him that this post would mark the nadir of his career. As Williams recalled in a 1979 interview in *Texas Coach,* the argument was based on a commonly accepted "fact"—that "the Valley was 80% Mexican American, and everybody knew Mexican Americans were poor football players." Some figures do seem to bear out this perception. Of the ten high schools with the greatest number of winless seasons (as of 1990), four (San Antonio Lanier High School, Crystal City High School, Laredo Martin High School, and El Paso James Bowie High School) are located in predominantly Hispanic areas.⁷

That perception of the caliber of football and football players in South Texas continues to the present. Each year, before the start of the fall gridiron campaign, thousands of Texas football fans reach for the sport's bible, *Dave Campbell's Texas Football* magazine. One recurring feature is a discussion among writers from various parts of Texas contending that their region produces the best teams, players, and level of competition. In the 2000 issue, Bill Hart (from the *Abilene Reporter-News)* argued that the western section of Texas (roughly from Fort Worth west to the New Mexico state line, south to the Rio Grande, and north to the Oklahoma boundary) produces the best football in the Lone Star State. Hart dutifully listed the various West Texas teams that won state titles during the 1990s and maintained that the squads lie at the heart of community life in this area of the state: "Football is king in small town Texas, and the team is the chamber of commerce come playoff time. Football is more than sport in west Texas. It's king! Oil wells and a lot of money have changed hands, and the fans will tell you that their team winning the championship means more than the money [wagered]."[8]

Writers Dave McNabb (of the *Dallas Morning News,* representing the Dallas metropolitan area and north central Texas to the Oklahoma line), Brian McTaggart (of the *Houston Chronicle,* representing the greater Houston area), Olin Buchanan (of the *Austin American-Statesman,* representing the central section of the state), and Louie Avery (of the *Texarkana Gazette,* representing the northeastern part of Texas) all contend that their region produces the best athletes and the highest level of competition. Not surprisingly, the one region of Texas that does not merit a representative in this debate is South Texas. Still, there have been some impressive moments over the years, and none more so than the victory by the Donna Redskins over the heavily favored Quanah Indians in the 1961 Class AA state title game played at the University of Texas' Memorial Stadium. A 1999 article in the *Dallas Morning News* summed up the unexpected triumph as "the Valley's best stand."[9]

At the start of a decade that would witness unprecedented social, political, and economic upheaval in many South Texas communities, the young men of the Donna squad provided the Valley's Spanish-speaking population with a focal point of pride and self-esteem. Over the past two decades, a long roster of historians of other minority groups and oppressed populations have noted the importance of sport to both an individual and a communal sense of worth in the United States and around the world.[10] The majority of the research in U.S. minority sport history has focused on the African American experience; notable among these are studies by Robert Ruck, David K. Wiggins, John M. Carroll, the late Arthur R. Ashe Jr., Jeffery T. Sammons, Elliott J. Gorn, and Sandy Tolan.[11]

During the 1980s and 1990s, historians and social scientists who were interested in other minority groups began focusing on the impact of sport on neighborhoods and school settings throughout the United States. Students of the Native American experience, for example, have provided numerous examples of how athletic competition has impacted these communities and schools. In a recent article on the Carlisle Indians, for example, David Wallace Adams argues that success on the gridiron helped some of the team members to believe that "if we could succeed on the field, we could do anything."[12] Gerald R. Gems's fine study of Native American and African American football players similarly notes that such competition (at all levels) "allowed subordinate groups to challenge the Social Darwinian beliefs and stereotypes that characterized them as 'others.'. . . [These] social evolutions took place on the high school teams . . . as disparate groups found some common ground in the popular culture of football."[13]

Likewise, Joel S. Franks, Roberta J. Park, Samuel O. Regalado, and Susan G. Zeiff have noted the impact of sport upon Asian Americans living in various locations in the American West. They describe how people of Japanese, Chinese, and Pacific Islander heritage in the United States have used success on baseball diamonds, football gridirons, and basketball courts to challenge the majority population's notion that Asian people are naturally "unathletic" and specifically that Asian males are "unmanly."[14] Further, Peter Levine, Steven A. Riess, and William M. Simons have studied the communal and personal implications of athletic accomplishment among the children of Jewish immigrants, primarily in the large metropolitan areas of the northeastern United States.[15] Finally, inquiries by Gary Ross Mormino and Anthony A. Yoseloff have summarized the impact of sport on Italian American neighborhoods from New York City to St. Louis and Tampa (the Florida materials examine both Italian American and Cuban American neighborhoods such as Ybor City). This chapter probes the existence of such circumstances among a minority population, the Mexican Americans of South Texas, that historians of sport have until recently almost completely ignored.[16]

Although the participation of Mexican Americans (and other Spanish-speaking people) in U.S. sport has not received much attention, one scholar, Samuel O. Regalado, has almost single-handedly brought Hispanic sport to an academic audience. His voluminous research scrutinizes important issues such as the significance of baseball leagues *(ligas)* to neighborhood (barrio) life in Los Angeles, the societal consequences of the Los Angeles Dodgers' Spanish-language broadcasts, and the majority population's perception of Hispanic major leaguers (especially the late Pittsburgh Pirate great, Roberto Clemente).[17]

My own work, published in 2002, focuses on the careers of two South Texas high school football stars, E. C. Lerma and Bobby Cavazos, between

1932 and 1965. In that article I note that the omission of the sporting contributions and experiences of Mexican Americans in Texas "leaves a gap in the historical understanding of sport and its impact on social relations." The success of such players and coaches, I argue, has had important repercussions, for while athletic competition did not eliminate all of the vestiges of racism, Lerma and Cavazos provided an effective counter to the stereotypical views many Texans held of people of Mexican descent.[18]

A limited number of other studies of the significance and value of Mexican American participation in various U.S. sports have appeared since the early 1970s. Donovan López's *Practice! Practice! Practice!: The History of the King Ranch Cowboys Baseball Team* is a slim volume that, like the works noted earlier, examines the impact of a mostly Mexican American team (although it included whites and African Americans) on social relations at the King Ranch and in the nearby city of Kingsville, Texas. López sums up the importance of the Cowboys' games by stating that athletic endeavor created "an environment that allowed ranch hands, councilmen, blue collar workers and corporate [ranch] managers to mix and mingle in the realm of sport." Further, López cites a 1997 *San Antonio Express-News* story that argues that these baseball games acted as "male icebreaker[s] and leveler[s] of class, race, and age. It's the democratic elevator conversation, the anonymous coffee shop exchange, the man-in-the-next-seat pleasantry. It's what many men who have little in common have in common."[19]

Three other publications, Jorge Prieto's *The Quarterback Who Almost Wasn't,* Mario (Mike) de la Fuente's *I Like You, Gringo—But!* and professional golfer Lee Treviño's *They Call Me Super Mex,* provide readers and researchers with firsthand accounts of Mexican Americans who used sport to break down stereotypes and achieve athletic, academic, and professional success. The Prieto and de la Fuente stories are particularly interesting because these men achieved success during an era (the 1930s) in which few Spanish-surnamed people in Texas and elsewhere in the West and Southwest even graduated from high school. A final contribution of note is Mario Longoria's thoroughly researched book, *Athletes Remembered: Mexican/Latino Professional Football Players, 1929–1970,* which focuses on the careers of Hispanic players in the National Football League (NFL) and the Canadian Football League (CFL), as well as notable Spanish-surnamed players from the collegiate ranks.[20]

The high school football experience of Mexican American students is not as well documented as that of other minority groups in Texas. The works of Ty

Cashion and Bill McMurray provide some coverage, but it pales in comparison with the attention given to the state's other large minority population, African Americans. To his credit, Cashion furnishes a cursory discussion of factors influencing the participation (or lack thereof) of *jugadores* (players) during the early twentieth century, but he presents limited material concerning the social significance of high school football for *comunidades* (communities) or the sport's impact on whites' perception of Spanish speakers.[21]

While the "Latin American" population of Texas did not face outright segregation on the gridiron, as did African Americans, there were substantial obstacles to athletic participation during the first half of the twentieth century. Poverty was the principal factor that kept jugadores off the field. Given the economic limitations of most families, the majority of young Mexican Americans did not even enter high school, much less have the opportunity to take part in athletic competition. A childish activity like football could not be permitted to keep a strong back and pair of hands from helping the family as it worked the cotton or vegetable fields.[22]

A second impediment was the perception by many in the educational system, as well as the general public, of both the intellectual and physical capabilities of Mexican Americans. An analysis of master's theses and doctoral dissertations produced by graduate students in education at the University of Texas (as well as other state institutions of higher learning) from the 1920s to the 1950s produces a litany of complaints about the shortcomings of "Mexican" pupils. Among the criticisms leveled were that they had little or no ambition, that they "lack[ed] pride in their schoolwork," and (ominously) that "their brains do not seem to work as rapidly as do the brains of English speaking students."[23] With regard to athletic ability, scholars were ambivalent. One noted that "Latin Americans" were "not as interested or eager to participate in physical education . . . particularly in inter-school competition, as are Anglo-American boys," while another argued that they "are fond of all sports, especially athletic contests . . . but they mar the [games] by being poor losers."[24]

In his monumental 1934 work on race relations in South Texas, *An American-Mexican Frontier: Nueces County, Texas,* Paul S. Taylor noted that some white children actively discouraged Mexican American youths from participating in sports. One of his informants recalled that classmates "didn't want us to play; they tell us to go away, not to play basketball and football. They wouldn't let me play very often.'"[25] Even "progressive" educational publications such as *Texas Outlook* assumed (during the early 1930s) that the academic circumstances confronting Mexican Americans had generated in them "feelings of inferiority . . . leading to suicide . . . [of] the instinct for self-improvement—the only really indispensable factor in the educating process."[26] Such characterizations hardly qualified these youths as prime candidates for success on the aggressive and spirited high school gridiron.

The Donna High School Redskins, and in particular the team's Mexican American players (10 of the 18 were of Mexican descent), battled such perceptions of inadequacy as they took the field in December of 1961 against the Quanah High School Indians in a contest for the Class AA state football title.[27]

Founded in 1907, the town of Donna is located in Hidalgo County, nestled right next to the Rio Grande, which serves as the border between the colossus of the North and los Estados Unidos de México. Because of its proximity to Mexico, the county was the scene of much cattle rustling and many other illegal activities. The jurisdiction also fits in nicely with the tradition of corruption and political chicanery common in South Texas during the early 1900s. Although Mexican Americans in Donna did not enjoy civil and social equality with their white neighbors, the political boss system then prevalent in the area provided a certain amount of protection from the worst ravages of racism experienced by some of their brothers and sisters in other parts of Texas. As long as corrupt Democratic Party machines needed "Mexican" votes, relations were amicable.[28]

The arrival of the St. Louis, Brownsville, and Mexico Railway in 1904, however, stimulated a land boom in South Texas and radically changed the area's racial dynamics. The arrival of Midwestern farmers during the late 1910s and early 1920s brought stricter segregation to Hidalgo and adjoining counties.[29] Donna split into two separate communities—one mostly white, the other almost all "Latin." The poorer side of town, East Donna, was the domicile of virtually all Mexican Americans, and the children of farm *trabajadores* (workers) often encountered humiliating and difficult circumstances in "their" school. During the early 1930s these students faced daily dirt and health inspections (specifically for lice infestation) and segregation for the first five grades because of perceived educational "handicaps." Due to such social and economic pressures, few of East Donna's pupils made it out of elementary school.

Because they were classified as "whites," however, those that did survive attended Donna High School (located on the west side of town), and, as one reporter noted in 1931, athletic ability could help increase Mexican Americans' acceptance among their white peers. "In fact, the Mexican children who can show their skill in art, music, scholarship, or physical prowess soon become favorites with the other white children and are wholeheartedly admired by them."[30] By the late 1950s, therefore, the Donna Redskins had a history of fielding competitive, ethnically mixed teams. The 1958 and 1959 squads produced records of eight wins and two losses but did not earn playoff appearances.

For the 1960 season Donna administrators hired Earl Scott, who had a proven record of succeeding with border area teams, in the hope of winning their long-sought-after district championship. The coach's credentials were impressive as, starting in 1955, he had guided the Eagle Pass (Maverick County) Eagles to a record of seven wins, two losses, and one tie (with a team that was 90 percent Mexican American) before moving on to Laredo (Webb County) in 1956. Prior to his arrival, Laredo school board members actually considered dropping football because, Scott asserts, many of them believed that the town's "kids could not compete in that league."

However, the new Laredo head coach proved the administrators wrong. After winning two games and losing eight in his first season, Scott's last two Laredo teams finished acceptable campaigns of six wins and four losses and nine wins and two losses. Both programs, though, lacked money, facilities, and winning traditions, and they generated only limited community support. Clearly, Scott was an able motivator and administrator who produced positive results under challenging conditions. Fortunately for Donna's bureaucrats, Scott purchased a small citrus farm in the community and accepted a junior high school teaching post in 1959. When the head coaching position came open, the veteran coach accepted the spot and guided the Redskins to eight wins and three losses in 1960, earning a district title and qualifying for the playoffs. The team's run ended when the squad lost to Sinton 12 to 0 in the first round of the state tournament.[31]

At the start of the 1961 season, Texas' sport media predicted that Donna would be respectable (selected to win its district, number 32AA), but the team was not perceived as a potential championship threat. In class AA, the pundits expected traditional powers Sweeny and Jacksboro to clash for statewide supremacy. The Redskins' early season schedule featured a scrimmage with San Benito (which fielded 45 players against Donna's 18), as well as two class AAA nondistrict teams, Rio Grande City and Mercedes. Injuries in the scrimmage and setbacks in the first two nonleague games (20 to 0 against Rio

Grande City and 12 to 8 against Mercedes) got the team's campaign off to a rocky start.³²

In addition to a grueling schedule, Scott also faced much the same situation as many Rio Grande Valley teams of that era: dealing with players who worked as migrants picking crops or performing agricultural and other types of labor in other states. A 1961 report by the *Corpus Christi Caller* stated that the (mostly Mexican American) population could "travel to approximately 38 other states on their journey . . . follow[ing] the cotton crops" and even trekking to "Colorado for sugar beets, Idaho for hops, Wisconsin for vegetables, Illinois for corn, and Illinois and Alabama for potatoes." Such circumstances made preparation for an upcoming season difficult since Coach Scott and his assistant, Bennie La Prade, never knew "what they had [with regard to talented players] going into any season."³³

For students such as running back Abel Benavides, playing conflicted with assisting in his family's economic survival. Benavides's father, for example, did not want his son to play and instead insisted that he toil in the fields until mid-September. "My dad didn't believe in sports, he believed in working all the time." Still, Benavides persevered, and his words buttress some of Gems's assertions regarding the value of football to the life of a minority student. "The migrant students had it especially tough . . . because their lack of English generally shut them out of school activities. For a young man struggling for a toehold in the mainstream, football worked wonders."³⁴

Quarterback Luz Pedraza faced similar circumstances since his family spent summers picking potatoes in northern Alabama and later in Illinois. Fortunately for Luz, his parents and siblings sacrificed some of their earnings and sent him home to Donna each year before the start of school. Other players, such as Richard Avila and Harry Lantz, shared similar experiences. When Avila's father, a Hidalgo County peace officer, died in 1955, the fifteen children in the family bagged groceries, delivered papers, raised livestock, and worked as migrants to generate income. Lantz's family traveled the nation as carnival workers, and the young Harry lived by himself in a trailer behind a local gas station for most of the school year.³⁵

Although they lost their first two games, the Redskins remained optimistic as they prepared for their third and final nondistrict game against the Mission Eagles. First, both Scott and La Prade were stern disciplinarians who insisted on strenuous conditioning (the Redskins started the first weight-training program in the Valley) to produce a team with stamina that played well through the fourth quarter of their games. Players recall that they "'didn't ever take [our] helmet off or sit during timeouts. . . . [We] sprinted on changes of quarter. We sprinted to the huddle. We ran everywhere.'" Second, tightly scripted practices were designed to perfect their offensive attack and eliminate mistakes. These efforts paid off handsomely during the playoffs as Donna totaled a minuscule fifteen yards in penalties during its last three games. Finally, unlike the situations Scott had faced in Eagle Pass and Laredo, the Donna community, both Mexican American and white, supported their team boisterously, with crowds of two thousand or more attending the junior varsity games. These factors, combined with a talented squad, generated eight consecutive victories (including holding opponents scoreless in four of their last five games), a perfect in-district mark, and a berth in the bidistrict (first round) playoff game.[36]

The Donna Redskins, the unlikely powerhouse from the Rio Grande Valley, marched into (and through) the tournament, defeating Refugio (32 to 0), Devine (12 to 7), Sweeny (32 to 14), and Brady (16 to 14) to reach the state title game with Quanah. In all five contests, they were considered the underdogs and were also the visiting team, which increased the difficulty of success. An examination of the Texas Class AA team polls from the 1961 campaign reveals that Donna never ranked in the top ten of the classification, while for the majority of the season Sweeny, Brady, and Quanah were all ranked in the top five.

Because of its racial undertones, the most noteworthy clash in the early rounds was the battle with Sweeny High School. Coach Scott never used race as a motivating factor for his team; during the regular season he certainly did not have to since most of the 32AA district teams also had substantial numbers of Mexican Americans. But the Sweeny game (which was played in the Gulf Coast city of Freeport) was different. One of the opposing coaches questioned the team's ability because of its ethnic composition. Prior to the game, he approached Scott and asked, "Can these pepper bellies play? I mean, you never hear of any of them in the Southwest Conference."[37] The Redskins' field general responded that his players would show their mettle between the sidelines and informed his squad of the commentary. Nick Padilla, who went out for the coin flip before the contest, endured one final insult when the Sweeny captain inquired whether he was a "real" player or the team's mascot. After battling to a tenuous 13 to 6 lead through three periods, the Redskins wore down their opponents in the fourth quarter, crossing the goal line three times in the final period to seize the victory.[38]

Donna's opponent for the title came in with highly impressive credentials. During a dominating season, the unbeaten and untied Quanah Indians tallied an astonishing 483 points, while permitting a mere 56.[39] The team from north central Texas had been classified as high as third in the state polls and had already eliminated top-ranked Jacksboro in the other state semifinal match. The Redskins' "Cinderella" season, prognosticators assumed, would meet an inglorious end on the turf of the University of Texas' Memorial Stadium on December 16, 1961. The Valley's representatives were apparently outmatched by their foes for the title game. In a 1999 interview, Luz Pedraza discussed some of the most glaring differences between Valley teams and squads from other parts of Texas. Although his commentary dealt with the 1961 team, it still holds true in many instances today (before the championship game one newspaper described the Redskins as being both "outweighed and outnumbered" by their opponent).[40] "We have mostly Mexican American kids. Other areas have more talent and speed, which you need as you go further and further in the playoffs."[41]

Donna's season had a happy ending, however, although the title game did not start off very well. Donna received the opening kickoff and quickly had to give up possession of the ball and punt to Quanah. The Indians marched down the field and scored to take a 7 to 0 lead after only five minutes of play. The scrappy Valley team responded with a drive of its own, although its offense lost possession of the ball near their opponents' goal line. The Redskins' defense then made a gallant stand, lead by Raul ("Chief") de la Garza and Fabian ("Outlaw") Barrera, who combined to sack the opposing quarterback, forcing Quanah to surrender the football. An appalling punt left the Redskins on the Indians' twenty-yard line, from where they quickly drove their offense across the goal line to make the tally 7 to 6 (Donna failed on a two-point conversion attempt).[42] The powerful Indian offense was unable to gain ground on their ensuing possession, and the Pedraza-led offense scored again with less than two minutes left in the second quarter. At halftime, surprisingly, the underdog led by a score of 12 to 7.

The second half began with an exchange of punts until Quanah pushed across the Donna goal line with about four minutes left in the third quarter. Uncharacteristically, the Redskins then turned the ball over on a Pedraza interception, and their opponents scored again to take a 21 to 12 advantage. The championship dream seemed to be slipping from the Redskins' grasp. Team member Joe González recalls that this was the only moment of panic for the squad. "Two or three guys started crying in the huddle, but Luz helped get them refocused on the task at hand."[43]

Atoning for his earlier miscue, quarterback Pedraza drove the offense down the field for a score and made a two-point conversion to narrow the deficit to 21 to 20. With less than six minutes to go, the Redskins' defensive unit stopped the Quanah offense and regained possession of the football. The Redskins' drive began on their opponent's 42 yard line and, with pinpoint passing and the hard running of Fred Edwards, scored a touchdown with about three minutes left. The Indians, in a final attempt to salvage victory, took the ensuing kickoff and drove down the field to make a tying score. Their last-ditch effort ground to a halt when Oscar Avila, one of five siblings on the Donna squad, sealed the title by intercepting a pass. The final score read 28 to 21 in favor of the Rio Grande Valley's representative.[44] The *Laredo Times* reported the triumph by stating that "Donna's Redskins were the only team to pull an upset. They brought the first state [football] championship in history to the Lower Rio Valley area."[45]

The Donna Redskins had done what many prognosticators thought impossible: A Rio Grande Valley team had become football champion of the state of Texas. Indeed, the "Mexicans" had shown "them" what they could do if given an opportunity. The task for the student of U.S. sport history is to uncover the significance of such an improbable triumph. What impact did the victory have on individual and community life? Sport reporters of the era noted the achievement but did not appreciate the social and historical significance of the victory. Harold Ratliff (in an article titled "The Latins Show Them") lavished praise on Coach Scott but voiced only faint approval for the sacrifice and talent of the Spanish-surnamed players. The championship "paid for all of the hard work the boys had done in showing that the Mexican boy can play football as well as anyone if he has the coach to tell him he can do it and show him how to prepare himself for the task at hand."[46]

The interviews conducted with members of the team provide insight into the sport's ability to engender social change. The Mexican American players asserted that competition offered them a setting where they could battle alongside and against whites and in which they were judged on individual merit, not their ethnicity. In part, football helped them stay in school, graduate, and pursue college degrees. As running back Abel Benavides reported, "'Football gave me a much better outlook on life. In football we all grew together. Coach treated everybody the same. . . . In this town, I went through the front door."'[47] Oscar Avila, whose interception sealed the Donna victory, supports this comment: "We never felt discriminated against and were always proud of who we were and were full of self-confidence. We were tough because of our fathers and the hard work we did and not because a coach told us we were."[48]

Non-Hispanics who were interviewed detailed similar circumstances and spoke of the camaraderie and friendships that formed while playing football and how all of the Donna residents stood by "their" Redskins during this run to glory. Still, Richard Avila mentions at least one barrier that even Mexican American athletes could not cross. In particular, he asserts, dating white girls was greatly discouraged. This did not mean that such rendezvous never took place, but they were clandestine. "Mexican American guys would meet Anglo girls at various places, but we would never go to Mr. Jones' house to pick up their [sic] daughter." He summed up his argument succinctly: "You did not notice many things forty years ago, but things did happen."[49] In an interview, Joe González noted both the benefits and the limitations of sport for the Redskins' Mexican American players. "Those who were not athletes were not as highly thought of," he said. He also recalled that, although the players were allowed certain advantages, in Donna, as elsewhere in the Valley, "we [Mexicans] knew that we had our place in life."[50]

These people's recollections support one scholar's contention regarding the benefits and limitations of sport as a vehicle to alter the majority's perception of minorities. As Gerald R. Gems states, "athletic feats and successes destabilized norms, expectations, and stereotypes . . . but socially they remained members of alternative cultures, marginalized with dual identities, and limited inclusion, particularly off the field."[51] The Mexican Americans on this team were privileged in certain ways, but at least some in the white community did not perceive them as social equals.

Part of the impact of Donna's victory on the town's Mexican American community can be gleaned from two unrelated events, roughly forty years apart. First, as Cathy Harasta notes in a story on the team written for the *Dallas Morning News,* the day after the triumph by the hometown squad in the championship game, many residents, with most of the team's players and coaches, "walked down old Highway 83 to San Juan, eight miles away, to a religious shrine [Our Lady of San Juan Shrine in Pharr]. The basilica had long been regarded as the site of a miracle."[52] What is significant is that the Donna comunidad used a mostly Mexican (and Catholic) way to commemorate victory in a mostly American (and Texan) ritual.

The second incident is apparent in an interview with Oscar Avila in May of 2002. Avila, who now lives outside the Valley, visits Donna frequently. During one of his sojourns an older gentleman approached him and inquired whether he was one of the "Avila boys" from the 1961 team. After indicating that he was, the individual turned to his wife and said, "Mira, viejita, este es uno de los Avilas que jugó en el equipo del '61 cuando les ensellamos a los gringos que nosotros tambien sabiamos jugar football" (My dear, this is one of the Avila boys who played for the '61 team *when we showed the gringos that we too knew how to play football*) (my italics).[53]

In a 1996 article, Samuel O. Regalado examined such connections through his research on baseball in Los Angeles barrios after World War II. He stated that sport and recreation "did more than help to preserve a strong sense of Mexican heritage . . . it wielded a sense of unity amongst the people. . . . Local baseball games were very much a part of the nucleus that held the community intact."[54] In 1990 filmmaker Rick Leal documented similar links between Rio Grande Valley high school football and Mexican Americans. In a documentary titled "Friday Night under the Lights," he describes some of the unique rituals that surround gridiron battles among South Texas' Spanish-surnamed population. Leal's work chronicles uniquely Mexican American rites such as the composing and signing of *corridos* (traditional ballads that tell a heroic story) about individual football programs around the Valley. The pilgrimage to the San Juan shrine made by Donna Redskin fans and the chance encounter by Oscar Avila with an elderly gentleman, it seems, are only two of the ways by which members of a Mexican American community have differentiated their participation as fans and players of Texas high school football.[55]

In November of 2001 the surviving members of the 1961 team gathered to commemorate the fortieth anniversary of their achievement. Part of that celebratory event included the presentation of championship rings to players or surviving family members. The group took time to remember their colleagues who had passed away: Assistant Coach Bennie La Prade (for whom the Donna High School stadium is now named), Tommy Stone, Raul ("Chief") de la Garza, and Fabian ("Outlaw") Barrera. Time has not dimmed the memory of that season, and Donna's permanent residents (now about thirteen thousand) still recall Coach Scott's squad. The community still has a water tower, visible throughout town, that proudly proclaims the Donna Redskins as "1961 AA State Football Champions." As *Dallas Morning News* reporter Cathy Harasta noted in 1999, "It looms as tall as ever, though its paint job shows its age, the maroon gone to a dusty rose and the gold [is] lacking sheen."[56]

Even more importantly, the season stands as a monument to the athletic and intellectual capabilities of an ethnic group that has suffered much discrimination throughout the history of Texas. For many Valley youths, the Redskins provided an example of what they could accomplish, both in the classroom and on the gridiron. A brief examination of the careers of the various Mexican American players on this team reveals that all of them have been able to move into middle-class, if not professional, employment. Two are educators: Luz Pedraza is currently the head football coach at Weslaco High School, and Alfredo Avila is athletic director for the Corpus Christi school system. Abel Benavides and Raul Alvarado work for Dupont in Corpus Christi. Joe González was an engineer with Boeing and is now an entrepreneur involved in Republican Party politics in Orange County, California. Richard Avila works in public relations for a San Antonio–based computer company. Nick Padilla works in the trucking supply industry, and Oscar Avila is retired from the postal service and owns his own roofing firm in San Antonio. Current Donna High School principal Fernando Castillo explains that the mystique of the championship season lives on even among those who were not alive to experience the events firsthand. "I was born in 1963 and heard about that team all of my life. That was the big talk. To be like that team was everyone's dream."[57] The success of these players permitted many of the Valley's Mexican American youth to envisage goals that previous generations could not.

In many ways, the improbable run of the Donna Redskins in 1961 parallels the accomplishments of another Texas-based team, the 1966 Texas Western (now the University of Texas–El Paso) Miners. This team, the first collegiate basketball team to play for a national title while starting five African American players, defeated the (all-white) University of Kentucky Wildcats for the national championship. According to Frank Fitzpatrick, who chronicled the Miners' season in his book *And the Walls Came Tumbling Down,* Texas Western's victory had a significant impact upon the outlook and lives of young African American men throughout the nation. One player recalled that the title run was a watershed and that "Young black players told me years later that it gave them confidence and courage." Fitzpatrick also quotes a Georgia senator (Leon Butts) who in 1957 foresaw the impact that athletic success could have on an oppressed population. "Where Negroes and Whites meet on athletic fields on a basis of complete equality, it is *only natural that this same sense of equality carries into the daily living of these people*" (my italics).[58]

Like the better-known anecdote of the Texas Western Miners, the story of the 1961 Donna High School Redskins provides scholars with an example of the promise and value of combining the history of sport and ethnic minorities. Over the past two decades the significance of such research has been amply demonstrated by scholars of groups such as African Americans, Asian Americans, Italian Americans, Native Americans, and Jews. Scholars have noted how sport helped build community pride and functioned as a way to generate communal cohesion, organize politically, and demonstrate the intellectual and physical capabilities of "others" before the broader, often biased, white population in cities and towns all over the United States. While much has been learned, there is still much to do since, until now, the athletic participation and history of the largest minority group in the United States, Latinos and Hispanics, have received only cursory attention.

Over the past thirty years, scholars of the history of Mexican Americans (and other Latino groups) have examined a variety of issues surrounding the daily lives of these Spanish-speaking peoples. Researchers have noted the class, religious, economic, and political diversity of the Hispanic communities in Texas, California, Illinois, and elsewhere. They have also examined topics such as labor, political organizing, and varied campaigns for social justice. This research has done much to expand our understanding of daily barrio life in the United States.[59] Until recently, sport had often been a missing element in the story of these communities. The account of the Mexican American players of the 1961 Donna High School football team and their impact on individual and community self-perception may help stimulate further research into the value, significance, and effect of sport as an integral part of Hispanic and Latino history and life in the United States.[60]

NOTES

1. A. O. ("Bum") Phillips, quoted in Ty Cashion, *Pigskin Pulpit: A Social History of Texas High School Football Coaches* (Austin: Texas State Historical Association, 1998), ix.

2. For a negative perspective on high school football in Texas see H. G. Bissinger, *Friday Night Lights: A Town, a Team, and a Dream* (New York: Harper-

Collins, 1990), and Douglas E. Foley, "The Great American Football Ritual: Reproducing Race, Class, and Gender Inequality," *Sociology of Sport Journal* 7 (1990): 111-35. Although the game of football initially took root in the Ivy League schools of the Northeast, it was not unknown in Texas in the years after the Civil War. Documentary evidence reveals that some of the larger cities in the state, such as the port city of Galveston, had "town" teams (not affiliated with high schools) before the 1890s. Many of the ambassadors of this sport were Ivy League graduates. This is the case with the "father of Texas football," James Perkins Richardson, a Yale University alumnus who accepted a position as a teacher of modern languages at Ball High School in Galveston in 1892. See David Baron, "The Birth of Texas Schoolboy Football," in *King Football: Greatest Moments in Texas High School Football History*, edited by Mike Bynum (Birmingham, Ala.: Epic Sports Classics, 2003), 26–39. Charles R. Frederick Jr., "A Good Day to Be Here: Tailgating in the Grove at Ole Miss," Ph.D. diss., Indiana University, 1999, 12, 16.

3. Frederick Jr., "A Good Day to Be Here," 17. While the majority of schools in Texas play the widely recognized style of football played with eleven players, smaller communities (particularly in the less-populated western sections of the state) have created their own version of the game: six-man football. Several writers, such as Harold Ratliff and Carlton Stowers, have documented the history and lore of the Texas high school gridiron. The most complete treatment of the sport's history is provided by Bill McMurray in *Texas High School Football* (South Bend: Icarus Press, 1985).

4. Mitchell Krugel, *Texas Football Trilogy: A Season in the Lone Star State* (Champaign: Sports Publishing, 1999), 1.

5. Cashion, *Pigskin Pulpit*, 14, 2; Myron Cope, "Texas Football: Fierce, Frantic, Fabulous," *Saturday Evening Post* (Sept. 24, 1966), 83–87, 84.

6. "All-time Football Records," *Texas Coach* (Oct. 1990): 56; Krugel, *Texas Football Trilogy*, 10.

7. Charlie Williams, "South Texas Football," *Texas Coach* (Apr. 1979): 37, 60; "All-time Football Records," 56.

8. Bill Hart, "West Texas: Same as It Ever Was," in *Dave Campbell's 2000 Texas Football*, 150.

9. David McNabb, "D-FW/North Texas: Size Matters"; Brian McTaggart, "Greater Houston: Black and Blue Division"; Olin Buchanan, "Central Texas: Westlake, Westlake, Baby"; and Louie Avery, "East Texas: Speed Thrills"—all in *Dave Campbell's 2000 Texas Football*, 152, 154, 155, 156. For competitive purposes, the high schools of Texas are grouped according to the number of students in their populations. For football, there are five different classifications of teams (from AAAAA, for the largest schools, with several thousand students, to A, for the small-

est schools, usually with fewer than one hundred students). Cathy Harasta, "Grande Memories: '61 Donna Team Remains Valley's Only State Champ," *Dallas Morning News*, Oct. 27, 1999, 44-48. This article is part of the series "100 Years of Texas High School Football."

10. Numerous works could be cited here. Among the most significant are C. L. R. James, *Beyond a Boundary* (1963; reprint, Durham, N.C.: Duke University Press, 1993); Allen Guttmann, *Games and Empires: Modern Sports and Cultural Imperialism* (New York: Columbia University Press, 1994); G. P. T. Finn and R. Giulianotti, eds., *Football Culture: Local Contests, Global Visions* (London: Frank Cass, 2000); T. J. L. Chandler and J. Nauright, eds., *Making the Rugby World: Race, Gender, and Commerce* (London: Frank Cass, 1998); J. Arbena, ed., *Sport and Society in Latin America: Diffusion, Dependency, and the Rise of Mass Culture* (New York: Greenwood, 1988); M. Cronin and D. Mayall, eds., *Sporting Nationalisms: Identity, Ethnicity, Immigration, and Assimilation* (London: Frank Cass, 1998), and J. A. Mangan and L. P. Da Costa, eds., *The Latin American World: Sport in Society* (London: Frank Cass, 2001).

11. Rob Ruck, *Sandlot Seasons: Sport in Black Pittsburgh* (Urbana: University of Illinois Press, 1993); David K. Wiggins, *Glory Bound: Black Athletes in a White America* (Syracuse: Syracuse University Press, 1997); John M. Carroll, *Fritz Pollard: Pioneer in Racial Advancement* (Urbana: University of Illinois Press, 1992); Arthur R. Ashe Jr., *A Hard Road to Glory: The African American Athlete in Football* (New York: Amistad, 1993); Jeffery T. Sammons, "'Race' and Sport: A Critical, Historical Examination," *Journal of Sport History* 21 (Fall 1994): 203-78; Elliott J. Gorn, ed., *Muhammad Ali: The People's Champ* (Urbana: University of Illinois Press, 1995); and Sandy Tolan, *Me and Hank: A Boy and His Hero, Twenty-five Years Later* (New York: Simon and Schuster, 2001).

12. David Wallace Adams, "More than a Game: The Carlisle Indians Take to the Gridiron, 1893-1917," *Western Historical Quarterly* 32 (Spring 2001): 25-53, 36. For a similar argument, see John Bloom, *To Show What an Indian Can Do* (Minneapolis: University of Minnesota Press, 2000).

13. Gerald R. Gems, *For Pride, Profit, and Patriarchy: Football and the Incorporation of American Cultural Values* (Lanham, Md.: Scarecrow Press, 2000), especially chap. 4, "The Huddle: Multicultural Football," 140.

14. Joel S. Franks, *Crossing Sidelines, Crossing Cultures: Sport and Asian Pacific American Cultural Citizenship* (Lanham, Md.: University Press of America, 2000), and *Whose Baseball?: The National Pastime and Cultural Diversity in California, 1859-1941* (Scarecrow Press, 2001); Roberta J. Park, "Sport and Recreation among Chinese Americans of the Pacific Coast from the Time of Arrival to the 'Quiet Decade' of the 1950s," *Journal of Sport History* 27(3) (Fall 2000): 445-80; Samuel O. Regal-

ado, "Incarcerated Sport: Nisei Women's Softball and Athletics during Japanese-American Internment," *Journal of Sport History* 27(3) (Fall 2000): 431-44; and Susan G. Zieff, "From Badminton to the Bolero: Sport and Recreation in San Francisco's Chinatown, 1895-1950," *Journal of Sport History* 27(1) (Spring 2000): 1-29.

15. Peter Levine, *Ellis Island to Ebbets Field: Sport and the American Jewish Experience* (New York: Oxford University Press, 1992); Steven A. Riess, *Sport and the American Jew* (Syracuse: Syracuse University Press, 1998); and William M. Simons, "The Athlete as Jewish Standard Bearer: Media Images of Hank Greenberg," *Jewish Social Studies* 44 (Spring 1982): 95-112.

16. Gary Ross Mormino, "The Playing Fields of St. Louis: Italian Immigrants and Sports, 1925-1941," *Journal of Sport History* 9 (Summer 1982): 5-19; and Anthony Yoseloff, "From Ethnic Hero to National Icon: The Americanization of Joe DiMaggio," *International Journal of the History of Sport* 16 (Sept. 1999): 1-20. For an examination of the importance of sport to other minority communities see the following: Franks, *Crossing Sidelines, Crossing Cultures;* Steven A. Reiss, "A Fighting Chance: The Jewish American Boxing Experience, 1890-1940," *American Jewish History* 74 (Mar. 1985): 233-54; Adams, "More than a Game"; Nicholas P. Ciotola, "Spignesi, Sinatra, and the Pittsburgh Steelers: Franco's Italian Army as an Expression of Ethnic Identity," *Journal of Sport History* 27 (Summer 2000): 271-90; Gerald R. Gems, "The Construction, Negotiation, and Transformation of Racial Identity in American Football: A Study of Native Americans and African Americans," *American Indian Culture and Research Journal* 22(2) (1998): 131-50; and Gems, *For Pride, Profit, and Patriarchy,* especially chap. 4, "The Huddle: Multicultural Football."

17. Samuel O. Regalado, *Viva Baseball!: Latin Major Leaguers and Their Special Hunger* (Urbana: University of Illinois Press, 1998); "Baseball in the Barrios: The Scene in East Los Angeles since World War II," *Baseball History* 1 (Summer 1996): 47-59; "Dodgers Béisbol Is on the Air: The Development and Impact of the Dodgers' Spanish-language Broadcasts, 1958-1994," *California History* (Fall 1995): 282-89; "'Image Is Everything': Latin Baseball Players and the U.S. Press," *Studies in Latin American Popular Culture* 13 (1994): 101-14; the preceding articles are all by Samuel O. Regalado.

18. Jorge Iber, "Mexican Americans of South Texas Football: The Athletic and Coaching Careers of E. C. Lerma and Bobby Cavazos, 1932-1965," *Southwestern Historical Quarterly* 55 (Apr. 2002): 616-33, 618, 632.

19. Donovan López, *Practice! Practice! Practice!: The History of the King Ranch Cowboys Baseball Team* (Kingsville, Tex.: privately published by Donovan López, 1998), 31.

20. Jorge Prieto, *The Quarterback Who Almost Wasn't* (Houston: Arte Publico Press, 1994), and Mario (Mike) de la Fuente with Boye De Mente, *I Like You, Gringo—*

But! (Phoenix: Phoenix Books, 1972). Prieto played his collegiate football in Mexico. For more information on U.S. football in Mexico see the following websites: http://www.onefa.org/ and http://tackleo.com/. See also Lee Treviño and Sam Blair, *They Call Me Super Mex* (New York: Random House, 1982), and Mario Longoria, *Athletes Remembered: Mexican/Latino Professional Football Players, 1929-1970* (Houston: Arte Publico Press, 1997).

21. Cashion, *Pigskin Pulpit*, 100-102.

22. For an overview of the circumstances surrounding Mexican American education in Texas throughout most of the twentieth century, see Guadalupe San Miguel, *"Let Them All Take Heed": Mexican Americans and the Campaign for Educational Equality in Texas, 1910-1981* (Austin: University of Texas Press, 1987).

23. For an example of some of these studies see the following: James Kilbourne Harris, "A Sociological Study of a Mexican School in San Antonio, Texas," master's thesis, University of Texas, 1927; Genevieve King, "The Psychology of a Mexican Community in San Antonio, Texas," master's thesis, University of Texas, 1936; Clyde Ira Kramme, "A Comparison of Anglo Culture with Spanish Culture Elementary Students in Physical Development as Determined by Height, Weight, and Vital Capacity Measurements," master's thesis, Texas A&I University, 1939; Andrew Lee Habermacher, "Physical Development of Anglo and Spanish Culture Boys and Girls Ages 13-18, Inclusive," master's thesis, Texas A&I University, 1940; and Albert Folsom Cobb, "Comparative Study of the Athletic Ability of Latin American and Anglo American Boys on a Junior High School Level," master's thesis, University of Texas, 1952. For a more thorough discussion of this topic, see Iber, "Mexican Americans and South Texas Football."

24. For a more recent examination of the educational establishment's view of Mexican Americans during the early decades of the 1900s, see Carlos Kevin Blanton, "'They Cannot Master Abstractions, but They Can Often Be Made Efficient Workers': Race and Class in the Intelligence Testing of Mexican Americans and African Americans in Texas during the 1920s," *Social Science Quarterly* 81(4) (Dec. 2000): 1014-26. See King, "The Psychology of a Mexican Community in San Antonio, Texas," 62; Harris, "A Sociological Study of a Mexican School in San Antonio, Texas," 96-97; and Cobb, "Comparative Study of the Athletic Ability of Latin American and Anglo American Boys on a Junior High School Level," 2.

25. Paul S. Taylor, *An American-Mexican Frontier: Nueces County, Texas* (Chapel Hill: University of North Carolina Press, 1934), 211.

26. Dorothy M. Kress, "The Spanish-speaking School Child in Texas," *Texas Outlook* 18 (Dec. 1934): 24.

27. The seventeen students who played for the 1961 team were Tommy Stone, Luz Pedraza, Abel Benavides, Oscar Avila, Richard Avila, Fred ("Flex") Edwards,

Alfredo Avila, Jim Hulme, Joe ("Rock") González, Raul Alvarado, Raul ("Chief") de la Garza, Jackie Roberson, Bill Brumley, Harry Lantz, Verle Hooper, Fabian ("Outlaw") Barrera, and Johnny Badeaux. This information is taken from Harasta, "Grande Memories," 48.

28. Ibid.

29. Alicia A. Garza, "Donna, TX," *The Handbook of Texas Online,* http://www.tsha.utexas.edu/handbook/online/articles/view/DD/hfd5.html, and "Hidalgo County," *The Handbook of Texas Online,* http://www.tsha.utexas.edu/handbook/online/articles/view/HH/hch14.html.

30. For an overview of the economic and social changes that took place in this part of Texas as a result of the land boom, see David Montejano, *Anglos and Mexicans in the Making of Texas, 1836–1986* (Austin: University of Texas Press, 1987).

31. Gladine Bowers, "Mexican Education in East Donna," *Texas Outlook* 15 (Mar. 1931): 29–30.

32. Earl Scott, interview with author, Feb. 15, 2002. See also Roy Hess, "Memories of Donna's State Championship Live On," *Associated Press Newswires,* Dec. 27, 2001.

33. Emil Tagliabue, "South Texas Teams Open Football Drills," *Corpus Christi Caller,* Aug. 13, 1961, 3C; "Schoolboys Open Football Drills," *Corpus Christi Caller,* Aug. 14, 1961, 5B; Ray Collins, "Sinton, Bishop, Flour Bluff Picked to Win Openers," *Corpus Christi Caller,* Aug. 31, 1961, 4C. Earl Scott interview.

34. Harasta, "Grande Memories," 46.

35. Ibid.

36. Earl Scott interview; Richard Avila, interview with author, Feb. 18, 2002; Harry Lantz, interview with author, Feb. 8, 2002; and Luz Pedraza, telephone interview, Sept. 5, 2001.

37. Harasta, "Grande Memories," 46; Earl Scott interview; Richard Avila interview.

38. The Southwest Conference (SWC) was one of the premier college football conferences in the United States, especially during the 1950s. The league was unusual in that seven of its eight member teams (Baylor, Texas, Texas Tech, Rice, Texas Christian, Southern Methodist, and Texas A&M) were located in the Lone Star state. The other squad that played in the SWC was the University of Arkansas. The SWC folded in 1996 when the member teams joined other conferences.

39. Earl Scott, interview with author, Feb. 8, 2002. For a look at a late-season Class AA ranking (before the start of the playoffs), see *Corpus Christi Caller-Times,* "Bucs Slip to tie for 10th," Oct. 31, 1961, C1.

40. "Rain, Mud Threaten Schoolboy Grid Playoffs," *Laredo Times,* Dec. 15, 1961, 12.

41. "Donna Wins State Championship," *Edinburg Daily Review,* Dec. 17, 1961, 4.

42. Harasta, "Grande Memories," 45.

43. In U.S. football, a touchdown is followed by a "try for extra point." This is done by kicking the ball through the uprights from a distance of twenty yards. The scoring team also has another option. Instead of kicking the ball, the offense and defense can line up on the defensive team's three yard line, and the scoring team has one play to either run or complete a pass into the opponent's end zone for two points. Joe González interview, Sept. 10, 2002.

44. This description of the game comes from game footage provided to the author by Oscar Avila. Videotape in author's possession.

45. *Laredo Times,* "Wichita Falls, Dumas, Albany, Donna Champs," Dec. 18, 1961, 11.

46. Harold Ratliff, *Autumn's Mightiest Legions: History of Texas Schoolboy Football* (Waco: Texian Press, 1963), 158.

47. Ibid.

48. E-mail from Oscar Avila to author, Apr. 24, 2002. Copy in author's possession.

49. Richard Avila interview.

50. Joe González interview.

51. Gems, "The Construction, Negotiation, and Transformation of Racial Identity in American Football," 145.

52. Harasta, "Grande Memories," 48.

53. The word "gringo" is a derogatory term used by many Spanish-speaking people in the United States and Latin America to refer to white Americans. Oscar Avila and Johnny Badeaux, interview with author, May 14, 2002.

54. Samuel O. Regalado, "Baseball in the Barrios: The Scene in East Los Angeles since World War II," *Baseball History* 1(2) (Summer 1996): 47–59, 57.

55. Rick Leal, "Friday Night under the Lights," video, KGBT, 1990.

56. Harasta, "Grande Memories," 44.

57. Ibid., 46.

58. Frank Fitzpatrick, *And the Walls Came Tumbling Down* (New York: Simon and Schuster, 1999), 27, 45.

59. The literature on Mexican Americans, their daily lives, community organizing, and organizations is extensive. Some of the most important works published (which provide an effective introduction to the latest historiographical trends in the field) in recent years include George J. Sánchez, *Becoming Mexican American: Ethnicity, Culture, and Identity in Chicano Los Angeles, 1900–1945* (New York: Oxford University Press, 1993); Lisbeth Haas, *Conquest and Historical Identities in California, 1769–1936* (Berkeley: University of California Press, 1995); Jorge Iber, *Hispanics in the Mormon Zion, 1912–1999* (College Station: Texas A&M University Press, 2000); Richard A. Garcia, *Rise of the Mexican American Middle Class:*

San Antonio, 1929-1941 (College Station: Texas A&M University Press, 1991); and David Montejano, ed., *Chicano Politics and Society in the Late Twentieth Century* (Austin: University of Texas Press, 1999).

  60. For an examination of the potential of this research, see José M. Alamillo, "*Peloteros* in Paradise: Mexican American Baseball and Oppositional Politics in Southern California, 1930-1950," *Western Historical Quarterly* 34 (Summer 2003): 191-211.

READ ALL ABOUT IT!
The Spanish-language Press, the Dodgers, and the Giants, 1958–1982
SAMUEL O. REGALADO

"Fernando was born to win," crowed Rodolfo García, sports columnist for the Los Angeles Spanish-language newspaper *La Opinión*.[1] In 1981 few, if any, major league rookies had received the type of national attention given to Mexican lefty pitcher Fernando Valenzuela of the Los Angeles Dodgers. Indeed, no other Latino player before that time had hit the majors with such force, a force that fueled the "Fernandomania" euphoria and propelled it into the national limelight and the annals of baseball history. To be sure, since the immediate postintegration years, which saw the Latin presence in the major leagues become a permanent fixture, only four players from Latin countries had won Rookie of the Year honors. And none of them captivated the type of national attention seen in 1981. Even the great Roberto Clemente, whose achievements and contributions unquestionably paved an important path for Latino progress in professional baseball, found his greatest fame only after his untimely death in 1972.

The demographic chemistry in Los Angeles and its adjacent communities in 1981 also contributed mightily to Valenzuela's immediate prominence. By the time of his arrival, 27.48 percent of that city's nearly three million residents were listed as having a "Spanish surname."[2] To the credit of their organization, the Dodgers had, since 1958, provided Spanish-language radio broadcast coverage of their games. Moreover, the Dodgers allowed the Spanish-language presses full access to the players and coaches. Hence, *La Opinión,* the largest and most prestigious daily in both the region and the country, enjoyed a sound relationship with the National League club. And, to no one's great surprise, the staff members at *La Opinión* were among Valenzuela's most jubilant supporters.

Nevertheless, while the left-hander from Sonora, Mexico, earned the greatest immediate notoriety among Latinos, particularly in the Southwest, he was not the first Latin player of distinction to play for a West Coast team. The San Francisco Giants, who, like their counterparts to the south, also settled in the West in 1958, had produced several players from Latin America, players whose impact in the majors won them statistical prominence. In their prime, Orlando Cepeda, Juan Marichal, and Felipe Alou, among others, were major league standouts. The impressive credentials of these athletes notwithstanding, their notoriety fell far short of the fame that later landed on Valenzuela. And though Los Angeles and San Francisco were home to large Spanish-speaking communities, newspaper coverage and the promotion of Latin players on their teams revealed a curious portrait of contradiction.

The story of California's Mexican Spanish-language press in relationship to Latin American professional baseball players in the Los Angeles and San Francisco regions characterized another component of the larger story involving sport and the Hispanic experience. Though the lens of scrutiny now includes closer examinations of ethnic Americans as a key factor in athletics in the United States, the path to this point was a long one. Since history fine-tuned itself as a profession in the late nineteenth century, athletics in the American experience had remained an invisible topic in the scholarly community. Serious study of sport in the American saga, in fact, did not even surface until the mid-1970s. Moreover, many of those early works leaned heavily on Eurocentric perspectives.

Baseball history, too, fit within this paradigm. However, by the 1980s, scholars were taking important steps to reconstruct the ethnic and cultural chemistry that made up the game and characterized its impact on the national scene. Jules Tygiel, Donn Rogosin, and Rob Ruck, for instance, produced works that more closely examined the link between the black community and the national pastime.[3] In addition, their revelations established with greater clarity the paramount role of ethnicity within the scope of the American saga. In the 1990s these works in turn spawned the production of scholarly studies that examined the case of Latins in baseball. As the Spanish-language demographic and cultural influence increased in the United States, authors such as Samuel O. Regalado, Alan Klein, and Roberto González de Echevarría produced monographs that highlighted not only the performance and struggles of the players but also their historical significance as a major factor in the development and establishment of an identity for the Hispanics in the United States.[4]

Arturo J. Marcano Guevara and David P. Fidler added to this growing list with an examination of baseball's questionable labor tactics in its recruitment of young Latino prospects.[5] Other scholars, such as José Alamillo and Richard Santillán, produced outstanding studies (in the form of articles) that keyed in on the relationship between Mexican semiprofessional baseball and the working class.[6] In addition, by the end of the 1990s, thanks to the works of historians Jorge Iber (on football) and Gregory S. Rodríguez (on boxing), the examination of sport within the Latin community expanded still further.[7] Not surprisingly, the Spanish-language (or "immigrant") press in the United States served as an essential tool of research from which historians could better view the fascinating saga of athletics in Hispanic America.

Before the twentieth century—long before the Dodgers and the Giants ventured westward—182 Spanish-language papers operated throughout the Southwest. Forty-two of these were in California alone.[8] Though most of them died after a brief existence, their missions were similar: Report local activities relevant to their readers and promote cohesion within a community still feeling the pain of annexation.[9] By the 1890s a substantial portion of people of Mexican descent living in the Southwest were either recent Mexican nationals or part of a generation raised in the years immediately following the 1848 Treaty of Guadalupe Hidalgo, the pact in which Mexico ceded much of its northern territories to the United States. Still others belonged to a generation that was born before the treaty. In any event, all of these groups experienced a critical socioeconomic transition that largely deprived them of any opportunities for advancement in the Anglo world that, by then, surrounded them. Faced with these difficult circumstances and channeled into barrios and *colonias* (communities), they hoped to plant the seeds of advancement and turned inward for strength and support.

As the Spanish-language newspaper industry expanded, their various editors sought to plant their stake in the new social environment. Some papers took on a position as advocate for Mexican American interests. Still others saw themselves as mouthpieces for Mexican nationals. Most importantly, all of them, in an effort to galvanize communities, accepted and promoted their role as "the most vocal instruments of cultural and linguistic resistance to assimilation [into Anglo society]."[10] As early as 1892, Hispanic journalists in the Southwest formed La Prensa Asociada Hispano-Americana (Press Association of Hispanic America), whose chief purpose was "to protect and promote the interests of Mexican Americans and preserve Hispanic culture."[11]

However, there was more to this mission. Along with the social and economic transition came the emerging negative stereotypes of Mexicans, accompanied by racial discrimination. Animosities that surfaced after the U.S.-Mexican War, anti-Catholicism, and prejudice toward people of dark skin all contributed to Anglo perceptions of Mexicans as simply unwanted "greasers." "Local and national hostilities toward Mexican-Americans influenced issues such as statehood, public education, land ownership as well as social contacts," observed writer Doris L. Meyer.[12] Alarmed by the growth of these elements, the perceptive Spanish-language journalists of that era also made it part of their mission to denounce "disparaging portrayals of Mexicans in the United States and to paint a more positive image of Mexicans."[13]

Between 1900 and 1930, several events occurred that impacted the Mexican borderland communities. First, vast economic development, particularly in irrigation, agriculture, and the railroad industry, took place in the southwestern region of the United States. Second, political instability in Mexico exploded into a civil war. As a result, during this period—an era that historians of Mexican American history refer to as the "Great Migration"—approximately one million Mexicans crossed the border into the United States. Having joined nearly half a million others already in residence there, they realized the need to establish an identity. *El Heraldo de México,* a Los Angeles–based paper founded in 1915, saw itself as a voice for Mexican nationals, particularly the working class, in "El Norte." To that end, the daily happily amplified all of the symbols and celebrations that promoted Mexico to its readers.[14] The self-proclaimed "Defender of the Mexicans in the United States," *El Heraldo* often ran columns that reported on "the role played by labor contractors and American employers in mistreating the immigrant workers."[15] But it was *El Heraldo*'s Los Angeles counterpart, *La Opinión,* that eventually led the charge in the promotion of Mexican culture.

Ignacio Lozano founded *La Opinión,* not coincidentally, on September 16, (Mexican Independence Day), 1926. Lozano, who came from an upscale family in the Mexican state of Nuevo León, entered the United States in 1908 and, five years later, started *La Prensa,* a daily in the San Antonio, Texas, area. The early success of *La Opinión* came as a result of the publisher's shrewd journalistic sense. Lozano "brought to Hispanic journalism in the United States a professionalism and business acumen that resulted in longevity for his ... papers."[16] His goal was to promote Mexican history and traditions, both of which resonated on an emotional level with many of the recent arrivals from Mexico who longed for their homeland.[17] By the midtwenties, after having "set up a network of correspondents throughout the United States," the publisher noted the increase in West Coast subscriptions and decided to open up operations in the Los Angeles area.[18] In fact, between 1920 and 1930, Los Angeles witnessed a rise in its Mexican population from approximately 29,000 to 190,000.[19] By 1930, a year into the Depression, *La Opinión* boasted a circulation rate of more than 25,000, with subscriptions that reached into several Midwestern states and San Francisco.

Interestingly, Lozano originally viewed *La Opinión* as "a Mexican paper published in the United States."[20] This "'México de afuera' [Mexico on the outside] campaign was markedly nationalistic and militated to preserve Mexican identity in the United States."[21] As the years went by, the paper took the lead in carrying on the mission set forth by the nineteenth-century Press Association of Hispanic America to "promote" and "preserve" Hispanic culture. All of the events and personalities whose achievements expanded Mexican awareness found a ready ally in *La Opinión.* Entertainers provided especially good print. Actress Dolores del Río, for instance, received immense coverage not only because of her fame but also because of her outspoken patriotism. That patriotism aside, the fact that the successful actress also came from a family of means reinforced the accurate perception that a Lozano paper catered to "the views of the elite."[22] Hence, del Río and others like her provided perfect fodder for Lozano's goals, one of which was to urge "readers to emulate the example of the better Mexican classes in the United States."[23]

From its start, sport had been a favorite item of interest to the paper. During the 1940s Rodolfo García, a staff sports writer, contributed much to the popularity and impact of the paper's sports section. García, who joined *La Opinión* in 1942, covered the city's boxing and baseball activities. Boxing, indeed, was a major interest to a community often emotionally torn between Mexican nationals and Mexican Americans. "The sport," argued historian Gregory S. Rodríguez, "represented the dreams of ethnic Mexicans of all colors, classes, generations, and sexual and political orientations."[24] As such, García's "Esquina Neutral" (Neutral Corner), which profiled boxers such as Lauro Salas, Bert Colima, and Art Aragón, was an exceedingly popular column. His clever prose, which often captured the steamy atmosphere and enthusiasm found in the Los Angeles Olympic Auditorium, appeared on a weekly basis.

Baseball also drew much of García's attention. Prior to 1958, the year that major league baseball moved to the Pacific Coast, both the Hollywood Stars and the Los Angeles Angels of the Pacific Coast League played in *La Opinión*'s backyard. "I used to go back and forth between Gilmore Field and Wrigley Field to cover the teams," recalled the late sports writer.[25] Though García reported the activities of the local clubs, he also did what he could to promote the activities of Latin players at the minor and major league levels. Roberto Francisco ("Beto") Avila of the Cleveland Indians was a particular favorite on two counts: First, in 1954 he was the first Latin to win a major league batting championship, and, second, he was a Mexican national—an especially important item for *La Opinión*. At the minor league level, Memo Luna, another Mexican national, who, in the midfifties, pitched for the San Diego Padres (minor league at that time), also attracted García.

Major league baseball's move to the West Coast in 1958 represented a new era not only for Los Angeles but for *La Opinión* as well. "Baseball will help the city become one of the most prestigious in the country," the daily reported following the 1957 announcement of the move. In the months preceding the first game of the 1958 season, *La Opinión* prepped itself for the task of handling major league coverage. A survey of its initial reports reveals two apparent goals: Promote the Spanish-language media and, at all costs, profile the Latin players, particularly those from Mexico. Indeed, García wasted little time in reminding the Dodgers that, because "Los Angeles has a large Spanish-speaking population, it would do the Dodgers much good to tap into LA's rich Latin section. Two or three good Latin players would gain the Dodgers millions in sales [of seats] and tequila."[26] That Cuban Sandy Amoros had come with the club from Brooklyn was not enough for *La Opinión*. García continued to trumpet the call for Latinos, particularly Mexicans, to join the Dodgers' roster since "most Latin fans in Los Angeles come from Mexico."[27]

In the meantime, San Francisco's Spanish-language community responded to the Giants differently from their counterparts to the south. By the time the Giants arrived from New York, San Francisco's Spanish-language media were nonexistent. In fact, the *Alta California,* which ran from 1849 to 1891, was the area's longest-running press. Though Los Angeles clearly received the lion's share of Mexican migrants in the early twentieth century, the San Francisco region attracted more than a handful of Mexicans. Most of them settled into the bay town of San Jose farther south, where, in the early twentieth century, they had migrated to work in the fruitful Salinas Valley. As in Los Angeles, the World War II defense plants served as a magnet for Mexicans in the southern Bay Area, too.[28]

Although the Mexican community developed and became more politically assertive in the years after World War II, there were no more Spanish-language papers in the area until 1972. Only *El Tecolote,* which began operations in 1972, lasted for more than a few years. Others, like *El Mundo* and some of its affiliates, often came across as propaganda pieces rather than dailies devoted to delivering community, state, and national news. And as the sixties' "movimiento" took hold, Bay Area Spanish-language papers gave almost exclusive coverage to events dealing with the social activism of that period.

Latin players in the Bay Area, however, were not entirely omitted. Even though nothing written about them came close to matching the type of coverage *La Opinión* provided, some San Francisco Spanish-language writers did offer slight impressions of the Latin plight in professional baseball. For instance, *El Informador* criticized the Giants for not having promoted more of its Latin minor leaguers to the big club. "The Giants have no excuses because their [Latin] players would be worth a lot on other teams, instead of just being on farm clubs," claimed the Berkeley-based weekly.[29] The author went on to suggest that the Giants had, in their entire time in San Francisco, been negligent in the promotion of Latins onto their major league roster.[30] However, his accusations had holes. The Giants, as most observers by then knew, had been among the leaders of the major league clubs, which routinely had Latin players on their team rosters. Moreover, regardless of whatever shortcomings the accusations legitimately revealed, the Bay Area Spanish-language press itself was virtually invisible when it came to reporting on any Latin players in the vicinity.

Finally, the *El Informador* piece appeared in December, at a time when baseball was hardly in the forefront of anyone's mind. In fact, the article, as it turned out, was the only one that ever appeared on the topic of Latin players. Still, from time to time, other presses profiled Latin players as a casual reminder that they did exist in the Bay Area. For instance, in advance of that year's baseball season, *La Prensa Libre,* a Berkeley paper that appeared sporadically in 1969, featured a piece on Juan Marichal's career.[31] Additionally, brief press reports on Jesus Alou, a Giants' player, and pitcher Miguel Cuellar, a member of the Baltimore Orioles who, in 1969, was a co–Cy Young award winner, appeared. Nevertheless, the paper produced not much else on the topic of Latin players.[32] As for *El Informador,* its last issue ran in 1970.

Bay Area Latino players, many of marquee quality, had no way to achieve recognition among northern California's Spanish-speaking community. Hence, only via the writings of the San Francisco English-language press did they attain any notoriety from journalists in the region. Interestingly, the Spanish-language press had many opportunities to report Latino success (in this case through baseball) during the late 1950s and the 1960s. For instance, having earned the 1958 National League Rookie of the Year award, Orlando Cepeda, whose popularity with San Franciscans resulted in part from not having been affiliated with the Giants during their New York days, began his distinguished major league career. From that point on, the feared Puerto Rican slugger, who in later years was inducted into the Hall of Fame, continued to shine. In 1962 he led the National League in home runs and runs batted in. One year later, three brothers from the Dominican Republic—Felipe, Mateo, and Jesus Alou—all appeared on the Giants' roster and made important contributions to the club's success.

During that period their teammate Juan Marichal also established himself as one of the greatest competitors of all time. In the sixties, the future Hall of Fame pitcher won twenty or more games six different times while wearing the Giants' uniform. And Latin talent also appeared in Oakland. There, as a member of the Athletics, Cuban Dagoberto ("Bert") Campaneris not only led the 1968 American League in hits but also twice captured the stolen base championship. Ironically, though, whatever fame these players achieved with the Spanish-language press did not originate from any journalism in the area but came from a source three hundred miles south of San Francisco Bay.

In 1958 the sports staff of *La Opinión* had, of course, been quite excited about major league baseball in their backyard. While the daily remained vigilant in its mission to report on the Latin achievements in baseball, its clear hope was to see a Latin star, particularly one with Mexican ties, emerge in the home club. Yet, throughout the 1960s and into the 1970s, the paper had few candidates on which to report. Ironically, though the Dodgers had pioneered Spanish-language media access, a move that saw season-long radio coverage as well as a seat in the press box for the print journalists, the organization's Latin presence on the field had been sparse. In fact, not until 1968 did the Dodgers hire its second Latino, Vicente Romo from Mexico. Romo's tenure with the team, however, was extremely short lived. He pitched only one inning before the team shipped him off to Cleveland. There was, of course, another major league team in the vicinity that carried a Latin standout. Cuban Marcelino López, who, in 1965, pitched his way to a fourteen-win season for the California Angels, a club that played at Dodger Stadium until 1966, won some raves. However, the writers at *La Opinión,* like many of their baseball aficionado subscribers, were not drawn to the American League club as they were to the more popular Dodgers.

As the decade matured, so did the frustrations at *La Opinión.* "We fought a lot with the Dodgers to get Latin players," Rodolfo García recalled. "In the Los Angeles area, you had Latin people from countries other than just Mexico, and they wanted to see their countrymen play ball."[33] The writer also argued that Mexicans had their own stars whose popularity bled into Los Angeles. Indeed, as early as 1962, García began to goad the Dodgers with his campaign to see more Latinos grace the home diamond. A "Latin will add a 'flavor' to the majesty of Chavez Ravine," he wrote as the club prepared to move from the coliseum into its new quarters high above the downtown area.[34]

Apart from the scant Latin-born representation on the team, the Dodgers did, in 1960, bring an American-born Hispanic on board. Phil Ortega, from Arizona, pitched for the Dodgers from 1960 on into 1965. But because he spoke only of his proud Yaquí Indian heritage and did not speak Spanish, he proved not to be an attractive feature for *La Opinión.* In fact, the daily rarely reported anything on their sole Latin representative. Given the paper's philosophical mission to promote Mexican attributes, Ortega's characteristics most certainly alienated him from Spanish-language writers like García, who was hungry to find a hero for the paper's subscribers. Oddly enough, the Dodgers, not entirely inattentive to the cultural demographics of Los Angeles, tried to market the Arizonan as a bona fide Mexican. "I wish you guys would stop calling him an Indian. He's Mexican," Dodgers' vice president Buzzie Bavasi routinely advised the press writers of both cultures.[35] During the 1965 baseball season, *La Opinión,* at long last, ran a feature on the mediocre pitcher, but the story was in reality a "farewell" item to announce Ortega's trade to the Washington Senators.[36]

Given the dearth of Latin players in the Dodgers' club, *La Opinión*'s writers ran stories and kept track of Latinos in other organizations. However, even this proved to be an exercise in frustration as Mexican players in the sixties and seventies were few and far between. Still, the paper maintained its vigilant support of Latin players and relied heavily on the accomplishments of those who played for the Giants. Rodolfo García, who had, since the 1940s, run a nearly one-man campaign on behalf of Latinos in professional baseball, rarely failed to find a suitable picture or positive attribute that he could include in his "Esquina Neutral." Even when Puerto Rican slugger Orlando Cepeda went hitless, the San Francisco team almost always appeared in print as the "Cepeda-led Giants."[37] The team's success, as seen through García's copy, was a result "de los muchachos de Alvin Dark."[38] García was always careful to properly identify the players he covered as "el dominicano," "el puertorriqueño," or "el cubano," among others.

Ironically, *La Opinión*'s sports staff found themselves in an awkward situation when, on August 22, 1965, during a critical Dodgers game in San Francisco, Giants' pitcher Juan Marichal clubbed the Dodgers' Johnny Roseboro with a baseball bat in a skirmish at home plate. Television cameras beamed the entire action to an attentive Los Angeles audience. Not surprisingly, the English-speaking press in Los Angeles lambasted the Dominican pitcher. García, on the other hand, treated the fiasco as simply a case of "confusion" attributed to the heated rivalry between the clubs. He went on to print the entirety of Marichal's apology for his actions.[39] In a gingerly written piece, the columnist for *La Opinión* went so far as to suggest that the Dodgers might write an admission of guilt for their own role in the brawl.[40] Following a brief report on September 7, no further mention of the incident appeared.

The 1970s saw a distinct increase in the number of Latins in the major leagues. Hence, the new era presented both the Los Angeles and San Francisco Spanish-language press with ample opportunities to expand their coverage of those players. Luís Tiant, Tony Pérez, and Miguel Cuellar were but a few of a number of talented stars that graced the majors. The Dodgers had also expanded their list with key players such as Pedro Guerrero and Manny Mota, but neither one was deemed the type of marquee player whom the press might rave about. Rodolfo García thus continued his vigil in the hope that a Mexican star might soon emerge. In 1981 the long wait came to an end.

Fernando Valenzuela, a Mexican national whom the Dodgers had promoted to their major league roster in September of 1980, stepped into the limelight. That month, the lefty threw eighteen innings and surrendered no earned runs. For this outstanding performance, Dodgers' manager Tommy Lasorda picked the young player to pitch on opening day. Valenzuela delivered a win for his club on that occasion, which turned out to be the first of eight consecutive victories. Having tied a major league record for consecutive wins at the outset of a season, Valenzuela became the darling of the English-speaking press, who dubbed his popularity with baseball fans as "Fernandomania." As for *La Opinión,* the daily could not have asked for a better scenario for their mission. Since the paper's birth in 1926, *La Opinión*'s writers sought to "preserve Mexican identity" and "paint a . . . positive image of Mexicanos" in the United States.[41]

Additionally, Valenzuela's background represented another interesting component of the ever-growing dichotomy of *La Opinión*'s mission. The paper's founder—Ignacio Lozano—openly expressed his desire "to serve as the voice of the Mexican exile community and to defend and represent the views of the Mexican elite."[42] The star pitcher, however, had impoverished roots. Moreover, his formal education ended at an early age, so he hardly fit the portrait of a refined socialite. Nevertheless, those very qualities proved to be attractive to both the Mexican community of the Southwest and mainstream Americans across the nation. As such, the paper, which in the sixties was forced to promote Latin players well beyond the scope of its region, in 1981 had as its biggest sports star a product of the campesino class to help preserve and forge the Mexican identity in the United States.

Fernando Valenzuela's success answered that call. He became an international celebrity, and, for many, his propensity to speak only Spanish during press conferences galvanized their sense of Mexican identity. Said one Los Angeles television commentator, "[T]here is the feeling among Hispanics that Valenzuela has succeeded without selling out."[43] For Rodolfo García, Valenzuela's success had been satisfying, indeed. In the young pitcher, García had not only a ballplayer who fit in perfectly with *La Opinión*'s intended mission but also a Mexican athlete of distinction whom he viewed as a pioneer. "I used to argue with [Dodgers' vice president] Al Campanis about Mexican players, and he said that they weren't good enough. But scouts never looked for them. Once [the Dodgers] went to Mexico, they found a talent like Fernando, [and] they learned that Mexicans, too, had big league skills," proclaimed the proud writer.[44]

At the conclusion of his first full season, Valenzuela was chosen as Rookie of the Year and was presented with the Cy Young award. Throughout the decade he maintained his position among the leading pitchers of the major leagues. Interestingly, in 1982 *La Opinión* found itself caught up in yet another cultural paradox. When, in an effort to tap into his newfound success, Valenzuela attempted to renegotiate his contract with the Dodgers, his efforts created a firestorm of controversy in the Los Angeles Mexican community. Torn between its support for the pitcher and its decades-long elitist position, the paper assumed a stance that came across as paternal. "We're not against Fernando, but he's asking for too much money," they chided.[45] Again cornered in an awkward situation on an issue regarding the major leagues, *La Opinión,* unwilling to further criticize the popular star, tempered its subsequent comments on the contract issue. By altering their tack, they maintained strong relations with an international sports icon who lived and worked in their locale, won greater notoriety as the leading Spanish-language daily for baseball coverage, and were better able to trumpet the achievements of Mexicans in the United States.

The tale of the Mexican Spanish-language press and its relationship to baseball on the West Coast encountered various scenarios in its efforts to "promote and preserve" the Hispanic culture. Ideal in purpose, that message—many discovered—proved difficult in delivery and practice. The life of many presses was short. Some papers focused on selected classes; some adopted assimilationist tendencies, while others downplayed them. Most of all, perhaps, they reported on items that they hoped readers would find inspirational and advantageous to their cause.

Sport, as it turned out, contributed to the fulfillment of their purpose. Mexicans in the United States, particularly those in the working class, followed the accomplishments of their local sports stars in the boxing arenas and on baseball and football fields with a degree of identity and pride. In the late 1950s, major league baseball's westward expansion, which brought it into the heart of California's Mexican communities, afforded the Spanish-language press an opportunity to magnify the message of Latin achievement in an otherwise Anglo world. But the voices that were able to deliver that message by then were few, and only one, *La Opinión,* maintained enough longevity to trumpet its views on behalf of patrons who clung to their Mexican values. To do so, its sports writers found it necessary to adjust and expand their mission to include profiles of Latinos who did not fall within gentry class lines. To that end, between 1958 and 1982, they featured players who belonged to all Latin nationalities. The Los Angeles paper also promoted Latinos who toiled in other locations, such as San Francisco. And to mainstream America in 1981, they championed a star whose rags-to-riches roots galvanized Mexicans across class lines. By the end of the eighties, *La Opinión*'s patience and flexibility in its practice and philosophy ultimately proved successful. As a consequence of these efforts, the paper lived up to the mission that its predecessors, nearly a century before, had set forth: to "protect and promote the interests of Mexican Americans and preserve Hispanic culture."

NOTES

1. Samuel O. Regalado, *Viva Baseball!: Latin Major Leaguers and Their Special Hunger* (Urbana: University of Illinois Press, 1998), 179. I would like to thank Jorge Iber and Richard Santillán for their careful scrutiny and helpful suggestions, which made this work possible. I would also like to acknowledge Michelle French, my student assistant, who dutifully and cheerfully wore out the pathway between my office and the Interlibrary Loan Office (whose staff was most helpful) at California State University–Stanislaus securing various articles for this chapter.

2. U.S. Bureau of Census, *County and City Data Book* (Washington, D.C.: Government Printing Office, 1977, 1983).

3. Jules Tygiel, *Baseball's Great Experiment: Jackie Robinson and His Legacy* (New York: Oxford University Press, 1983); Donn Rogosin, *Invisible Men: Life in Baseball's Negro Leagues* (New York: Atheneum, 1983); Rob Ruck, *Sandlot Seasons: Sport in Black Pittsburgh Leagues* (Urbana: University of Illinois Press, 1987).

4. Regalado, *Viva Baseball!;* Alan M. Klein, *Sugarball: The American Game, the Dominican Dream* (New Haven, Conn.: Yale University Press, 1991) and *Baseball South of the Border: A Tale of Two Laredos* (Princeton, N.J.: Princeton University Press, 1999); and Roberto G. Echevarría, *The Pride of Havana: A History of Cuban Baseball* (New York: Oxford University Press, 1999). As of 2003, conventional histories of the various Latin groups in the United States have continued to ignore the impact of sport. The lone exception to this is Louis A. Pérez Jr., *On Becoming Cuban: Identity, Nationality, and Culture* (Chapel Hill: University of North Carolina Press, 1999). Also, Milton Jamail, in the early 1990s, conducted several interviews on the topic of baseball and Latin adjustment in the major leagues, which appeared in various popular journals and magazines. Among them is "Culture Adjustment Takes Time," *USA Today Baseball Weekly* 1(18) (Aug. 2–8, 1991): 35.

5. Arturo J. Marcano Guevara and David P. Fidler, *Stealing Lives: The Globalization of Baseball and the Tragic Story of Alexis Quiroz* (Bloomington: University of Indiana Press, 2002).

6. José M. Alamillo, "Mexican American Baseball: Masculinity, Racial Struggle, and Labor Politics in Southern California, 1930–1950," in *Sports Matters: Race, Recreation, and Culture,* edited by John Bloom and Michael Nevin Willard (New York: New York University Press, 2002), 86–115; Richard Santillán, "Mexican Baseball Teams in the Midwest: The Politics of Cultural Survival and Civil Rights," *Perspectives in Mexican American Studies* 7 (2000): 131–52.

7. Jorge Iber, "Mexican Americans of South Texas Football: The Athletic and Coaching Careers of E. C. Lerma and Bobby Cavasos, 1932–1965," *Southwestern Historical Quarterly* 55 (Apr. 2002): 616–33; Gregory S. Rodríguez, "Saving Face, Place, and Race: Oscar de la Hoya and the 'All-American' Dreams of U.S. Boxing," in *Sports Matters,* 279–98.

8. Francine Medeiros, *"La Opinión,* A Mexican Exile Newspaper: A Content Analysis of Its First Years, 1926–1929," *Aztlán* 11(1) (Spring 1980): 65–87.

9. David G. Gutiérrez, *Walls and Mirrors: Mexican Americans, Mexican Immigrants, and the Politics of Ethnicity* (Berkeley: University of California Press, 1995), 36. In spite of the brief life span of many of these papers, at the close of the nineteenth century, the Spanish-language presses ranked third among all foreign-language newspapers. Roberto R. Treviño, "Prensa y Patria: The Spanish-language Press and Biculturation of the Tejano Middle Class, 1920–1940," *Western Historical Quarterly* 22 (Nov. 1991): 452.

10. Nicolás Kanellos, "A Socio-historic Study of Hispanic Newspapers in the United States," in *Recovering the U.S. Hispanic Literary Heritage,* edited by Ramón Gutiérrez and Genaro Padilla (Houston: Arte Publico Press, 1993), 126.

11. Richard Griswold del Castillo and Arnoldo De León, *North to Aztlán: A History of Mexican Americans in the United States* (New York: Twayne, 1996), 49.

12. Doris L. Meyer, "Early Mexican-American Responses to Negative Stereotyping," *New Mexico Historical Review* 53 (Jan. 1978): 77.

13. Ibid., 56.

14. George J. Sánchez, *Becoming Mexican American: Ethnicity, Culture, and Identity in Chicano Los Angeles, 1900–1945* (New York: Oxford University Press, 1993), 108–109.

15. Nicolás Kanellos with Helvetia Martell, *Hispanic Periodicals in the United States, Origins to 1960: A Brief History and Comprehensive Bibliography* (Houston: Arte Publico Press, 2000), 35.

16. Kanellos, "A Socio-historic Study of Hispanic Newspapers in the United States," 84.

17. Michael R. Ornelas, *Beyond 1848: Interpretations of the Modern Chicano Historical Experience* (Dubuque: Kendall/Hunt, 1999), 84.

18. Ibid.

19. Albert Camarillo, *Chicanos in California: A History of Mexican Americans in California* (San Francisco: Boyd and Fraser, 1984), 34.
20. Medeiros, "*La Opinión,* A Mexican Exile Newspaper," 68.
21. Kanellos, "A Socio-historic Study of Hispanics Newspapers in the United States," 110.
22. Roberto R. Teviño, "Prensa y Patria," 455.
23. Griswold del Castillo and De León, "North to Aztlán," 81.
24. Rodríguez, "Saving Face, Place, and Race," 280.
25. Rodolfo García, interview by author, Los Angeles, Aug. 6, 1982.
26. *La Opinión,* Apr. 17, 1958.
27. Ibid., Apr. 19, 1958.
28. Although no exact figures concerning Mexican Americans living in San Francisco are available prior to 1970, historians estimate that approximately 12 percent of all San Franciscans fit into this category. In 1970, 14.2 percent of the 715,674 residents were people of "Spanish surname." U.S. Bureau of Census, *County and City Data Book.*
29. *El Informador* (Berkeley), Dec. 2, 1967.
30. Ibid.
31. *La Prensa Libre* (Berkeley), Mar. 7, 1969. Interestingly, the profile did not address Marichal's 1965 melee with Dodgers' catcher John Roseboro.
32. The report on Jesus Alou appeared in *La Prensa Libre* on June 12, 1969. The profile on Miguel Cuellar appeared in the same paper on Nov. 13, 1969.
33. Rodolfo García interview.
34. *La Opinión,* Apr. 6, 1962.
35. Regalado, *Viva Baseball!,* 176.
36. *La Opinión,* July 8, 1965.
37. Ibid., Apr. 7, 1960.
38. As a point of interest, Alvin Dark, manager of the Giants from 1961 to 1964, had several difficult encounters with the Latin players of his club. His relationship with Orlando Cepeda was among his most intense. Yet, while the English-speaking press reported on some of those problems, García's columns never mentioned them.
39. *La Opinión,* Aug. 23, 1965.
40. Ibid., Sept. 3, 1965.
41. Kanellos, "A Socio-historic Study of Hispanic Newspapers in the United States," 110; Griswold del Castillo and De León, *North to Aztlán,* 56.
42. Treviño, "Prensa y Patria," 455.
43. Regalado, *Viva Baseball!,* 188.
44. Rodolfo García interview.
45. Regalado, *Viva Baseball!,* 184.

RAZA BOXING
Community, Identity, and Hybridity in the 1960s and 1970s in Southern California
GREGORY S. RODRÍGUEZ

On April 30, 1964, Al Díaz attended his first prizefight in his official capacity as the newly appointed California boxing commissioner. Along with ninety-four hundred other fans packed into the Olympic Auditorium in the city of Los Angeles, Díaz witnessed a fast-paced, bloody, twelve-round fight between Mexican Efrén "Alacrán" (the Scorpion) Torres and Japanese Hiroyuki ("the Japanese Beetle") Ebihara. At the fight's end, as both gladiators motioned signs of victory, jubilant mariachis clambered into the ring and broke into song as the crowd awaited Jimmy Lennon's announcement of a split decision. According to *La Opinión,* when the popular Lennon announced the victor to be Ebihara, he gave the signal "to set Troy ablaze."

The "mutiny" and "bloody melee" that ensued were, according to the newspaper, "the greatest demonstration of protest in the annals of angeleño pugilism." As a rain of bottles, beer cans, pieces of cement, and other projectiles showered onto the ring and floor below, the three judges, mariachis, reporters, broadcasters, and spectators at ringside took refuge in the crowded space under the ring. "It was worse than being in a foxhole," said one writer whose face was bloodied by a broken bottle. According to the *Los Angeles Times,* "Only a bombing raid could have wreaked so much havoc.... The scene was unparalleled in Los Angeles sports history." From all corners of the auditorium protestors yelled in Spanish, "Vamos a destruir el lugar" (Let's destroy the place), "Robarón al Alacrán, vamos a quemar la arena" (They robbed the Scorpion, let's burn the arena), and "No se van a salir con la suya" (They won't get away with it). Heavy steel chairs were ripped up in the balcony and hurled down onto the main floor. Two four-hundred-pound advertising billboards were torn off the balcony and sent crashing down. Angry fight fans ripped out water pipes in the balcony, letting loose a stream that cascaded down the main flight of stairs. Someone turned a fire hose on the spectators, drenching them as they tried to escape through the main entrance. A number of fires were started but quickly extinguished. One Olympic official had his shirt torn off in the row. "An unsung hero of the riot was an unidentified Mexican fan," observed a *Los Angeles Times* correspondent, "who bravely climbed into the center of the ring and tried to quiet the demonstrators. While he appealed for reason, the angry mob took aim and fired away at him with bottles and wadded paper and anything they could get their hands on. Miraculously he escaped being hit." In a more detailed account, *La Opinión* pointed out that the "unsung hero" was Al Díaz, the first Mexican American prizefighting commissioner, who, in attempting to calm the demonstrators, was indeed hit by a flying piece of concrete that opened a gash on his leg.

The Ebihara-Torres bout that sparked the rebellion exemplified the intense excitement over boxing as U.S. Mexicans (Mexicans residing and fighting in the United States without regard to their citizenship) came to dominate the lighter-weight championships in the 1960s. Boxing competition continued to highlight differences among groups by bringing them together in what had truly become a transnational industry. Boxing had become a ritual in which Mexicans from south of the border participated by the thousands, making the sport into a symbol of national affiliation. In the 1960s and 1970s the Los Angeles boxing industry produced Mexican and Chicano world champions at an unparalleled rate, one that virtually guaranteed these groups' hold on championship belts. In the bantamweight division (118 lbs.), U.S. Mexicans produced 12 world champions between 1960 and 1980 (10 of these were all in the 1970s). In the same period, Mexicans and U.S. Mexicans accounted for 9 featherweight champions (125 lbs.); 6 lightweight champions (135 lbs.); and 3 welterweight champions (147 lbs.) but no middleweight champions (160 lbs). In 1969, Efrén Torres, el alacrán, became the first Mexican to win the flyweight championship, marking the beginning of Mexican and Latino dominance in the 112-lb. category. The modern flyweight title dated to 1913, with the division originally dominated by U.S. Jews, ethnic Italians, and Filipinos until the 1950s, when the title was won primarily by Japanese, Chinese, and Southeast Asian athletes. In the 1960s Mexican-descent boxers took control; between 1969 and 1999 more than 20 Mexican-descent flyweights became world champions.[1]

Al Díaz represented not just the continuity of boxing in the lives of U.S. Mexicans in Southern California but also the emergence of a small Mexican American middle-class presence at the fights. In the 1960s and 1970s, although Mexican Americans and Mexican nationals continued to share the cheap seats in the arena galleries, the movement of Mexican Americans closer and closer to the ring symbolized the class mobility that increasing numbers of them were experiencing. Although arena seating reflected a community increasingly fragmented by class, ethnicity, and nationality, these divisions were not always reflected in boxing rivalries. Otherwise divided groups—Mexican Americans, Chicanos, and Mexican nationals—nonetheless continued to find common ground and at times shared heroes in the boxing industry. Much of what follows is an exploration of community change as refracted through the lens of Southern California's transnational boxing industry. Beginning in the 1960s, professional prizefighting's metaphorical allure—as a cultural practice in which more and more groups joined together to emphasize their self-perceived "differences"—spoke to the real-life concerns of groups who found themselves increasingly distanced from each other on some fronts, while sharing certain interests on others.

Rather than arguing that the relationship between Mexicans (regardless of their citizenship) who attended fights in the United States and boxing in the 1960s and 1970s was part of a capitalistic process of assimilation, U.S. Mexican, or *raza* (terms I use interchangeably), boxing can be understood only in its historical context. Some would maintain that Mexican Americans became absorbed into a corporate world of mass consumption and were thereby duped into thinking that "winning was the only thing that mattered." However, boxing in that era is more appropriately understood as the continuing evolution of "identity" and "community" among Mexicans, Mexican Americans, Chicanos, and other less-powerful groups that formed the fabric of Southern California. That story is manifested through historical changes in the sport, which in turn helped shape the continuing evolution of social hierarchy and integration among these social groups. It is a tale of community integration but not necessarily of assimilation—in its normative definition, as a process of the shedding of "foreignness" by members of distinct groups—though certainly these people were actively engaged in shaping the terms of their integration.

Although U.S. Mexican boxing dramas had always been linked to inter- and intragroup conflicts associated with the immigrant, ethnic, and assimilation experiences, in the 1960s and 1970s the conflict between groups defined by "descent" and those defined by "consent" produced new ethnicities that were expressed in new boxing rivalries and fan allegiances.[2] Largely as a result of successive waves of Mexican immigration, U.S. Mexicans had long-standing success in holding on to their descent relations emphasizing national and ancestral origins in Mexico. The growth of Mexican culture represented the successful formation of community consensus that sustained a vibrant ethnicity that encompassed increasingly diverse groups. In the 1960s and 1970s the meaning of boxing evolved in the context of this new cultural environment, an uncanny, liminal state as old structures were dissolving and redefinitions of community were emerging to take their place.

In their observations of the circulation of populations between Mexico and the United States, Chicano historians have long problematized the seemingly bipolar conflict for ethnic Mexicans between identification with aspects of U.S. culture and the maintenance of "Mexicanness" in the United States. In 1964, the year marking the end of the twenty-year-long Bracero Program, more than one hundred thousand braceros were forced to leave California alone. The program created both a dependence on Mexican agricultural labor and an expanding transnational Mexican community. That same year, Mexico instituted foreign export assembly plants known as *maquiladoras* along the Mexican side of the border. These were designed in part to employ families of braceros who were forced to return to Mexico.

Jobs in U.S. agriculture, in *maquila* manufacturing, and in the expanding metropolitan regions on both sides of the border, coupled with economic downturns in the interior of Mexico, facilitated the rise of communities of "transmigrants." Transmigrants maintained multiple relationships—familial, economic, social, organizational, religious, and political—that spanned the U.S.-Mexico border. The changing connection between U.S.-born Mexicans and Mexican nationals, expressed in boxing beginning in the 1960s, revealed new multistranded social relations that linked Mexican societies and U.S. settlements. The increasing dependence on boxing audiences from Tijuana, Mexico, reflected the exponential growth of that city's population. In the 1960s and 1970s boxing emerged as a transmigrant sport that crossed geographic, cultural, and political boundaries. In the most lucrative Los Angeles arenas, boxing promotions came to be sustained as much by transmigrant Mexicans as by Mexican Americans or any other group. Transmigrant/Mexican American/Chicano (raza) boxing challenges common conceptions of space, culture, identity, and community. The pressures that brought about Mexican transmigrant and Mexican American boxing force us to reconceptualize older notions of "sender" versus "host" nations, "immigrants" versus "migrants," and "alien" versus "citizen" groups.

The contributions that Mexican Americans, Mexican transmigrants, and openly politicized Chicanas and Chicanos made to a redefinition of boxing during this period is an example of how transnational people and their practices have been transforming the national cultures of Mexico and the United States. As a form of serious play connected to the everyday lives of raza on both sides of the border, boxing in the 1960s and 1970s also provides a rare glimpse into nascent cultural relations that have helped shape current discussions in Mexico centered on new conceptions of "nation" and "citizen." Emerging from these discussions are notions of a Mexican national community that include as citizens those who live within the boundaries of the United States but maintain social, economic, and political ties to Mexico. A focus on boxing in the period helps us to see yet another dimension of the problematics of these discrete nation-states in an evolving global and political economy.[3] In boxing we see hegemonic contention between core and periphery, between capitalists and workers, and between first- and third-world nations as much as we see cooperation, communication, and consensus.

An examination of pugilism builds on recent and ongoing historiographical recognition of Mexican transnationalism in the region ceded by Mexico to the United States in 1848. Scholars of the ethnic Mexican experience have used concepts such as "borderlands," "Greater Mexico," and "México de afuera" (Mexico on the outside) to capture regional and cultural processes that can be thought of as transnational. An explanation of the social changes in recent history that have given rise to this concept will help us understand the transformations in boxing that resulted from the new complexity in the lives of U.S. Mexicans and from the development of new spheres of experience, influence, and social relations.

U.S. Mexican boxing in Southern California in the 1960s and 1970s was, in large part, about globalization. Although boxing had always been an international sport, its growth in Asian and Latin American nations expanded dramatically in the period, making boxing in Southern California all the more international in structure as a center of worldwide boxing power. This movement coincided with the growing communities of new immigrants who entered the United States after 1965. The emergence of boxing as a national pastime in Mexico (largely as a result of the exportation of the sport from the United States), coupled with the increasing transnational character of Greater Mexican communities along the border, meant that boxing came less to simply signify the issues of growth and incorporation of groups into United States society.[4]

Indeed, the international boxing industry is a prime example of the shaping of culture by processes that no longer belonged to the framework of one national culture. This is not to suggest that ethnic Mexican boxing practices represented global processes of cultural homogenization but rather that a new local and global rearticulation of the sport's social import was under way beginning in the 1960s. Different kinds of Latino and Asian social groups encountered each other more frequently in boxing, much as they did in other realms of Southern California life. Boxing rivalries exemplified the way that globalizing pressures were being lived locally. As a form of cultural enunciation, prizefighting rivalries revealed global conditions of positioning, identity, cultural traditions, and histories.

For a time, boxing continued as a pastime of groups yoked together in the working classes, although between 1960 and 1990 an income gap began to widen between Mexican Americans and Mexican nationals living in the United States. The modest income gains that the Mexican Americans made over time did not come close to keeping pace with those made by comparably situated whites. While it is true that small middle classes expanded within Mexican American communities in the 1960s and 1970s, the manufacturing industries of the 1940s and 1950s, which provided the basis for Mexican American middle-class mobility, were, by the 1970s, being rapidly eliminated by regional deindustrialization, union busting, a growing service economy, and the feminization of the labor market. Deindustrialization meant that social segregation at all levels was becoming more entrenched in these years. By the late 1960s, the cumulative effects of postwar highway and housing policies had subsidized suburban growth at the expense of ethnic Mexican enclaves, thereby exacerbating racial and class polarization and encouraging residential segregation.[5]

Thus, the boom times of the fifties and sixties produced a generation of socially incorporated Mexican Americans and new waves of unassimilated Mexican immigrants. Compared to other European immigrant groups of the same generation, the Mexican Americans continued to be augmented by new Mexican immigrants. More recent ones tended to be less well off than those ethnic Mexicans whose families had been in the United States since the twenties and thirties. The demographic and economic changes of the late seventies and eighties—notably mass immigration and the decline of well-paid, stable manufacturing jobs—progressively removed the conditions for middle-class mobility, thus confining ethnic Mexicans, particularly the foreign born and their children, to lower-level economic positions that often straddled the border.[6]

For Mexican Americans, a rising standard of living, increased migration from Mexico, and continued discrimination against Mexicans within a segmented labor market all combined to help create a new consciousness.[7] By 1970 there were close to three million jobs in Southern California, nearly a threefold increase within thirty years. Virtually all social groups benefited from the sustained boom of the 1960s, with whites making the greatest gains.[8] The disparity between the white middle-class and Mexican American communities was not lost on Mexican Americans, whose experiences of rising middle-class aspirations or steady working-class dissent combined to spark urban unrest, violence, and crusades for civil rights. Mexican American civil rights movements, which gained momentum in the 1960s and 1970s, were struggles to protect middle-class gains as much as to end social discrimination. Both middle- and working-class ethnic Mexicans had a stake in finding solutions to problems with discrimination, education, housing, street gangs, police repression, and drugs.

As I revisit this history and in light of recent scholarship and social change along the U.S.-Mexico border, I have to ask, what role have Mexican immigrants played in boxing? Boxing rebellions, such as the one I began with, became increasingly common, and boxing authorities—promoters, journalists, state officials, even Mexican American and Chicano fans—held Mexican nationals responsible for the melees. What were the causes of these uprisings, and what lessons might we learn from them in the evolving relationships that came to constitute identity and community?

To answer these questions I draw on the work of recent scholars who have altered my thinking and who see themselves as part of social movements intent on changing explanatory models that tend to be bound by a focus on the nation-state—especially the ethnic and cultural groups. In the past, it would have been easy to argue that boxing was a ritual practice that Mexican people used as a means of assimilating, acculturating, or incorporating themselves into U.S. society. Boxing may also have been a means of resisting assimilation into the U.S. polity and society. These are the basic tenets of understanding processes of ethnicity—that is, the means by which immigrant or racialized groups of people gradually move from the margins of a society to its center. This process almost always involves the movement of individuals and their families along cultural lines of deracination, perhaps generationally, until they finally arrive at the center of society, having shed their cultural differences to become like other citizens of the United States who compose the nation's "melting pot." Within this framework, ethnic people (in this case, U.S. Mexicans) might just as easily resist assimilation. This outcome is evinced in the evocation of culturally nationalistic formations of community signified in the assertion of Chicana and Chicano identities. The framework for explaining this type of social change over time I call "ethnic studies," although it is much too simple an explanation of the kind of work that scholars of ethnic studies do today.

On the other hand, we might think of raza boxing as a phenomenon more readily explained by the theories and explanatory models of cultural studies. Within this cluster of paradigmatic approaches, the emergence of the raza boxing industry and its transformation over the course of the twentieth century might represent the power of ordinary consumers to symbolize or enact positive cultural changes in their lives. Before this, we might have thought them to be powerless to do so, assuming that the capacity for cultural change lay only within the grasp of elite producers and consumers. This latter group remains critical of and refuses to give in to the mundane, uncritical circumstances that shape the lives of participants in popular (or, even worse, mass) consumer culture.

So why not? What's wrong with thinking of raza boxing as a way in which people resist assimilation and perhaps make use of ordinary mass consumer culture to do so? A few years ago I would have responded, "nothing." In fact, I might have argued that boxing provided a form of agency (if not political agency, at the very least a rehearsal of political agency) that could be established as a register of Chicano and Latino sentiments. At any moment these feelings threatened to burst into full-blown political movements aimed at reshaping the purpose of national projects in the United States and Mexico from which these people had been shut out. Of course, I was never sure of this—that raza boxing indicated a way for ethnic people to express radical identities in a form of mass popular culture from which a few (like Oscar de la Hoya) could benefit (with benefits possibly extending to the female fans who supported him)—and I am even less sure of these benefits today.[9] Today I think raza boxing poses even more radical possibilities for measuring social change. Scholars who are part of an emerging school of thought that I call Latina/o critical studies influence my thinking. So, what's new?

First, although orchestrated for the most part as contests for championship belts in the United States, raza boxing has always been international in composition. In the Southwest, the competition between Mexican nationals and Mexican Americans has driven the sport at least since the 1950s. This rivalry, any boxing promoter will tell you, is the most lucrative in the fight game, guaranteeing sell-out crowds who pack arenas and private homes and spend upwards of fifty dollars to get the fight on pay-per-view. To a lesser degree, at least in the western United States and in Latin America, lucrative rivalries have included those between boxers of Mexican descent and any other Latino, although a Puerto Rican–Mexican (or Mexican American) contest is particularly useful for bringing in the profits. This internationalism in the boxing industry confounds any simple understanding of its use for ethnic assimilation or resistance. Moreover, it disrupts a simple sense of its place as being part of a singular national culture. Second, although the major boxing venues are in the western United States, the fanfare and the boxers themselves in this country are often transmigrant people who, although residing and working in this country, might think of home as being somewhere south of the border.

Following Gustavo Esteva and Madhu Suri Prakash, I would like to think of the history of U.S. raza boxing as the development of a form of grassroots postmodernism that has been busy remaking the national cultures from which it has sprung. Although raza boxers, their promoters, managers, fans, and others who have a stake in the industry might be part of a wide-scale promotion of a consumerist mentality (and as such might be thought of as reinforcing the control of social minorities over the social majorities), we might just as easily think of the industry as registering opposition to this kind of state control. We might see it as an opposition to state authority born of the processes of social dislocation and hence a way of finding fulfillment of desires that emerge from the alienation of migrant groups—*recien llegados* (recent arrivals)—from state formations in a specific region. Remittances from transmigrants in the United States that have exceeded the revenue from tourism generated in Mexico might be thought of as a use of funds in spite of state sanctions. Similarly, raza boxing and all of its symbolism and practices spring from civil society according to the willfulness of a people who act despite what this or that state might sanction. Moreover, raza boxing, although a form of cultural representation in the United States, has historically represented (at least since the 1970s) a nascent transnational public sphere that indicates a new sense of hemispheric citizenship linked to the destinies of an increasingly transmigrant—and illegal—Mexican labor force that challenges national states and their global capitalist faces.

Numerous examples from raza boxing history support the claim that its participants have actively established strategic alliances in the formation of their social circuits. Boxing history had long been part of constructing an essential "Mexican" subject, but the problem with this process in the Mexican or U.S. context was its very hybridity. The experience of boxing in the United States brought into play the recognition of the immense diversity and differentiation of the historical and cultural experience of Mexicans and Mexican Americans. Just at the moment that Chicanos came into existence in the 1960s and 1970s, boxing revealed a politics that marked the end of the essential Mexican subject that chicanismo was busy attempting to recover. In this respect, boxing emerged as a form of antiracism to the extent that it revealed that not all "Mexican" people were good or even the same.

In the 1950s the career of the brilliant Art Aragón demonstrated how the morality of ethnic and national identification depended on the historical specificity of group positions.[10] As the social bases for individual and group identification changed, so did the possibilities for strategic community formations based on new identifications and desires. For example, some of Southern California's most famous champions came from a diverse community of longshoremen who worked at the Port of Los Angeles in San Pedro. Chicanos and Mexicans took advantage of a particular union brother, Jackie McCoy, a boxer since the 1930s and a successful manager since the 1950s. As one reporter put it in 1972, "The nicest thing you can say about a Los Angeles fighter is that he's a McCoy man. In 1953 or 1972 [the time of the article] it means something special."¹¹ Ethnic Mexicans in the region remembered McCoy as a courageous fighter who battled with one of the greatest Mexican American world champions from the 1940s and 1950s: Manuel Ortiz.

In 1951 Ortiz took off his gloves for the last time as a professional after losing to Corky Gonzales, who later became a leader of the Chicano movement (see chapter 5).¹² In the 1970s McCoy joked with Chicanos, on the one hand, about remembering Gonzales when he was nothing more than a tough pug and with whites, on the other, about being retired as a boxer by "a nobody." "You remember Corky," he once joked with columnist John Hall. "He's big in the news these days as one of the militant Chicano leaders." When Hall admitted "the memory of Corky was gone," McCoy quipped, "that's why I quit. When you start losing to somebody nobody knows, it's time to go."

McCoy became a card-carrying longshoreman and "bumped bundles" on the docks with ethnic Mexicans who recognized him as a resource for advancement in the world of boxing. Precisely because he came into close contact with ethnic Mexicans on the docks and in the world of boxing, McCoy had access to insider knowledge. Thus, he, like few whites at the time, knew Corky Gonzales as a "militant Chicano" as well as a tough pug. Precisely because he came into contact with ethnic Mexicans on the docks, McCoy went on to train and manage five U.S. Mexican world champions. "Some of the great Mexican American champions came off the docks," remembered sports editor Bud Furillo. "Seems like all the fighters came from the docks, and the docks always took them back and took care of them. Longshoremen stick together."

Such allegiances in boxing emanated from urban spaces like Long Beach, where ethnic Mexicans established intercultural forms of communication that gave rise to new hybrid social arrangements and interactions. A heterogeneous culture made the performance of Mexican identity at the fights possible. The relationship between McCoy and his fighters is but one example of the hybrid conditions of U.S. Mexican identity as expressed in 1960s' and 1970s' boxing. McCoy handled three world champions who worked with him at various times as longshoremen—Chicanos Raúl Rojas and Armando ("Mando") Ramos and Mexican Rodolfo González.

Although each of these lightweight champions emerged from the same community of Long Beach longshoremen, in the eyes of fans they were distinctly different. All three were extremely popular among Mexicans and Chicanos because of their fighting skill. Nevertheless, fans had reason (or so they believed) to be fickle. For example, when Mando Ramos, who some consider "the best Mexican American champion or fighter in LA history," fought Carlos ("Teo") Cruz twice (in 1968 and 1969) for the lightweight title, Mexicans from both sides of the border gave him their full support. Nevertheless, Ramos—who had always been cocky, earning the nickname "Super Teen" in the English- and Spanish-language media—began to lose favor in the eyes of fans. "Mando was a legitimate lightweight champion," recalled *Times* editor Bud Furillo, "but had all the problems of drinking and drugs."[13]

News of Ramos's partying (which often involved spontaneous trips to Las Vegas), his decisions not to train or listen to his trainers, his determination to move from the "old neighborhood" in Long Beach to luxurious Belmont Shores, and his flamboyant self-portrayals in the English-language press all served to draw the ire of some fans. Still others admired Ramos as a high-school dropout who had made it. In many ways, Ramos was to Chicanos what O. J. Simpson was to the African American community. In fact, the two became close friends, supporting each other at the Olympic Auditorium and at USC football games. Together they became the darlings of sports columnists because, as a *Times* correspondent put it, "Both of them came out of a rough background and are forging bright futures in athletics."[14] Ramos had grown up playing Sunday football in the ethnically mixed neighborhoods of Long Beach with kids such as Earl McCullouch, Gene Washington, Marv Motley, and Oscar Brown. His father had introduced him to weekly raza boxing rituals at Olympic Auditorium, where they always sat in the gallery. "I was 11, 12, 13 years old. That's where I watched those great boxers," he recalled. "I learned that boxing was beautiful. It's a ballet."[15]

Ramos became a block-busting draw at the Olympic Auditorium. From 1970 to 1974 he fought only "Hispanics"; that is, he fought four Mexicans, three Chicanos, and one Spaniard, almost all in title fights. Some of the most memorable bouts in LA boxing history involved Ramos and other local heroes, such as Ultiminio ("Sugar") Ramos or Raúl Rojas. The fans' loyalties were diverse and ambiguous. Of these three, only Sugar Ramos was a Mexican national, although he was formerly a Cuban exile. Yet, as one of the youngest ever to fight for the title (at age nineteen), Ramos had captured the imagination of Mexican fans enough to win their support early in his career. For example, although most Mexican nationals apparently supported Sugar Ramos in his fight with Mando in August of 1970, when in the end the latter was handed the decision, Mexican nationals accepted the call in good faith and even applauded Mando as he left the ring. Two months later he would stage "a monumental battle of attrition" and take "a bloody decision victory" from his stable mate, former lightweight champion Raúl Rojas. That was in December of 1970.[16]

Over the next two years Ramos won the title but fought only three times in Los Angeles. Becoming a bona fide celebrity did not bode well for Ramos, who was now making headlines in the tabloids as much as in the sports pages. *La Opinión* now referred to him as "El Bibelot de Long Beach" and covered in detail his refusal to train and his cocky predictions of fight outcomes. In the meantime, Mexican nationals scoured the ends of the earth for a Mexican capable of unseating Ramos, a fighter who was now seen as a self-absorbed individual, not giving enough back to the community even in symbolic terms and perhaps overly assimilated. Finally, on September 15, 1972, *el noche del grito,* the eve of the celebration of Mexican independence, Mando Ramos was scheduled to meet Mexican national Eudibiel Guillen Chapin (aka Erubey "Chango" Carmona) in one of the most sensational fights in LA and Greater Mexican history. Interestingly, for the first time in California's boxing history, boxing competed for the hearts and minds of Mexicans as a means of officially celebrating Mexican patriotism. "Some say it's a bad date to fight," noted *La Opinión* columnist Rodolfo B. García. "These are people who supposedly have patriotic obligations. Those who favor boxing believe that any ceremony of celebration tomorrow night will only intensify the great program in the [Los Angeles] Coliseum. No matter what, there certainly will be thousands of *gritos*. . . . The majority will be in favor of Carmona[,] who was born beyond the Rio Bravo. . . . If the three fights end in a KO, there will be time to attend the ceremony *del grito* at City Hall or watch the events from Mexico via TV."[17]

On the day of the fight *La Opinión* reported that even "fickle Mexicans" would support their national champion, Chango Carmona. "Los Angeles's incomparable hospitality means the doors will be wide open to receive the legions of Mexicans coming here from Tijuana and elsewhere along the border who are convinced they will be on firm ground for the coronation of Erubey Chango Carmona as Lightweight Champion of the World."[18] The same day, Mando Ramos threatened not to fight if promoter Aileen Eaton did not reschedule the bout for an earlier hour. Ramos had made plans for an elaborate victory party in Las Vegas following the fight. Yet when the match finally came to pass, Ramos, "who had wanted to spend the wee hours of the morning at a party in Las Vegas, was hustled off to a hospital instead after being knocked out in the eighth round." According to one observer, a crowd of 20,113 paid $218,650 to see the fight in the coliseum. They "seemed mostly in favor of the challenger, who gave up height and reach to the two-time champion." Down a total of six times in the contest, Ramos "was a bloody mess when it ended." One boxing writer recalled the scene: "He gamely got up after each time, but his nose was bleeding as early as the third round and his eyes were nearly closed. He had a deep laceration near the corner of his left eye. He crumbled into a corner after the fight was stopped and after receiving first aid, Mando tried to arise. He didn't have any legs, so a stretcher was brought into the ring. Mando was placed on it and an ice pack was applied to his head and he was wrapped in blankets."[19]

In the ring, Ramos was diagnosed as having a concussion and liver damage. Meanwhile, Chango Carmona, the new world lightweight champion, "was carried on the shoulders of his thunderstruck rooting section, a tidal wave that swarmed the ring, lifted Carmona to the sky and gave him a victory ride half way around the Coliseum running track before depositing him up the tunnel in his dressing room." Back at ringside, fans formed a barrier that did not allow Ramos access to his waiting ambulance. Ring announcer Jimmy Lennon pleaded with the mob to make way. "They had to carry Ramos down from the ring on his stretcher and through hundreds of gawking fans, statues who refused to budge even in the face of the obvious emergency," noted one columnist. "It took more than 20 minutes to get the stricken fighter out of the ring and into the ambulance. . . . It was a sad, strange night."[20]

As Ramos was being placed into the ambulance, the situation deteriorated further. Unlike other rebellions in which fans violently attacked the built environment, these enthusiasts wanted Ramos himself. One veteran observer at ringside was shocked to see "Mexican nationals . . . throwing rocks at the ambulance as it left. . . . I could never get over all those people throwing rocks and everything, they hated him."[21] Although we cannot be sure why the fans expressed their disgust with Ramos by throwing rocks, what seems clear is that Ramos's cocksure demeanor had angered even his managers. As Leo Prlia, a tough moneylender from the docks who had "a piece" of Ramos, put it, "You can't be in fighting shape when you call all your own shots in training, when you don't pay attention to anybody but yourself and when you think you know it all."[22] The day after the fight, the newspapers published pictures of Carmona visiting Ramos in the hospital in a demonstration of prizefighting sportsmanship.

In any case, Ramos's career demonstrated that, although the forging of fan alliances in boxing contests depended on a variety of circumstances, the general trend was an open-ended dialogue among diverse Mexican-descent groups that came to be represented in the sport. For example, Chango Carmona's very next fight, less than two months after his bout with Ramos, would be a title defense against one of Ramos's fellow dockworkers, Mexican national Rodolfo ("El Gato") González. Originally from Guadalajara, Mexico, González had become a permanent resident of Long Beach, where he learned to box under Jackie McCoy's tutelage. González was a big favorite of both Chicanos and Mexicans. Unlike Ramos, González was fluent in both English and Spanish, which made him accessible to a wide audience. After winning the title from Carmona, González boasted before a cheering crowd that the title "remained Mexican" but that he was also happy that it "was again McCoy's," thus proving that the specific conditions of everyday life—at least for González—were as important in organizing group identity as were conceptions of "nation," "race," or "blood."[23]

In boxing, ethnic Mexican fans began to work with and through racial and national differences, establishing a basis on which to build forms of solidarity and identification in common support of diverse Latino groups without suppressing the real heterogeneity of interests and identities. In boxing, fans drew lines of solidarity without fixing permanent boundaries but often only for particular boxing contests. The sport as practiced in Southern California was becoming less a ritual "war of manoeuvre" by essential groups and more a "war of position," in which diverse groups formed specific unities. It was less easy for boxing fans to think about identification with their boxing idols as a simple process structured around fixed selves, which boxers and fans tended to be or not be. Experience constructed the self, and often experiences were so varied and yet so delimited by relationships of economic and cultural power that people failed to think or act singularly as racialized or gendered or sexualized or classed subjects and instead made themselves in multiple and complex ways.

The kind of intergroup communication via boxing, which emerged in the 1960s and 1970s, differed from earlier periods to the extent that it reflected a social structure under transformation that fostered such contact and communication in the wider world. In the pre–World War II era, fighting heroes affirmed their identities by accentuating their differences. The exclusive group solidarities that shaped boxing rivalries in the first half of the twentieth century gave way by the 1960s and 1970s to more inclusive—and more complex—formations. These competitions reflected Mexican American and Mexican national communities that were being transformed under pressures brought from more open exchanges of knowledge and populations in the western hemisphere. The career of welterweight champion José Angel Nápoles illustrates this point.

Born on April 13, 1940, in Santiago, Cuba, Nápoles became a Mexican national after fleeing the Cuban Revolution. Fighting as a pro in Cuba from 1958 to 1961, Nápoles became a refugee in 1961 and then acquired Mexican citizenship. He continued his boxing career when he was accepted into the stable of fighters managed by Carlos ("Cuco") Conde, who operated out of Mexico City but had strong ties to the big-time raza boxing industry in Southern California. Typical of Mexican national boxers, Nápoles not only worked his way up in the boxing world but also gradually moved northward to the United States.

Starting out in Mexico City, Nápoles took on fights in Culiacán, Los Mochis, Hermosillo, Reynosa, Juárez, Tijuana, and finally Los Angeles. After winning the welterweight title in 1969 in Los Angeles, Nápoles made that city his home for title defenses until he retired in 1975. Just as Nápoles had adopted Mexico as his nation, Mexican nationals adopted him as their boxing hero in Los Angeles, nicknaming him "mantequilla" (which means "butter" and referred to his ultrasmooth style). When Nápoles regained his title from Italian American Billy Backus, *Sports Illustrated*'s Robert H. Boyle marveled at the way in which "a dispossessed Cuban now operating out of Mexico City" could muster "a volatile crowd behind him, a Forumful of Mexicans who rhythmically chanted, Meh-hee-coe, Meh-hee-coe, Meh-hee-coe." Nápoles pranced into the ring amid tremendous applause, as well as cheers and shouts of "Viva Mantequilla!" Backus drew jeers and boos. "The south-of-the-border theme continued," noted Boyle for *Sports Illustrated*, "as a señorita dressed like Rio Rita sang seemingly every verse, punctuated with applause, of the Mexican national anthem, leading a few gringos to conclude they had bought tickets to a concert instead of a fight. By contrast the crowd remained mum and Backus glum after the mod-suited, hirsute ring announcer invited everyone to sing *The Star-Spangled Banner*."[24]

The hybrid celebration of ethnic Mexican popular nationalism that Nápoles's fights enacted forced other groups to ponder the meaning of their own ethnic identities. "I don't care if they got half the Mexican army in there," exclaimed Backus's manager, Tony Graziano. "We got that dago blood in us and we don't give a hoot how tough he is. When that fight starts, fans can't help him in the ring." Yet, after Nápoles scored an eight-round knockout, *Sports Illustrated* observed, "Maybe the crowd didn't jump in the ring with him, but the fervor certainly helped."[25]

Yet Nápoles did not always receive uniform backing at the fights. For example, when he fought Ernie ("Indian Red") López, fans were divided not only along ethnic, national, and regional lines but also along the more complex fault lines created by an increasingly complicated Latino population in Southern California. Chicanos and other fans of locally developed boxers saw Indian Red López and his younger brother, Danny ("Little Red") López (who would become a featherweight champion), come up in Los Angeles arenas. Although the López brothers were born on a Utah Indian reservation, when it was made known that they "had some Mexican in them," they immediately attracted a following of Mexicans and Mexican Americans. In two sell-out championship fights in Los Angeles—one in 1970 and another in 1973—the *cubano nacionalizado mexicano* managed to keep his title from the American Indian/Chicano. On both occasions, however, López earned standing ovations even from Nápoles's most partisan fans.[26]

In the 1960s and increasingly in the 1970s, the mixing of allegiances became common practice in the popular culture of boxing. Nápoles was not the only Cuban ex-patriot to become a Mexican boxing idol in Los Angeles. Other champions who won support from ethnic Mexican fans in the transborder region were Ultiminio ("Sugar") Ramos and Luís Rodríguez, who, like Nápoles, were Afro-Cuban expatriates. Moreover, although a string of Mexican and Mexican American boxers became champions in Los Angeles in the 1960s and 1970s, these groups often came together in support of other Latinos, Asians, and African Americans. It became commonplace in the 1970s for ethnic Mexican fans to boo favorable decisions they felt were given unfairly even to "Mexicans." For instance, the great French Algerian bantamweight champion, Alphonse Halimi, who fought two famous Mexican-descent champions—Raúl ("Ratón") Macías (1957) and Joe Becerra (1959, 1960)—became a legend in Mexican boxing circles long after he had retired. Halimi was a toe-to-toe slugger similar to the "Mexican" style, which described a boxer who was never on his toes and therefore had the leverage to throw powerful combinations to the head and body. He had absolutely no defense except to duck, and he took punches with haughty disdain. If you could stay out of his way, you could outpoint him, but in the eyes of fans the boxer could lose only if he was outbludgeoned. Alphonse Halimi was this kind of boxer. Mexican-descent people remembered him as one of the greatest body punchers in the business. More importantly, they honored him because he was considered a champion of poor people everywhere. His reputation was celebrated in Los Angeles fanfare as it was in other places he fought.

The youngest of eighteen children of an impoverished family, Alphonse Halimi was born in Constantine, Algeria. At age seven he set out on his own and was taken in by a family in Algiers, where he was raised as the younger brother of a nineteen-year-old named Marcelle. When Marcelle married, she adopted Alphonse as her son. Alphonse became a tailor's assistant but decided to take up boxing when he saw the success of another North African Frenchman, 1940s' middleweight champion Marcel Cerdan. When Halimi climbed into the ring, it was a well-known fact that he did so to support his foster mother, who used to be his foster sister. When Halimi fought and badly beat ex-champion Ratón Macías, the latter's fans, who had trooped over the border to cheer him on, became fickle. When the bout was over, they applauded Halimi and booed referee Mushy Callahan's incomprehensible vote in favor of Macías. One youth who attended would later become a boxer and assume the name Halimi Gutiérrez. Halimi became a popular nickname among Mexican and Mexican Americans boxers as a tribute to the boxer who earned it, to the memory of the tough Algerian, and to the spirit of postcolonial cooperation supposedly engendered in the sporting spirit of the day. The sense of fairness or fair play cultivated in sport reflected parallel developments of intercultural communication among diverse groups in everyday life. For example, the hybridity of boxing meant that, by the 1960s, even some whites had come to be revered by ethnic Mexicans, even becoming celebrated as "honorary" mexicanos and Chicanos.

Boxing matchmaker and promoter George Parnassus was such a figure. Much like Johnny Otis, the music promoter who had become so integrated into African American life in Los Angeles that he was often thought of and "recognized" as black, Parnassus was often mistaken for being "Mexican." Both men, in fact, were of Greek descent. They represented the kinds of ethnic and class interactions common to industrial cities such as Los Angeles that gave meaning to shared popular cultural and commercial pursuits like sports and music.

Parnassus had emigrated from Methone, Greece, to Los Angeles in 1915 because he thought his brother was well-to-do. On arrival, Parnassus discovered that his brother was actually struggling just to make ends meet. He realized that, to get by, he had to seek whatever unskilled work he could. Immediately he came into contact with U.S. Mexicans who were washing dishes for a dollar a day in downtown Los Angeles and working with pick and shovel on rail lines. "I learned about the Mexicans," he once said, "and liked them and they learned to like me. When I was still trying to speak English, I tried to speak their language, too." Later he tried to make it on his own selling watermelons on the Venice pier and running a hotdog stand.[27] "I saved my money and got a checkroom concession in a nightclub," he recalled. "Years ago it was a tremendous business, because everybody used to wear a hat."

From checking hats Parnassus went into the restaurant business and eventually bought a place in Phoenix, Arizona, across the street from a fight gym, where most of his customers were Mexicans and Mexican Americans. There he met Rosalie Montez de Ocas, a manicurist, married her, and learned to speak Spanish. "Like any self-respecting Greek in the 1920s," recalled LA *Times* columnist Jim Murray, "George thought he was going to make his fortune selling pie and hot roast beef sandwiches to truck drivers."[28] Instead, Rosalie and George made themselves integral parts of the Mexican community. They tailored their establishment to the interests of their Mexican and Mexican American constituents, most of whom worked in the flourishing cotton fields in the years following World War I. At one end of the Parnassus café was a diner, at the other end a pool hall, and at all ends were mexicanos. It was there that Parnassus earned his reputation for speaking Greek-accented Spanish and Greco-Mexican-accented English.[29]

In the 1910s and 1920s raza prizefighting was a booming business in Arizona, as it was elsewhere in the Southwest. U.S. Mexican boxers and their fans patronized Parnassus's restaurant and pool hall, making it into a place to hear boxing broadcasts, set odds, and celebrate victories. "If one of the boys in the place was fighting, I bet a few dollars on him. If he won, I give him a free meal ticket. Before I knew it, if anybody asked them who was their manager, they would say Parnassus." When the bottom dropped out of the cotton market in the 1920s, Parnassus agreed to help the boxers devote themselves full-time to the profession. He would eventually handle some of the most successful U.S. Mexican boxers around. By the mid-1920s Parnassus had moved to Los Angeles and made his profession as a manager of "Mexican" fighters. He attracted them to his stable with Spanish-language advertisements in *La Opinión,* and he published endorsements he somehow obtained from raza ring idols such as Bert Colima and Baby Arizmendi, whom he did not manage. At one time before World War II, Parnassus had forty-three fighters, plus a Studebaker and a seven-passenger Hudson. "I'd put 10 fighters in each, go somewhere and put on the whole night's show," he boasted.[30]

In the 1920s and 1930s Parnassus was truly a "people's manager." At a time when boxing management in Los Angeles was dominated by Hollywood actors, wealthy eccentrics, and organized criminals, he became a favorite not just among U.S. Mexicans but also among Filipinos. By 1934 he found his first world champion in Filipino Ceferino García, who was deserted by his Filipino manager. By 1944, along with Jimmy Fitten (with a Mexican mother, another bilingual, bicultural boxing entrepreneur), he had maneuvered Juan Zurita, a Mexican, into a world championship, and, by 1956, another Mexican, Raúl ("Ratón") Macías, into a bantamweight championship. By 1957 Parnassus had established himself as one of the premier managers of local U.S. Mexican boxers. In the same year, when the Olympic Boxing Club's notorious matchmaker, Babe McCoy, lost his license for fight fixing, Aileen Eaton enlisted Parnassus to replace him. Although he staged bouts at the Olympic until 1968, he also arranged matches internationally, especially in Mexico, but also in Wales, Japan, Thailand, Argentina, Italy, and England. During this period he helped establish and finance the World Boxing Council (WBC), which remains a powerful sanctioning body. In 1968, after a bitter falling-out with Aileen Eaton, Parnassus contracted with Jack Kent Cooke, owner of the Fabulous Forum, to be the establishment's sole promoter, making him a larger operator than he was at the Olympic Auditorium.

Raza fight fans praised Parnassus for his personal etiquette and comportment as much as for his emphasis on the "positive" aspects of boxing: its discipline, fitness, and instillation of respect for authority. "He was boutonniere-in-the-lapel, handkerchief-in-the-breast-pocket dapper, he got his shoes shined once a day," noted Jim Murray. "In front of strangers, to my fighters I was always Mr. Parnassus," Parnassus claimed. "I never was drunk in my life. I went to bed at five o'clock, and if I had to be somewhere at six o'clock I'd be there, a little bit ahead of time," he retorted. "I ask fighters and ex-fighters: When did you feel worse—the day after a real tough fight or the day after a real drunk?"

U.S. Mexican prizefighters made Parnassus a household name among Southern California Mexicans in the post–World War II era. He graciously acknowledged that, had it not been for the Mexican fighters, his two sons would never have had the chance to become the doctor and monsignor they became. Indeed, his reputation as a father to young raza boxers became part of the regular fanfare of Los Angeles boxing, even after Parnassus gave up managing to be a promoter. In the 1970s stories began circulating about the ways he protected fighters, the ways he fought boxing's underworld, and the ways he paid fighters higher-than-average rates.

One particularly telling story along these lines was not made public record until fourteen years after the fact, when *Sports Illustrated* asked Parnassus to confirm it in 1971. As a match promoter at the Olympic Auditorium in 1958, Parnassus fought the world's most powerful boxing monopoly, Jim Norris's notorious International Boxing Club. As Parnassus explained it, in 1958 he guaranteed Carmen Basilio $60,000 for a nontitle fight with Art Aragón in Los Angeles's Wrigley Field. "The Norris people brought all kinds of pressure to bear trying to get Basilio to pull out, give them the fight," he recalled. "Between Madison Square Garden and Chicago Stadium they had millions of dollars, and here I am with a roast biff [sic] sandwich. But they can't take the fight away. Then somebody come up with Floyd Patterson and Roy Harris, a title fight, in Los Angeles 18 days before the Basilio fight. I protest to the state athletic commission, but they let it go. So I stand up in the commission meeting and bet the other promoter $5,000 I would out-draw him whatsoever—I peel it off in $100 bills right there and embarrass him. He got to bet. And I won."[31]

Over the course of a career extending through the 1970s, Parnassus was a central figure in the expansion of a transnational boxing community between Mexico and the United States. Ironically, it was only after Mexican nationals became world champions in Los Angeles arenas that boxing flourished in Mexico. By the 1930s boxing had become something of a national pastime. In the 1960s and 1970s Parnassus became a respected person among boxing fans in Mexico, even befriending Mexican presidents such as Gustavo Díaz Ordaz in the mid-1960s.

It was not just that Mexico was in the midst of preparations for the 1968 Olympics that explained why Ordaz embraced Parnassus as a friend; in fact, Parnassus was part of the larger forces originating on both sides of the border that had made sport so important to Mexican national identity. For example, in 1932 the *Los Angeles Times* marveled at this phenomenon. "Fighting for the glory of Old Mexico but boosting Southern California with every punch," the newspaper noted, "[e]very one of the twenty-two [Mexican] boys has been developed this year through the medium of Southern California amateur boxing clubs which, in a sense, is quite a laugh on the clubs[,] for their advertised purpose was to develop boys for the Yankee team."[32]

By the 1960s, as a result of both the increasing prestige of boxing clubs in Mexico and the elimination of mob control in the United States, it became easier for Mexicans to fight for world titles in their homeland. The first of these champions was featherweight Vicente Saldívar, who won the world title from Ultiminio ("Sugar") Ramos in September of 1964. Saldívar would defend his title four times in Mexico, once in Los Angeles, once in London, and once in Wales. As the first world champion ever to win and defend his title more times in Mexico than in Los Angeles, Saldívar became a national treasure.[33]

In the 1970s Parnassus boasted that "Even the dogs know me in Mexico." In 1971 *Sports Illustrated* named him "the world champion fight promoter" and "boxing's hottest matchmaker." The magazine hailed Parnassus for "his ability to draw astonishing gates with bantamweights—bigger gates than Madison Square Garden tends to draw with heavyweights, except in fights of the century—due largely to his Mexican connections." Indeed, of all of the fights Parnassus promoted in ten years at the Forum, only one did not feature a Mexican or Mexican American in the main event. According to *Sports Illustrated,* "as much as half of a top Forum turnout of 15,000 to 17,000 is likely to be Latin, including thousands of Mexicans who have taken buses up from as far as 500 miles away."

In 1969, counting only gate receipts, Parnassus grossed $1,086,400 in eight Fabulous Forum attractions featuring U.S. Mexicans, an average of $135,800 per event. In contrast, Madison Square Garden, which relied on heavyweights, where all the money was thought to be, grossed $1,531,500 for fourteen bouts, an average of only $109,392. In 1970 the Forum's average for six shows was $150,000.[34] Parnassus's success is even more astounding when one considers that he was not the only show in town. His promotions coincided with Aileen Eaton's weekly bouts at the Olympic Auditorium, which also continued to rely on ethnic Mexican fanfare. This was a very bitter, though obviously lucrative, rivalry indeed.

Coming from Phoenix to Los Angeles, then extending links to boxing centers in Mexico, Parnassus drew not only on aspects of regional complexity in the expanding transnational culture of boxing but also on the cultural and regional connections and the complexity of groups and individuals that had evolved in the U.S.-Mexico transborder region. Responding to fresh interest in boxing by a generation of U.S. Mexicans that was increasingly aware of sources of oppression, limits on social mobility, and the need to mobilize as mexicanos and Chicanos, Parnassus, Eaton, and others involved in local boxing promotions publicized fights with new strategies aimed directly at U.S. Mexican boxing fans. For example, before and after big prizefights Parnassus strategically advertised the arrival and departure times of Mexican champions to ensure the mobilization of Mexican American community leaders, journalists, mariachi bands, and cheering sections. At these times Parnassus would throw elaborate dinner parties at restaurants in the Olvera Street district, a part of downtown dedicated to nostalgic representations of the Mexican and Spanish past.

Parnassus hired ethnic Mexican champions from the past to plump for the fights. Jim Murray of the *Los Angeles Times* noted that the theory behind this procedure was that, "if your palookas can't get space in the papers, Joe Louis always can." But instead of Joe Louis, Parnassus often hired Art Aragón, a man with a proven track record in stirring up interest, if only in himself. For example, in 1965, when asked to visit the camps of Vicente Saldívar and Raúl Rojas before their lightweight title fight, Aragón exclaimed, "I don't know who's going to win, but I know I'm going to make a comeback and challenge the winner. That is if either of them *can.*" When Parnassus asked Aragón to explain to Rojas how to fight a left-hander (knowing full well that Aragón had lost to almost every southpaw he had ever fought), Aragón pronounced grandly, "The best way to fight a left-hander is to fix the fight."[35]

Although there was significant class mobility for segments of ethnic and racial groups between 1945 and 1970, relative to whites, the majority of Mexican Americans and African Americans remained for the most part on the low end of the occupational wage ladder. At the bottom of the unskilled labor market were the newest waves of recent immigrant Latinos. Although boxing and other professional sports seemingly heightened awareness of conflict among groups, and while certain individuals used sport to express an explicit politics of difference, the case of U.S. Mexican boxing in the 1960s and 1970s marks the introduction of unprecedented mutualism among increasingly diverse groups in upholding a sporting life based on the shared experience of boxing. The hybrid unities of ethnic and racial populations that formed in Southern California boxing are an extension of cultural communication and collaboration brought about in other evolving realms of the social structure.

The Greater Mexican community out of which boxing emerged and ultimately transcended casts new light on the global positioning of the U.S. Mexican community in Southern California and of the U.S.-Mexico region that includes communities of origin for migrants *wherever* they exist in Mexico and their flourishing communities of support in boxing wherever they exist in the United States. In the 1960s and 1970s, transformations in the everyday lives of Mexican Americans and Mexican nationals living in Greater Mexico gave boxing its determinate shape. Although both groups continued as the main constituents of the lucrative LA boxing market, their experience of the fights differed to the extent that their everyday lives had changed. Fans and boxers were now Chicano or Mexican American, transmigrant mexicano or refugee Cuban Mexican national, Indian or *indio,* Latino or Latin, or any number of performative possibilities that composed the local rearticulations of global identities expressed in boxing.

With Mexican philosopher and poet Octavio Paz as our guide we could argue that the rise of sensational and transnational commercial boxing in the 1960s and 1970s was a kind of reaction to the social alienation that "Mexicans" experienced within or in relation to life in the United States. Yet, as Edward Said insists in his introduction to *Orientalism,* "one never ought to assume that the structure of [cultural identity] is nothing more than a structure of lies or of myths which, were the truth about them to be told, would simply blow away."[36] It has not been my concern nor do I believe it was the concern of those described in these pages to use boxing to unmask or resuscitate the essential figure of some "real Mexican." The mass culture of boxing was not masked culture but rather an example of how Mexican ethnic and national groups constantly fashioned identities in a form of cultural expression appropriate to their evolving realities. These groups pursued boxing as a strategy for individual and group presentation that brought their distinctive and evolving cultural traditions into the mainstream of mass popular culture as part of creating a new tradition. In order to do so, they drew upon the experiences and cultures of other groups, at times forging hybrid unities with those whose experiences, alienations, and ideas resonated with their own but came to light in the world of boxing.

Beginning in the 1960s and 1970s and continuing through the 1980s and 1990s, the expanding scope of the mass media intensified the cultural crisis that U.S. Mexicans faced. Although Mexican immigration was on the rise, Mexican Americans faced increasing underrepresentation in positions of social power and in the popular imagination. Media representations continued to erase or distort the Mexican American world, serving to legitimate dominant white hegemony. The exception was boxing, where U.S. Mexicans had cultivated a tradition of reaching out to other groups in order to imagine and claim space of their own.

As a result of the failures of liberal social programs and because of the lack of real opportunities for ethnic Mexican mobility, boxing in Southern California continued to be a way for fighters to advance their own interests and at the same time a place where Mexican Americans and Mexican nationals could come together in a ritual that symbolized their relatively subordinate positions in the larger society while maintaining differing degrees of community identity. In this way, boxing became a sort of borderland, an interstice within which ethnic Mexicans have gone about defining their cultural milieu in Southern California and in which they both acknowledged and contested their ties to one another. Its says something more about the shifting nature of identity and community as these terms become increasingly disconnected from older, official narratives of citizenship and community in the evolving and intersecting discursive spaces of nation-states.

NOTES

1. These world titles are recognized by either the World Boxing Council (in Mexico City) or the World Boxing Association (in Manila).

2. Werner Sollors, *Beyond Ethnicity: Consent and Descent in American Culture* (New York: Oxford University Press, 1986).

3. For an exploration of this problem see Saskia Sassen, *The Mobility of Labor and Capital* (New York: Cambridge University Press, 1994); David G. Gutiérrez, "Migration and Ethnic Politics in a Transnational Age: Reflections on the California-Mexico Border," in *Su voto es su voz: Latino Politics in California,* edited by Aníbal Yañez-Chávez (La Jolla: University of California–San Diego, Center for U.S.-Mexican Studies, 1995), 121–39.

4. My use of the concept "Greater Mexico" follows that of Américo Paredes, who saw ethnic Mexican communities on either side of the international border as sharing common cultural practices and historical memories. Américo Paredes, *Folklore and Culture on the Texas-Mexican Border,* edited by Richard Bauman (Austin: Center for Mexican American Studies, University of Texas, 1993). For a recent explication and application of Paredes's concept see José Limón, *Dancing with the Devil: Society and Cultural Poetics in Mexican-American South Texas* (Madison: University of Wisconsin Press, 1994).

5. For a history of race and space in Anglo-Mexican relations in Los Angeles see Edward J. Escobar, *Race, Police, and the Making of a Political Identity: Mexican Americans and the Los Angeles Police Department, 1900–1945* (Berkeley: University of California Press, 1999); Raúl Villa, *Barrio-logos: Space and Place in Urban Chicano Literature and Culture* (Austin: University of Texas Press, 2000); Douglass S. Massey, Jorge Durand, and Nolan J. Malone, *Beyond Smoke and Mirrors: Mexican Immigration in an Era of Economic Integration* (New York: Russell Sage Foundation, 2002).

6. For an exploration of these social changes, see Vilma Ortiz, "The Mexican-origin Population: Permanent Working Class or Emerging Middle Class?" in *Ethnic Los Angeles*, edited by Roger Waldinger and Mehdi Bozorgmehr (New York: Russell Sage Foundation, 1996), 247–78. Also see Edward W. Soja, *Postmodern Geographies: The Reassertion of Space in Critical Social Theory* (New York: Verso, 1989), chap. 8–9; Barry Bluestone and Bennett Harrison, *The Deindustrialization of America: Plant Closing, Community Abandonment, and the Dismantling of Basic Industry* (New York: Basic Books, 1982).

7. Ian F. Haney-López, *Racism on Trial: The Chicano Fight for Justice* (Cambridge: Belknap Press of Harvard University Press, 2003); Ian F. Haney-López, *White by Law: The Legal Construction of Race* (New York: New York University Press, 1996); Raymond Rocco, "Citizenship, Culture, and Community: Restructuring in Southeast Los Angeles," in *Latino Cultural Citizenship: Claiming Identity, Space, and Rights*, edited by William V. Flores and Rina Benmayor (Boston: Beacon Press, 1997).

8. John H. M. Laslett, "Historical Perspectives: Immigration and the Rise of a Distinctive Urban Region, 1900–1970," in *Ethnic Los Angeles*, 63; Ortiz, "The Mexican-origin Population," 252–61.

9. Gregory S. Rodríguez, "Boxing and Masculinity: The History and (Her)story of Oscar de la Hoya," in *Latino/a Popular Culture*, edited by Michelle Habell-Pallán and Mary Romero (New York: New York University Press, 2002).

10. Gregory S. Rodríguez, "'Palaces of Pain'—Arenas of Mexican-American Dreams: Boxing and the Formation of Ethnic Mexican Identities in Twentieth-century Los Angeles," Ph.D. diss., University of California–San Diego, 1999.

11. John Hall, "The Real McCoys," *Los Angeles Times*, Apr. 27, 1972, sec. 3, 3, col. 1.

12. F. Arturo Rosales, *Chicano! The History of the Mexican American Civil Rights Movement* (Houston: Arte Público Press, 1996).

13. Bud Furillo, interview by author, May 1, 1993, West Sacramento, Calif.; tape recording in author's possession.

14. Dwight Chapin, "Ramos Awaits Title Bout, Wedding," *Los Angeles Times*, Dec. 8, 1968, sec. D, 14, col. 7.

15. Tim Kawakami, "Olympic Comes Off the Ropes," *Los Angeles Times*, Mar. 4, 1994, sec. 1, 1, col. 1.

16. Ibid.
17. Rodolfo B. García, "Esquina Neutral," *La Opinión*, Sept. 13, 1972.
18. "Ramos es 7 a 5 favorito para imponerse a Carmona," *La Opinión*, Sept. 15, 1972.
19. Dan Hafner, "Carmona Flattens Ramos, Wins Title," *Los Angeles Times*, Sept. 16, 1972, sec. 3, 1, col. 5.
20. John Hall, "Coliseum Fans, Fighters Get Carried Away," *Los Angeles Times*, Sept. 16, 1972, sec. 3, 1, col. 6.
21. Furillo interview.
22. Hall, "Coliseum Fans, Fighters Get Carried Away."
23. Gabriel S. Hernández, "'El título también es de México!—dijo González," *La Opinión*, Nov. 10, 1972.
24. Robert H. Boyle, "Everything's Rosy with José," *Sports Illustrated*, June 14, 1971, 22–23.
25. Ibid.
26. Gabriel S. Hernández, "Nápoles fulminó a López; Chacón ganó por KOT en 3," *La Opinión*, Mar. 1, 1973, 10, col. 6; "Nápoles KO's López in 7th to Retain Title," *Los Angeles Times*, Mar. 1, 1973, sec. 3, 9, col. 1.
27. "Parnassus, Veteran Fight Promoter, Dies," *Los Angeles Times*, Feb. 26, 1975, sec. 3, 6, col. 4.
28. Jim Murray, "50 years in Boxing," *Los Angeles Times*, Apr. 19, 1973, sec. 3, 1, col. 1.
29. Jim Murray, "He Knew the Ropes," *Los Angeles Times*, Feb. 27, 1975, sec. 3, 1, col. 1.
30. Roy Blount, "'Out of This I Am Getting Not a Nyickl [*sic*]': So Says George Parnassus, but Dollars Flow around the Man Who Is the World-champion Fight Promoter," *Sports Illustrated*, 34(22) (May 31, 1971), 63.
31. Ibid., 64.
32. "Ringsters Battle for Old Mexico: Fast Little Boxers in Olympic Tournament on Monday Developed Here," *Los Angeles Times*, July 10, 1932, sec. 6a, 6, col. 2.
33. When Saldívar went to London in 1965 to defend his title, the sensational bout took on international significance as if the world had been entirely unaware that Mexicans could demonstrate proficiency in any sporting endeavor. President Ordaz announced that he would watch the fight and, following Saldívar's victory, phoned the champion to congratulate him for his "brilliant victory for Mexican sports." Newspapers in Mexico City devoted space to nothing else but the fight on their front pages. This was because "it was a great day," the *New York Times* reported, "[f]or a country that does not often shine in the sports world." The newspaper went on to explore the reason that Mexicans seemed incapable of athletic prowess: "It's the food," noted one commentator. "You cannot expect to build ath-

letes on tortillas and beans." The paper went on to explain exactly what a tortilla was, then noted that "The beans are prepared in a variety of ways, but together the two food items do not make for a balanced diet." When questioned about these issues, the newspaper reported that "The president preferred to attribute the lack of athletic development to the fact that Mexico has had to overcome many other problems to become a developed nation. These problems 'have prevented the athletic preparation and the physical improvement of her youth.'" If the role that Mexicans played in prizefighting was any indication of athletic prowess, then the assessments by Ordaz and the *New York Times* were inaccurate, to say the least. What these accounts obscure is the important distinction between professional and amateur sports. The increasing dominance of Mexicans in the lighter weights revealed profit motives, a bottom line that made prizefighting seem a logical means of escaping poverty. "Saldívar Victory Hailed in Mexico," *New York Times*, Sept. 9, 1965, sec. L, 50, col. 6.
34. Roy Blount, "Out of This I Get Not a Nyickl," 67, 63.
35. Jim Murray, "A Work of Art," *Los Angeles Times*, May 7, 1965, sec. 3, 1, col. 1.
36. Edward Said, *Orientalism* (New York: Pantheon, 1978), 6.

BEATING THE ODDS
Mexican American Distance Runners in Texas, 1950–1995
ALEXANDER MENDOZA

Reubén Reina entered the final lap of the men's 5,000-meter semifinal in the 1992 Olympic Games in fourth place. The capacity crowd of more than eighty thousand people cheered as Ethiopia's Worku Bikila led Kenya's Paul Bitok and Morocco's M. Brahim Boutayeb by a few meters at the bell lap. Running slightly behind the top three, Reina led the remaining group of runners in the event's second semifinal heat. Suffering from anemia, the San Antonio, Texas, native could not muster a strong last lap and finished in fifth place, a mere two seconds away from making the final. Despite the near miss, Reina acknowledged the greater significance of even making it to the Olympic Games, a dream he had had since attending Glenn Elementary and later Jay High School in his hometown. Reina, a veteran of national-class competitions and the European track circuit, could not help but feel overwhelmed by his experience in Barcelona. "Walking into the stadium, they marched us around the track, and I remember looking at the crowd," he recalled. "Among all the thousands of people in the coliseum, all that stood out was an American voice yelling out, 'Go USA!'" Reina confessed that, despite being focused on his race that day, the enormity of representing his country at the pinnacle of track and field competition broke his concentration just slightly. "I couldn't help but smile," he reminisced.[1]

Although Reina became only the fourth Mexican American distance runner to represent the United States in the Olympic Games, his path to Barcelona took him through stiff competition in Texas and later in the Southwest Conference, where he earned All-American honors at the University of Arkansas. His seven state titles for Jay High, however, do not stand alone in the annals of Texas state high school championships. Since 1950, Mexican American distance runners have amassed an impressive array of accomplishments in Texas. Since the formation of the University Interscholastic League (UIL)—the governing body for Texas high school athletics—in 1909, *tejanos* have won 77 state titles in the 1,600 meters and the mile, 32 in the 3,200 meters, and 56 state championships in cross-country. In addition to winning state championships outright, Mexican American runners have also amassed a remarkable number of silver and bronze medals in each of the aforementioned events. In the 1,600-meter/mile run, 123 Mexican Americans have graced the awards podium with second- or third-place finishes, while 56 medalists have earned the same honors in the 3,200-meter race, and 95 have done so in cross-country. The success at the high school level is paralleled at the collegiate level, as tejano runners have earned All-Conference and All-American honors in various universities, and two students have won National Collegiate Athletic Association (NCAA) championships.[2]

In spite of the success that Mexican Americans have had in the long-distance running events, the paucity of historical literature on the subject is staggering. Scholars have neglected U.S. distance runners by failing to examine the lives and careers of the numerous athletes who have accomplished significant feats in national and international competition. The present literature on distance runners focuses primarily on two people who have earned legendary status in the U.S. running community, Jim Ryun and Steve Prefontaine. Two works that analyze the life and running career of the country's first high school runner to run a sub-four-minute mile are Cordner Nelson, *The Jim Ryun Story* (1967), and Ryun's autobiography, *In Quest of Gold: The Jim Ryun Story* (1984). *Pre: The Story of America's Greatest Running Legend, Steve Prefontaine* (1977), written by Tom Jordan, examines the life of arguably one of the country's finest distance runners, who held every U.S. record between 3,000 and 10,000 meters during the early 1970s, before a car accident ended his life in 1975. Prefontaine's legendary status continued to grow even after his death as two films, *Fire on the Track: The Steve Prefontaine Story* (1995) and *Prefontaine* (1997), told the story of the University of Oregon alum and his running career. Although the works on Ryun mention Ricardo Romo, a native of San Antonio who later ran at the University of Texas–Austin as a fierce competitor and a rival of Ryun's, they fail to examine Romo's own contributions to the sport. Carlton Stowers and Wilbur Evans's history of the University of Texas' track and field program, *Champions: University of Texas Track and Field* (1978), also mentions Romo, the first Mexican American to run the mile in less than four minutes, but the study fails to thoroughly examine the two-time Southwest Conference champion.[3]

While the two most successful distance runners in the United States have earned the attention of the mass media and the cinematic world, scholars have failed to examine the role of Mexican American runners and their contributions to the Hispanic and Latino society. Studies of distance runners have focused more on the training and the physiological aspects of the sport than on the impact the athletic achievements have had on the community. The few biographical works on prominent U.S. distance runners are complemented by general studies offering biographical sketches of different runners. Works such as *The Silence of Great Distance* (2000) by Frank Murphy provides historical perspectives of the running careers of prominent female distance runners at the collegiate and professional levels. Richard Benyo's *Masters of the Marathon* (1983) also falls into this genre by providing brief descriptions of well-known distance runners, including U.S. record holder Alberto Salazar, a Cuban American runner from Massachusetts and a two-time Olympian.[4] Ultimately, the only resources for scholars seeking information on prominent Mexican American distance runners are magazine and journal articles. Periodicals such as *Runners World, Runner, Sports Illustrated, Track and Field News*, and various other regional publications remain the only source of perspective and insight into the lives of these athletes.

Nonetheless, the lack of publicity or recognition did not deter Mexican American athletes from competing against the best competition the state of Texas had to offer. As early as 1937, Lee Montes from Nacogdoches won a state championship in the mile run. Javier Montes from El Paso Bowie High School (1947, 1948), S. B. Escoto from Alice (1948), and Alberto Estrado from Bowie (1949) later replicated Montes's accomplishments.[5] Not until the 1950s did Mexican American distance runners begin to make their presence known in state competition. That decade witnessed four state champions in the mile run and an additional eleven silver and bronze medallists.

In addition to the track competition, the second annual Texas State high school cross-country championships in 1955 saw its first Mexican American champion, Humberto Adame, a senior from Laredo Martin High School, who won the overall state title in a run of 9:45, a state record at that time. Adame, who came from a small town on the U.S.-Mexico border, overcame his naïveté in a sport that was still in its infancy in the mid-1950s. Homero Adame, who competed alongside his brother in both high school and college, recalled that training and racing opportunities were few and far between before 1960. "There were no road races in Laredo," Adame pointed out. "Instead, I had to race in Nuevo Laredo, Mexico, to get in shape for the long-distance events."[6]

By the 1950s Mexican Americans were beginning to continue their running careers at the collegiate level. The success of El Campo native Inocensio Cantú, who achieved All-American status at the University of Texas (UT), encouraged runners like the Adame brothers to pursue a collegiate running career after high school. Although Cantú's path to Austin took him through Victoria Junior College for two years, he knew that running was his calling. Despite his parents' wishes, Cantú left the family farm in east Texas to pursue his dream. "I knew I had a certain skill in running that would take me places," Cantú recalled. "I wanted to try out at Victoria Junior College, but my parents wouldn't let me because I was needed on the farm." Despite his family's opposition, Cantú chased his dream and earned a scholarship to the Austin school after a successful junior college career that proved he could compete with the best runners in the Southwest Conference. The highlight of Cantú's years as a Longhorn was his eleventh-place finish at the NCAA cross-country championships in East Lansing, Michigan, earning him All-American status. He was the first tejano to earn this distinction.[7]

Cantú's success had a significant impact on some of the Mexican American runners in the state since they saw in him an athlete with a similar background succeeding at the collegiate level. Homero Adame, for instance, recalled that, in the 1950s, the University of Texas track team traveled to Laredo's Border Olympics, one of the premier high school and collegiate track meets in the spring, and made an impressive showing in front of the border crowd. "Texas seemed to win all of the meets and dominated the other schools," Adame pointed out. "Because of that I fell in love with the school . . . [when] I was in grade school." In addition to watching runners like Cantú compete at the collegiate level, the younger Adame had another motivating factor influencing his decision to attend the Texas school: the desire to explore the world beyond the Texas-Mexico border. For Homero, that meant taking advantage of the educational opportunities at a large university such as the state's flagship school in Austin. There he would be exposed to a more culturally diversified environment, something that life on the border had not prepared him for.[8]

Although runners like Cantú and the Adame brothers recalled no racial discrimination at the high school or collegiate level, they all claimed their focus was solely on competing, and thus they disregarded the subtle nuances that can imply racial prejudice.[9] However, other Mexican American athletes competing in various sports in the 1950s sometimes found the English language a formidable obstacle. According to Chevo Contreras, a member of the 1952 Laredo Martin baseball team, which competed at the UIL state championships in Austin, he and his teammates felt uncomfortable visiting the state capital as the only team consisting of Mexican Americans. "We used to go into places where no one spoke Spanish," Contreras remembered. "We would be asked what we wanted to eat. Ham and eggs, would say one, and soon everyone was saying 'ham and eggs,' 'ham and eggs.' At dinner we would do the same with everyone ordering chicken-fried steak."[10]

In the late 1950s Ricardo Romo, then a freshman at San Antonio Fox Tech High School, was determined to use his natural ability to excel in a sport in which success correlated with dedication and hard training. Growing up in San Antonio's Prospect Hill barrio in the city's West Side, Romo recognized the problems inherent in a neighborhood that had to contend with gang violence, unemployment, and low wages. Although Romo began his running career as a result of the encouragement of his junior high school coach, it did not take long for him to dedicate himself solely to the task of running, which would eventually earn him a college scholarship. The desire to succeed greatly motivated the young runner. "One time in an assembly at Tech they gave the results of a study they had made," Romo recalls. "It showed of 435 in the graduating class that only six planned to go to college. I made up my mind that I wasn't going to be one of the 429. It gave me a lot of drive."[11]

One result of Romo's desire to succeed was his wholehearted interest in following the athletic careers of other Mexican American runners in the state. In addition to keeping tabs on the accomplishments of fellow San Antonio native Richard Menchaca, an all-state runner from Lanier High School in San Antonio, Romo also kept up with other Mexican American runners. "When reading the newspapers, I was accustomed to looking for Mexican American names," Romo recalls. "There were so few role models that it was natural to do that. We needed heroes. We looked for heroes." Armed with a strong work ethic, the Fox Tech thinclad sophomore trained hard and soon qualified for the state championships, ultimately finishing in sixth place. "There wasn't anything more important to me than running," Romo remembers. "Not work, not girls, not my studies. It was the number one thing in my life. Everything else was secondary."[12]

Training with his coaches at Fox Tech, the lanky Romo became a peculiar fixture in his West Side neighborhood when he added extra workouts to improve his conditioning by running along San Antonio's San Pedro Creek. The extra training paid off when he returned to the state championships in 1961 and won the overall title. He replicated the feat the following year and added the cross-country title to his list of accomplishments. By the time Romo graduated from Fox Tech, he had won three state championships, held the best time in the nation for the mile (4:10), and proved to be one of the most highly recruited runners in the country.[13]

While Romo garnered the attention of the local press, his reputation extended throughout Texas. Some members of the media even suggested that a rivalry existed between the Fox Tech runner and another Mexican American thinclad from Crystal City, Ricardo Gallegos. As a sophomore in 1961, Gallegos won the UIL state championship in the AA division with a time of 4:28. The following year, Texas newspapers portrayed a rivalry between the two South Texas runners. "Back then, there weren't many Mexicans running track," Gallegos reminisced, "and the San Antonio newspapers made it seem as if we were enemies. In reality, we were *camaradas* [friends]."[14] At the 1962 state championships, the *Austin American* stressed the competition between the two athletes, despite the fact that they ran in different divisions. When Gallegos set the state meet record of 4:17.4 on Friday, May 4, reporters wrote of Romo's reaction to the new mark and suggested that it might not last too long in the record books if the San Antonio runner had a say in the matter. Romo, for his part, refused to speculate on the subject, simply answering that he "would run his own race."[15] The following day Romo ran a 4:17.9, a mere half second off the Crystal City runner's time. Romo bettered both marks a few weeks later at the national championships in California, running a personal best of 4:10.[16]

Gallegos did not return for his senior season due to the UIL's maximum age, but he recalls receiving many letters from fans throughout the state commending him and Romo for representing the Mexican American community at the state level: "People told me that they admired what I did. They were proud for Latinos to do well in running. We [Mexican Americans] had been successful in baseball, but track and field was a new sport for us to do well in. People were especially proud of Romo because he later went to a large university [the University of Texas–Austin] and was the first Latino to run under four minutes for the mile."[17]

Romo's running career flourished at the University of Texas, despite the fact that he missed an entire season because of a tendon injury that required surgery. Nevertheless, Romo won two Southwest Conference titles in the mile—one in the three-mile run and another in cross-country—during his tenure as a Longhorn.[18] Despite his collegiate honors, Romo's greatest impact on Texas running came in his final season at the University of Texas. On August 10, 1966, he became the first Texan and the first Mexican American to run the mile in less than four minutes.[19] After serving as the pacesetter for Jim Ryun's world record mark of 3:51.3 in July, Romo established the University of Texas school record for the mile a few weeks later.[20] "What Ryun did was finally convince me that the mile could be run under four minutes. I took what I had experienced from that race and won the following week [month] in a school record time," Romo stated.[21] Although Romo received more attention from the national media for his pace-setting responsibility during Ryun's world record race, his accomplishment proved a significant milestone for Mexican Americans in his home state. During the 1960s and later in the 1980s and 1990s Mexican American runners would note that Romo's feat motivated them and influenced the way they participated in the sport.[22]

Although Romo and Gallegos may have sparked a greater interest in and awareness of tejanos in the running community, two individuals from Falfurrias carried the success of Mexican American distance runners to new levels in the mid-1960s. Roberto González and Homero Martínez finished in first and second place respectively at the state championships for three consecutive years. After Martínez graduated in 1966, González lowered the state meet record the following year to 4:07.4, to earn a fourth consecutive state title. Referred to as the "Dynamic Mile Duo" from Falfurrias, the two runners from a small town sixty miles southwest of Corpus Christi astonished newspapers throughout the state at the way they dominated the event.[23] "People thought we were something special," recalled González. "I remember them asking my high school coach what we would eat, thinking we were something special."[24]

Despite the perceptions track and field fans had about the two Falfurrias runners, González and Martínez tied for the AAA state championship in 1964 before finishing in first and second place respectively in 1965 and 1966. Each year they both bettered the state meet record mark until González, who was a year younger than Martínez, ran a 4:07, a mark that still stands. In addition, the two runners also compiled an impressive cross-country record, finishing number one and two respectively in 1964 and 1965 and leading the Falfurrias team to the state championship in 1965, the first of nine state titles the Jerseys would win in the next fifteen years.[25]

While Texas track fans marveled at the accomplishments of González and Martínez and wondered whether the Falfurrias program contained any secrets to success, the two runners knew that they owed their performances to the synergy of hard work and their personal physiological attributes. "We were fortunate to have each other because we pushed one another to the maximum," noted González. "Homero is the type of individual who could run someone to the ground in distance training while I had better leg speed. We complemented each other."[26] For his part, Martínez attributes the success that he and González experienced to the background they shared. "Our upbringing allowed us to handle the heavy training," Martínez pointed out. "As soon as school was out, we picked cotton and watermelons on the farm. That is what made us tough. So, when we got on the track, it was not as hard as working on the fields."[27]

The diligence displayed by the Falfurrias thinclads remained a consistent theme with many successful Mexican American runners who grew up in the 1950s and 1960s. Inocensio Cantú remembered that he learned to deal with pain while working in the East Texas cotton fields as a child in the late 1940s and early 1950s.[28] Ricardo Gallegos stated that his father instilled in him a strong work ethic as a migrant farmworker who traveled to North Dakota to labor in the fields. "My father would prefer that I work for money rather than be in sports," recalled Gallegos. "He didn't think too much of education, and he made me work so I could be a man."[29]

In addition to working on the farms near Falfurrias, Martínez cited the fact that he and his teammates did not have a car and had to walk to get to various places. "Everything we did was done walking," he remembered. "Even after long workouts we would walk home." Gallegos concurred, stating that he had to run and walk a mile to and from school four times a day. "I had to eat at home because I didn't have any money to eat at school," he reminisced. "So I ran and walked to school every day and during lunch so I could get something to eat." For his part, Martínez noted how his notoriety gave him the opportunity to work in the cafeteria to get free lunches. "Back then [in the 1960s] there was no free lunch at school," he remembered, "but we were proud because we would get a free meal."[30]

Even those runners who did not come from agricultural towns found that their families still placed a strong emphasis on hard work. Homero and Humberto Adame recalled that their father, who owned a small grocery store in Laredo, would make them work in the family business. "My dad discouraged us from being in athletics because it took time away from earning money," Homero stressed.[31] Similarly, Ricardo Romo started working in his dad's grocery store in San Antonio at the age of six. He swept the floor, stocked the shelves, and minded the counter up until he graduated from Fox Tech High School in 1962. "Our parents were very hard-working individuals, and they instilled a work ethic in us," recalled Romo's brother, Henry. "If we weren't in school, we had to be helping them out at the store. There were always chores to do there—sweeping the floor, stocking shelves. It was tantamount to the old days when kids grew up on farms."[32] Henry Romo Sr., who ran that grocery store for more than twenty years, adhered to the belief that the key ingredients to success remained "plenty of work, plenty of sweat." Homero Martínez stated that, while the Falfurrias runners were quite successful in cross-country and track, he and his teammates took "pride in that we may not have been the best, but we did what was necessary, in terms of hard work, to win."[33]

Each of the dominant high school runners of the sixties earned track scholarships to various colleges in Texas. As Romo continued his success in Austin, Gallegos attended Sul Ross State University in Alpine, and González and Martínez became teammates once more at Texas A&I University in Kingsville. These athletic standouts found that college presented them with a whole new set of obstacles to overcome, the foremost being advanced curriculum. "I had trouble with school," acknowledged Gallegos. "They gave me tutors, but it didn't do any good." Unlike Gallegos, who ultimately left Sul Ross, González and Martínez completed their degrees but failed to significantly improve on the marks they had run in high school, despite the fact that they won several Lone Star conference titles. "In dealing with the class work," Martínez maintained, "it was tougher, and we didn't do as well in running as we should have done. It hurt us as far as developing [as runners]."[34]

González recalled that there were few scholarship opportunities for

Mexican Americans during the sixties and that what he and Martínez accomplished by running for four years and earning their diplomas was more significant than the enhanced economic opportunities the former athletes benefited from upon graduation. "Scholarships for Mexican Americans in the sixties was [sic] not very common," he pointed out. "The distance [running] programs of the sixties and seventies opened the doors for Mexican Americans of later generations to be as good as they would want to be." Martínez agreed that the runners of the 1960s proved to be groundbreakers in a sport that was ideal for the Mexican American community.[35]

Although no one athlete dominated the running scene like the runners of the 1960s, Mexican Americans continued to succeed in state competition throughout the following decade. Beginning in 1972, the first year that the University Scholastic League began to sponsor the Texas State high school cross-country championships, Mexican American runners won eight of the ten state cross-country titles in the first five years of UIL-sanctioned competition.[36] In addition, teams with Mexican American runners began to stand out in the state championships. While Falfurrias was a perennial favorite in the Class B division during the early part of the decade, the El Paso schools of West Texas soon dominated the competition in Class A, winning three state championships and five silver and bronze finishes during the seventies. Moreover, the girls' team from El Paso High School won two back-to-back state titles in 1978 and 1979. Other schools from the Rio Grande Valley also moved to the forefront of contenders for the state title, as schools like McAllen and Edinburg High also earned the top three spots in the team races. The Edinburg High Bobcats, coached by former Falfurrias star and Texas A&I alum, Homero Martínez, captured the overall crown in 1977.[37]

Like Martínez, many of the elite Mexican American runners of the previous decades returned to the sport in the 1970s—but not as competitors. This time, with the desire to give something back to their communities, the former runners were joining the coaching ranks. In Laredo, both of the Adame brothers returned from the University of Texas to coach high school cross-country and track teams at United and Nixon High Schools. Roberto González returned to his alma mater, Falfurrias High, while his former teammate, Homero Martínez, spent a few years in the San Antonio Independent School District before moving to Edinburg and taking charge of the track program there. Throughout Texas, the school districts filled still more coaching positions with Hispanic candidates as the state's Mexican American population made numerous advances in political representation. As the Chicano movement, which dominated the 1960s, came to an end in the midseventies, tejanos witnessed a significant increase in the growth of the Mexican American middle class.[38]

The development of the Mexican American professional class allowed the former athletes of the fifties and sixties to return to the sport they had left behind. "I felt I could contribute a lot more with the kids than I ever could while I was running," explained Homero Martínez with regard to his decision to assume a coaching career. Having Mexican Americans assume positions as football and track coaches was a striking departure from previous decades, when, for runners like Ricardo Romo, the majority of the teachers and coaches were Anglos.[39]

As Mexican American coaches took the helm in greater numbers during the seventies and eighties, tejano distance men soon reestablished their predecessors' dominance during the Reagan years. From 1980 to 1989 Mexican American runners won nineteen of thirty-eight state titles in cross-country. Moreover, with the introduction of the 3,200-meter run to the UIL state meet in 1981, the tejano thinclads added eighteen additional state crowns to the seventeen 1,600-meter titles.[40] The Falfurrias cross-country squad, coached by former Jersey standout Roberto González, highlighted the new decade by winning the 3A state title with a predominantly Mexican American team while another Martínez—José—won the individual title in 1980. The following year brought a resurgence of distance runners from the El Paso area, with Bobby Aguirre, from Riverside High School, winning two state titles in 1981 and 1983 and placing second in 1982. The team from El Paso High School also won the 5A title in 1983. In the early eighties, the *El Paso Times* boasted that the Sun City's schools had dominated the regional competition and maintained a leading presence in state competition.[41]

As Aguirre's high school career came to an end in 1984, Reubén Reina, a 5 foot 7 inch sophomore from San Antonio's Jay High, emerged as the new star of the 5A division, the largest and most competitive classification in UIL competition. Unlike some of his predecessors, Reina did not participate in the sport because a junior high coach had recruited him or because he had failed at another, more popular, sport like football or baseball. Instead, the young Reina came to be a distance runner because he had witnessed what his two older brothers, Randy and Roland, had accomplished in the late seventies and early eighties. Affectionately referred to as the "Running Reinas" by the

San Antonio media, Ralph and Emily Reina ultimately produced arguably the most talented running family in Texas. Led by oldest brother, Randy, a 1978 graduate of Jay High who ran a 4:19 mile, a total of five Reinas, including two sisters, Janice and Eileen, competed at the collegiate level. Roland, a 1982 graduate of Jay, also won that year's 5A state championship in the 3,200-meter run. Later, at the University of Arkansas, Randy and Roland accumulated two individual Southwest Conference titles and All-American honors for Coach John McDonnell's highly respected distance program. Randy remembered that he developed a serious interest in distance running because of "the love I had for the sport."[42]

Randy Reina's success had a significant impact on younger siblings Roland and Reubén, who chose to follow in his footsteps at Jay High School and later at the University of Arkansas. Roland pointed out that "Randy was a motivator all the way from Fayetteville," writing letters and taking a great deal of interest in his younger brothers and sisters.[43] Randy knew he had to pave a path for his entire family. The son of a third-generation Mexican American, Randy felt that going to college "was never a question," considering how strongly he felt about the sport and academics.[44] In 1979, after a year at Texas A&I University, Reina transferred to Arkansas to run for the Razorbacks, who had an emerging national distance program in the 1970s.[45]

While Randy was developing as a distance runner, he did not neglect his younger siblings in San Antonio. Even though he could not directly oversee Roland's and Reubén's training programs in the early eighties, he wrote to them frequently, offering encouragement and advice on training and racing. When Randy came home from Fayetteville, the entire Reina clan made running a family affair. "We'd all sit around and watch track meets as a family," recalled Roland. "Whenever there was a major track meet on television, Randy made sure we'd all sit around the living room and watch it as a family." Randy's enthusiasm for the sport affected even his father, Ralph, who provided his offspring with the food and nutrients that distance runners need for optimal performance.[46]

The strong family network evident in the Reina household in the early 1980s helped Roland and Reubén to win the state titles that had eluded Randy in the late 1970s. After Roland won the state 3,200-meter run his senior year and followed his older brother to Fayetteville, Reubén, the youngest of the "Running Reinas," became perhaps the most successful runner in Texas history. In addition to winning seven state titles at Jay High, Reubén was the first

Texan to win the Kinney National High School Cross-country Championship in 1985.[47] Running a course record of 14:36 for the 5,000-meter course, Reina secured a victory that made him one of the most highly recruited distance runners in the nation his senior year.

Despite the significance of his win at nationals, his accomplishments at Memorial Stadium in Austin, the site of the UIL state meet, made him a legend in the Texas track community. As a sophomore, Reubén became the first and only runner in Texas high school competition to win the 1,600- and 3,200-meter runs for three consecutive years. The "triple double," as Texas track fans referred to it, remains such a significant part of Texas track lore that runners competing more than fifteen years after Reubén's last race inevitably hear of the Jay runner's accomplishments.[48] As Randy sums it up, his younger brother's running career at Jay High was "perfect."[49]

Reubén Reina's successful high school career carried over to the collegiate level as he earned eight All-American honors and two NCAA championships in the indoor 3,000-meter run for the University of Arkansas. Although his two NCAA championships remain the most ever won by a tejano runner, his first victory came in 1990, five years after Aaron Ramírez, a native of Mission running for the University of Arizona, won the 1986 NCAA cross-country crown. Ramírez, a 1982 graduate of Mission High, won the Texas relays but never captured a state title. After a year at Texas A&M University, he moved west, where he resumed his running career for the Wildcats.[50] Like Reina, Ramírez also continued to run successfully after college. In 1991 he qualified for the World Track and Field Championships and, from 1990 to 1994, ranked among the top five Americans in the 5,000- and 10,000-meter events.[51]

Reina and Ramírez also shared another distinction that solidified their prominence in the tejano distance-running tradition—they each broke four minutes for the mile. Although the first American to run a mile in less than four minutes did so in 1957, the nation has always held a fascination with the elusive mark.[52] Reina became the second tejano to run the mile in less than four minutes in February 1989 with a time of 3:58.88. Four years later, Ramírez joined Reina on the U.S. all-time list, when he ran a 3:59.57. According to *Track and Field News*, of the 244 Americans who have conquered the elusive barrier, only five are Mexican American. Of those five, three are from Texas.[53]

The Reinas' accomplishments on the track were due in part to the strong family network that Ralph and Emily Reina cultivated. "The family is what made the Reinas great," Roland emphasized. "My mom and dad made sure that we were 'one.' They would go shopping for us to make sure that we had the fruits [and other food] to stay healthy."[54] The elder Reina even served as a motivating tool when he promised his children that he would run a 10-kilometer road race in San Antonio, despite never having trained for such an endeavor. The support and enthusiasm the Reinas exhibited while the five siblings ran competitively exemplified the new, more encouraging attitudes of Mexican American families in backing their children as young competitors. While runners such as Inocensio Cantú, the Adame brothers, Roberto González, Homero Martínez, and Ricardo Gallegos had to run competitively with minimal or no family support during the 1950s and 1960s, Mexican American families of later generations became more involved in the young athletes' activities. By the 1980s and 1990s, the parents of successful tejano runners often attended track meets, encouraged their sons and daughters to pursue running as an avenue to college, provided financial support, and bought needed equipment.

Mexican American runners, now bolstered by a stronger family support network, continued to succeed in the 1980s and 1990s. Crystal City runner Ricky Gallegos Jr. is an example of how tejano runners used the close-knit ties of their Mexican American families to succeed in athletics. The young Gallegos, who won seven state championships for the Javelinas, recalled that his father experienced no such support from his family while he was growing up in the 1960s. Ricardo Gallegos Sr., in fact, pointed out that his father had a low opinion of both education and sports. By the 1980s, the older Gallegos was training his son, offering coaching advice, and even sponsoring pasta parties for the Crystal City runners.[55]

Similar stories can be found throughout Texas as Mexican American families came together to support the young athletes. Gabriel Santa María, Laredo Nixon's 1989 silver medalist in cross-country, for instance, recalled that his father, a bartender in Nuevo Laredo, Mexico, would close his cantina at 5:00 A.M. so that he could return to Laredo, Texas, to watch his son run an early-morning cross-country meet. "My family would even throw pasta parties [for the team] despite the fact that we weren't in the best of economic situations," Gabriel stated.[56] El Paso High's Gilbert Contreras, who won the state title in the 800-meter run and placed second in the 1,600 in 1988, also experienced extensive familial support. His family made the more than 600-mile trek from El Paso to watch him run in Austin. Other runners like Eagle Pass's Luís Sánchez, the 1986 silver medalist in the 1,600-meter run, recalled that, despite his father's lukewarm response to his participation in track, "Dad was thrilled when I made it big."[57]

Even though runners in the 1980s and 1990s received greater support from their families, community support for tejano runners never wavered in the more than forty years of competitive racing. In the 1960s, when Roberto González and Homero Martínez were dominating the state's competition, the city of Falfurrias took a great deal of interest in the two runners who brought acclaim to the South Texas ranching community. "When we won state," Martínez recalled, "our names and a 'congratulations' were placed on the town theater's marquee sign to show how the community felt about us." Ricardo Gallegos Sr. remembered that his father was proud of the fact that he never paid for his own beer in the various bars around Crystal City while his son raced to victories in state competition. Reubén Reina said that the San Antonio community raised funds to send him to various national competitions he could not finance himself. In some cases, community support came after the tejano runners had graduated from high school and college. In the Rio Grande Valley, Rene Guillén, the 1986 4A state cross-country champion for Brownsville Pace, proudly recalled that the community of Brownsville and his adopted hometown of Laredo came to his aid and provided funding for him to attend the 2000 Olympic trials marathon in Pittsburgh, Pennsylvania.[58]

While community support for Mexican American runners often took traditional forms, in some cases the public's pride reached extraordinary levels. Luís Sánchez remembered that, after he won the national title in the Amateur Athletic Union's 1,500-meter run, he and his coach received a homecoming parade that took the young runner through the streets of Eagle Pass:

> Once we got to La Pryor, right outside of Eagle Pass, my coach turned the radio on, and I heard the DJ say "we are waiting for Luís Sánchez to arrive," and as soon as he said that, we came up on a usual speed trap, when a police car turns his lights on, begins to follow us, and then pulls up beside us. Although I first thought we got a speeding ticket. My coach started laughing, and the surprise was out. He confessed that the city had arranged a parade in my honor. We pulled up [to the city], and I hugged my mom and dad while the press was there. They put me on a fire truck, and they took me down Main Street to the Parks and Recreation building, with all the vehicles following along and honking their horns. People came out waving, yelling, "We are proud of you." The

whole motorcade came to a stop at the building, and it was just as crazy down there. I still get chills thinking about it.[59]

To Sánchez, the most important thing was that his parents would return to their blue-collar jobs the next day and all their coworkers would comment on their son's accomplishment. In other cases, media organs like the *Laredo Sports Journal (LSJ)* provided extensive coverage of local athletes, and fans from rival schools attended the state competitions to show their support. As Goyo López, the editor for the *LSJ* wrote in a 1998 editorial, "At this level of competition you represent more than your high school, you symbolize the athletic prowess of all Laredo [a predominantly Mexican American town]." His journal's coverage of Mark Contreras, who won that year's 3,200-meter run state title, inspired a group of Laredoans to make the trip to Austin's Memorial Stadium to shower *porras* (cheers) on Contreras.[60]

As community backing reached new levels in the 1980s and 1990s, Mexican American distance runners demonstrated a greater awareness of their ethnic identity than the runners of the fifties and sixties. Athletes like Roberto González and Homero Martínez cited their focus on winning races and running fast times as a reason for not examining the larger picture. "I never thought about being a Mexican American, just being a runner," said Inocensio Cantú. "It never crossed my mind." Roberto González, the Falfurrias standout, maintained that his success in cross-country and track never had a greater significance. "From what I understood from people, my running opened the door for other people to follow," he maintained. "I didn't see it that way. I was just doing something I was successful at." González's teammate, Homero Martínez, believed that the encouragement they received from both the Mexican American and the Anglo community in Falfurrias lessened any feelings that he and his teammates were distinct. Other runners like Homero Adame never felt a greater sense of accomplishment because of their ethnic background. Despite always considering himself a mexicano, Adame confessed that he "never paid much attention" to his ethnicity.[61]

As significant as the athletic achievements may have been for the runners of the 1950s and 1960s, their focus on running precluded any analysis of their identity as Mexican Americans and their position as role models. Runners of the seventies like Randy Reina placed greater importance on heritage. Consequently, his younger siblings, who grew up listening to their older brother talk about running and the importance of national-class runners like Alberto

Salazar and Rudy Chapa, viewed their ethnicity in a different light. "I started to see that I represented a group of people and that my success could motivate others from the Hispanic culture to strive to do the same," maintained Roland Reina. Reubén Reina concurred with his older brother: "Competing on the national scene, I felt that I was representing more than just myself," he affirmed. "I represented more of a community of Hispanic people."[62]

Rene Guillén, who ran at Brownsville Pace High School before running at the University of Texas–San Antonio (UTSA) and later UT–Pan American, made sure he never lost sight of his origins. "When I was at Pan Am, I always thought of representing Hispanics," Guillén pointed out. "I always wanted to show that Hispanics were able to succeed."[63] Living along the border prevented some tejano runners from realizing their ethnicity until they reached state competition or ran on a collegiate team. Laredoan Gabriel Santa María, who later ran at UTSA in the early nineties, remembered that, even though he lived in a city with a predominantly Mexican American population, he never placed much emphasis on his ethnicity. However, when he traveled to national competitions outside of the border area, "it meant a great deal more."[64]

Coaches sometimes taught their runners to have pride in their heritage. José Navarro, the boys' distance coach at Laredo Martin High School, describes the accomplishments of past tejano runners like the Reinas and emphasizes the importance of setting high goals. "One thing that I have done [as a coach] is . . . [to encourage] the athletes to believe in themselves," he points out. "I tell them about Roberto González, Homero Martínez, and Homero Adame, and I tell the athletes that education is the best way out of the *barrio*."[65]

Role models also became important to former runner Ricardo Romo, who, after his running career, earned a doctorate in history, taught at his alma mater (the University of Texas), and was named president of UTSA in 1999. "It is important that we serve as role models for our students. Taking even a passing interest in a person's talents can be tremendously important," he stated.[66] Homero Martínez, who, as a runner in Falfurrias during the sixties, never placed a strong emphasis on his ethnicity, has found that, as a coach and a leader of young men and women, his place as a role model has grown exponentially. "I take pride as a Mexican American coach," he says. "We pull for the Mexican American kids. I don't care where they are from, we all pull for each other." Martínez's approach to his position as a coach and role model has succeeded; in his thirty-one-year coaching career he has led one of his teams to a state title while coaching four individuals—all of Mexican American descent—to state championships.[67]

Two of the runners who won state titles under Martínez's leadership are female. Laura Vásquez and Sonia Sepulveda, both students at Edinburg High School, won 5 individual state championships and 3 silver medals for the Bobcats. The success of Mexican American female distance runners has not been as imposing as that of their male counterparts. Mexican American girls have won 15 individual state cross-country titles, 12 championships in the 1,600-meter run, and 15 crowns in the 3,200-meter run. The lower number of gold medals in state competition is partly attributable to the fact that the UIL did not recognize girls' championship events until 1975 in cross-country, 1977 in the 1,600-meter run, and 1981 in the 3,200-meter run.[68]

Unlike in boys' competition, no dominant runner like González in the 1960s, Reina in the 1980s, or Gallegos in the 1990s has reigned over the girls' ranks in the same fashion. Instead, Edinburg's Sepulveda, with a total of six state championship medals, bears the distinction of being one of Texas' most successful Mexican American female runners. Sepulveda continued her running career at Baylor University, where she earned All-Southwest Conference honors for the Bears. Returning to the Rio Grande Valley, she assumed a position as assistant track coach under her former mentor, Homero Martínez. Sepulveda concedes that she has taken her position as a role model more seriously now that she can help other athletes from the Texas-Mexican border reach their goals. "I always knew that, from early on, when I first started competing, . . . I carried a responsibility of being an example for the public," she maintains. "I carried that with me, and I was always aware of how I could encourage other kids."[69]

Although a slight gap remains between the success levels of male and female Mexican American distance runners in Texas, both have made notable strides in cross-country and track and field competition in the last fifty years.[70] The tejano runners of the fifties and sixties broke new ground for others to follow by challenging the state's best high school competitors and later running successfully at the collegiate and professional level. Mexican American distance runners of past generations, however, did not see themselves as pioneers or role models. Rather, they focused on training and on upcoming competitions. By the 1970s and 1980s, however, tejano runners viewed themselves in a different light. They seemed to have a greater awareness of those who came before them and the level of success those earlier runners had achieved. Consequently, the runners of the seventies and eighties felt a greater responsibility to act as role models for their community and placed a greater importance on their college education.

At the turn of the new millennium, tejano runners continue to grace the awards podiums at yearly state championship events in cross-country and track, and they are no longer a rarity in collegiate competition. Examination of Texas colleges and universities with track and cross-country programs reveals that almost every school has at least one Spanish-surnamed athlete competing on their squad.[71] For an ethnic group whose athletes once felt like a minority at the state championships and in collegiate competition, the tejano runners have accomplished truly impressive feats.[72]

NOTES

1. Reubén Reina, interview by author, tape recording, Fayetteville, Ark., Jan. 27, 2002; *San Antonio Express-News,* June 26, 2001; *Houston Post,* Aug. 7, 1992; Cordner Nelson, "5,000 Meters: Baumann's Big Kick," *Track and Field News* 45(10) (Oct. 1992): 26.

2. The first Mexican American runner was Javier Montes, who ran at El Paso Bowie High School before representing the United States in the 1952 Olympic Games in the 1,500-meter run. See the "2001–2002 University of Texas at El Paso Track and Field Media Guide." Copy of booklet in author's possession. In this chapter, "distance runners" are defined as those running at least 1,600 meters (one metric mile). Records for the state championships are given in the University Interscholastic League's *Historical State Tournaments and Champions Records, 1909–2001* (Austin: Bureau of Public School Service Press, 2001) and the *Austin–American Statesman,* 1950–1995. In 1911 the UIL first recognized the mile, which stood until 1979, when the UIL switched to the 1,600-meter run, or the "metric mile." The 3,200-meter run was first contested in 1981. Although cross-country was not recognized by the UIL until 1972, the Texas Parks and Recreation Department sponsored a "state championship" from 1954 to 1971. See Donald Jay, "History of Texas Track and Field," *Texas Coach* 23(8) (Apr. 1980): 59–64; *Austin–American Statesman,* Nov. 21, 1954. The number of state championships and medallists is derived from all of the divisions in the Texas State high school championships and the UIL. The two people who have won NCAA titles are Aaron Ramírez, a native of Mission, Texas, who won the 1985 NCAA cross-country championships, and Reubén Reina, who won both the 1990 and the 1991 NCAA indoor 3,000-meter runs.

3. Cordner Nelson, *The Jim Ryun Story* (Los Altos, Calif.: Tafnews Press, 1967); Jim Ryun with Mike Phillips, *In Quest of Gold: The Jim Ryun Story* (San Francisco: Harper and Row, 1984); Tom Jordan, *Pre: The Story of America's Greatest Running Legend, Steve Prefontaine*, 2d ed. (Emmaus, Penn.: Rodale Press, 1977); Joseph M. Turrini, "Prefontaine: The Legend Continues," *Journal of Sport History* (Summer 1998): 321–23. Other biographical works include Marc Bloom, *Steve Scott, the Miler: America's Legendary Miler Talks about His Triumphs and Trials* (New York: Hungry Minds, 1997); Frank Shorter's autobiography with Marc Bloom (Boston: Houghton Mifflin, 1984); and John C. Chodes, *Corbitt: The Story of Ted Corbitt, Long-distance Runner* (Los Altos, Calif.: Tafnews Press, 1982). See also Carlton Stowers and Wilbur Evans, *Champions: University of Texas Track and Field* (Huntsville, Ala.: Strode, 1978).

4. Frank Murphy, *The Silence of Great Distance* (Kansas City: Windsprint Press, 2000); Richard Benyo, *Masters of the Marathon* (New York: Atheneum, 1983).

5. *Historical State Tournaments and Champions Records, 1909–2001*.

6. Alex Mendoza, "The History of Laredo High School Cross-Country," *Laredo Sports Journal* 2(12) (Dec. 1998): 25–26; Homero Adame, interview by the author, tape recording, Laredo, Tex., Dec. 20, 2001.

7. Inocensio Cantú, interview by the author, tape recording, Richmond, Tex., Jan. 22, 2002; *Austin–American Statesman*, Nov. 23, 1954; "Texas Cross-Country, 1992," media guide, n.p., n.d., 12.

8. Adame interview, Dec. 20, 2001.

9. Ibid.; Humberto Adame, interview by the author, Laredo, Tex., Oct. 30, 1998; Cantú interview. Adame states that he "was fairly naïve in regards to racial tension." Cantú maintains that, despite the fact that he was the only Mexican American on the UT track team, he "never ran across any situation of racial discrimination." He adds that he "never had any difficulties with that, and it never crossed [his] mind."

10. Goyo López and Armando X. López, "What If . . . the Story of the 1952 Martin Tiger Baseball Team," *Laredo Sports Journal* 2(2) (Feb. 1998): 7.

11. Ricardo Romo, interview by the author, tape recording, San Antonio, Dec. 29, 2001; Tom Osborn, "Going the Extra Mile," *San Antonio Express News*, June 24, 2001; Ricardo Romo, quoted in *Austin–American Statesman*, Jan. 12, 1967.

12. Ricardo Romo, interview by the author, tape recording, San Antonio, Nov. 14, 2001. Romo points out that he had only one Hispanic teacher in his twelve years of public education. Ricardo Romo, quoted in *San Antonio Express News*, June 24, 2001.

13. *San Antonio Express News*, Jan. 27, 2002.

14. Ricardo Gallegos Sr., interview by the author, tape recording, Crystal City, Tex., Jan. 11, 2002.

15. *Austin–American Statesman,* May 5, 1962. For evidence of the rivalry between Romo and Gallegos as portrayed by the media, see the *San Antonio Express News, San Antonio Light,* and *Laredo Times* from March through May 1962.

16. Romo interview, Nov. 14, 2001.

17. Ricardo Gallegos Sr., interview by the author, tape recording, Crystal City, Tex., Jan. 31, 2002.

18. Ricardo Romo to Alex Mendoza, Jan. 4, 2002; *San Antonio Light,* Nov. 24, 1963; Romo interview, Nov. 14, 2001.

19. E. Garry Hill, "Chronological Listing of U.S. Milers Who Have Broken 4:00 in the Mile," *Track and Field News* (July 2, 2001):31–32. According to Hill, the official statistician for *Track and Field News,* Romo was the nineteenth American ever to run under 4:00. Further inspection of the list reveals that only five Mexican Americans have broken the four-minute barrier. Three out of those five are native Texans: Romo, Reubén Reina from San Antonio (1989), and Aaron Ramírez from Mission (1991).

20. For a description of Romo's pace-setting duties during Ryun's world-record-setting run of July 25, 1966, see Ryun's autobiography, *In Quest of Gold,* 47–51. Despite the fast pace required of Romo, the Texas native finished third overall with a time of 4:01.4. Prior to the race, Romo reportedly stated, "I would like to see the [world] record come back to the United States." Romo is quoted in "Richard Romo: All-American," undated biographical sketch in author's possession. I would like to thank Mario Longoria, a native of Helotes, Tex., and one of Romo's former students, for a copy of this article. Longoria is also a respected historian of Mexican Americans in sport, having published *Athletes Remembered: Mexicano/Latino Professional Football Players 1929–1970* (Tempe, Ariz.: Bilingual Press, 1997).

21. Romo, quoted in *San Antonio Express News,* May 18, 1997.

22. Interviews with Homero Martínez, Roberto González, Ricardo Gallegos, Homero Adame, Randy Reina, Reubén Reina, Danny Castro, Rene Guillén, Gabriel Santa María, José Navarro, Marc Contreras, Oscar Vela all attest to the significance of Romo's accomplishments among Mexican American runners. In January 2002 Romo was inducted into the San Antonio Sports Hall of Fame for his achievements on the track. See *San Antonio Express News,* Jan. 27, 2002. Homero Martínez, also state champion in the mile from Falfurrias and a two-year runner-up, stated that Romo would come to see him and teammate Roberto González, who won four state championships between 1965 and 1968, at various Texas meets in the 1960s. "We looked up to Richard," Martínez remembered. "He was our idol back then." Homero Martínez, interview by the author, tape recording, Edinburg, Tex., January 23, 2002.

23. Quoted in *Austin American,* May 6, 1966.

24. Roberto González, interview by the author, tape recording, Falfurrias, Tex., Jan. 21, 2002.

25. Ibid.; Homero Martínez, interview by the author, tape recording, Edinburg, Tex., Jan. 23, 2002; *Austin-American Statesman*, Dec. 12, 1965; Dec. 4, 1966; Dec. 3, 1967; Dec. 8, 1968; Dec. 14, 1969; Dec. 13, 1970; Dec. 11, 1971; Dec. 10, 1972; Dec. 9, 1973; Dec. 8, 1974. In the early 1970s the Falfurrias team was led by Bernave Martínez, Homero Martínez's brother, who won individual state titles in 1973 and 1974. The team returned in 1980, under the leadership of Roberto González, to win the championship team title.

26. Roberto González, interview by the author, tape recording, Falfurrias, Tex., Jan. 21, 2002.

27. Martínez interview.

28. Cantú interview.

29. Ricardo Gallegos Sr., interview by the author, tape recording, Crystal City, Tex., Jan. 31, 2002.

30. Martínez interview; Gallegos interview.

31. Homero Adame, interview by the author, tape recording, Laredo, Tex., Jan. 20, 2002.

32. Henry Romo, quoted in *San Antonio Express News*, June 24, 2001; Ricardo Romo interview, Dec. 29, 2001.

33. Henry Romo Sr., quoted in *San Antonio Express News*, Feb. 21, 2001; Martínez interview.

34. Martínez interview.

35. González interview; Martínez interview.

36. From 1954 to 1971, the Texas state championship was sponsored by the Texas Parks and Recreation Department and at one point included more than six different divisions based on school enrollment. In 1972 the UIL began to sponsor the state championships, albeit with only two divisions (Class A and Class B) based on school enrollment. In 1980 the UIL expanded the state championships into 3A, 4A, and 5A divisions and added 2A in 1984 and division 1A in 1988. See "University Interscholastic League 1988 State Championship Program," copy in author's possession.

37. For information on the 1970s, see the *El Paso Times*, Dec. 12, 1971; Nov. 12 and 19, 1972; Dec. 2 and 10, 1972; Nov. 2, 3, 4, 7, 10, and 11, 1973; Dec. 2, 5, 7, and 9, 1973; Nov. 15, 16, 17, 23, and 25, 1974; Dec. 7 and 8, 1974; Dec. 12, 1976; *Austin-American Statesman*, Dec. 13, 1970; Dec. 11, 1971; Dec. 10, 1972; Dec. 9, 1973; Dec. 7 and 8, 1974; Dec. 14, 1975; Dec. 11, 1977; Dec. 3, 1978; Dec. 2, 1979; Martínez interview.

38. See David Montejano, *Anglos and Mexicans in the Making of Texas, 1836-1986* (Austin: University of Texas Press, 1987), 288-307; Rodolfo Acuña, *Occupied America: A History of Chicanos* (New York: Harper and Row, 1988), 377.

39. Martínez interview; Ricardo Romo, interview by the author, tape recording, San Antonio, Nov. 13, 2001. Romo stated that, in twelve years of public education, he recalled having only one Hispanic teacher in his native San Antonio, despite the fact that the city's population remained predominantly Mexican American.

40. In 1980 the UIL switched from the mile to the 1,600-meter run, reducing the total distance by approximately 10 meters. For the records of the state champions, see the UIL's *Historical State Tournaments and Champions Records, 1909–2001* and the *Austin–American Statesman,* 1980–1989.

41. See the articles by Richard Luna, staff writer for the *El Paso Times,* Nov. 1, 7, 8, 13, 14, and 15, 1981; Oct. 30, 1983; Nov. 5, 6, 11, 12, and 13, 1983.

42. Randy Reina won the 1983 Southwest Conference 10,000-meter run; Roland won the 1985 Southwest Conference indoor two-mile run. Roland was also a two-time All-American, winning the honor in the 1984 and 1985 cross-country seasons. Roland Reina, interview by the author, Feb. 2, 2002; Randy Reina, interview by the author, tape recording, Helotes, Tex., Jan. 17, 2002; *San Antonio Express News,* June 26, 2001.

43. Roland Reina interview.

44. Randy Reina interview. Reina stated that he believes that "education is democracy."

45. Beginning in 1974, the University of Arkansas won twenty-six consecutive cross-country conference championships. See "University of Arkansas Cross-country Media Guide," 2001, copy in author's possession.

46. Roland Reina interview.

47. Reubén Reina was only the second tejano runner to run at the national championships. Mexican Americans from Texas who have run in the prestigious event include Tony Martínez (San Antonio), 1983; Reina; Alex Mendoza (Laredo), 1987; Michael Lara (El Paso), 1988; Ricky Gallegos (Crystal City), 1989 and 1990; and Andres Gómez (Bedford) and Joaquín Torres (Houston), 1992. See "Foot Locker National Championships" (media guide), copy in author's possession. The Foot Locker Cross-country Championships were formerly known as the Kinney Cross-country Championships until the name and sponsors were changed in 1993.

48. The term "triple double" has been used by various Texas sports writers as well as the coaching community. To gain a sense of Reina's accomplishments and their effect in later years, I discussed his performance with various present and former coaches in Texas, who all concur that Reubén Reina's state championships in the mid-eighties remain an impressive feat in Texas track history. Moreover, I submitted questionnaires to several South Texas high school cross-country teams, and a large majority of them recall hearing of Reubén Reina's state championships. For the opinion of present coaches, see my interviews with José Navarro (Laredo

and the same percentage of women chose softball as a recreational activity.[5] Still, little scholarship has focused on women's experiences in collegiate softball, especially those of Latinas.

V. L. Abell, a staff writer for the *NCAA News,* has suggested that the success of Olympic softball, coupled with the need to comply with Title IX, resulted in an explosive increase in the number of schools offering collegiate softball. For example, in 1984, 451 NCAA schools sponsored softball, and by 1998 that number had grown to 767. Opportunities for young women to get involved in softball have also expanded throughout the nation.[6]

Although this new era of increased opportunity for involvement in softball sounds promising, the sport is clearly not accessible to all young girls in all types of neighborhoods around the country. The ASA magazine has suggested that girls' fast-pitch tournaments are the most numerous and most profitable events for host cities.[7] Based on the numbers reported by the ASA, the estimated cost per person for a two-day tournament in 1998 was $250.00. Couple this prohibitive cost with the fact that, in Division I institutions in 1997, 80 percent of the student athletes in softball were recruited from ASA summer programs, and it becomes increasingly clear that collegiate softball is a structure of growing, yet disparate, opportunities.[8] In fact, despite the recent prominence of Olympic pitcher Lisa Fernández and professional slugger Crystal Bustos, collegiate softball remains pervasively white.

R. V. Acosta has examined the experiences of three Latinas who made their way first to athletics and later to careers in physical education. Her biographical studies reveal that, despite some shared family traditions, each woman received support in ways that were specific to the social location of their families. Acosta concludes that, while all women struggle to gain unconditional support for their sport involvement, Latinas may face additional challenges due to the absence of Latina role models, limited financial resources, and the ambivalent attitudes of family members toward higher education and sports.[9]

Related research reveals that high school athletics may have some holding power and offer significant educational benefits for Latinas in rural settings; however, this is not the case for those Latinas who live in urban settings.[10] Intercollegiate athletic participation rates reveal disproportionately lower numbers of Latinas in leadership roles and as student athletes, limited choices for sports participation, and differential chances of receiving athletic-related educational funds.[11]

Contrary to popular belief, Latina participation in sport is not a new phenomenon.[12] Some examples of Latina athleticism date back to the 1940s, when the All-American Girls Baseball League (AAGBL) began recruiting talented and experienced Cuban baseball players. Many Cuban women had been playing organized baseball in a league called Estrellas Cubanas (Cuban Stars), which was similar to the AAGBL. The first Cuban woman to play baseball in the AAGBL was Eulalia Gonzales, who played for the Racine Bells in 1947. Two years later, in 1949, Isabel Alvarez, Ysora del Castillo, Mirtha Marrero, and Migdalia Pérez joined the minor league ranks of the AAGBL.[13]

Additionally, the sport of professional tennis boasts a diverse field of Latina athletes. While not all U.S. natives, Gigi Fernández, Mary Jo Fernández, Aranxta Sánchez-Vicario, and Conchita Martínez have participated in multiple tennis events in North America. Moreover, in women's professional golf, Nancy López stands out among her peers, especially as the youngest inductee to the Ladies Professional Golf Association (LPGA) Hall of Fame. In the college ranks, Lisa Fernández, a softball pitcher for the University of California–Los Angeles, was named the top female collegiate athlete of the year in 1993 and pitched for the U.S. softball team, which won a gold medal in the 1996 Olympics. Most recently, a 1999 study by the U.S. Centers for Disease Control indicated that 44.5 percent of Hispanic female high school students played on a sports team, in comparison to 36.3 percent of black females and 50.5 percent of white females who did likewise.[14] Thus, a mixed bag of exclusionary practices and increasing representation makes it even more compelling for us to examine the experiences of Latinas who have made their way to elite levels of athletic competition.

THE STUDY

The following data and analyses are excerpts from interviews I conducted in the spring of 1998. The research design was a mixture of phenomenology (recording the unfolding of a particular event, moment, or experience) and case study (a thick description of the experiences of a single case or set of cases). Throughout the course of one month, 4 focus group interviews and 17 individual interviews were conducted for the purpose of better understanding how women make paths to collegiate softball. While the research focused on the ways these women navigated systems of inequality in their quest to make lives of their own, I paid specific attention to the influence of families, educational systems, and sport structures in shaping these paths.

Each of the 27 women interviewed was of Latin heritage. As a group, they were overwhelmingly of Mexican descent in their Latina ethnicity, but there were exceptions. Several of the women were of mixed racial or ethnic heritage, the most prevalent of which was a European and Latin mix (e.g., of Scottish and Puerto Rican parentage). Two of the women were of mixed African American and Mexican parentage, further complicating our understanding of Latina identities and experiences. As a group, they claimed varied sexualities and social class statuses. Additionally, 10 of the women were former collegiate athletes at the time of the interviews, while the other 17 were current in their collegiate athletic involvement. Some of the women participated in community college softball, while others took part in the more elite levels of NCAA Division I and II programs.

Not surprisingly, the majority (44 percent) of the women were at least third generation born in the United States; however, a good number were also first generation (37 percent). Generational status is significant in understanding access to resources, interaction with various social institutions, language, and general knowledge of U.S. culture and social structures. Thirty percent of these women began their collegiate careers at a community college, and 44 percent went directly from high school to Division I softball. A total of 59 percent eventually competed in Division I softball, showing successful transitions for some from lower levels of competition.

The most common Latino ethnicity among parents was Mexican (74 percent of mothers and 69 percent of fathers). Interestingly, 19 percent of fathers were white, while only one (4 percent of the total) mother was not of Latino heritage—important in terms of racial constructions, cultural values, and access to power in a white-dominated society. With regard to educational attainment, 55 percent of mothers had completed 12 or fewer years of formal education, 26 percent had completed either a 2- or 4-year degree, and 19 percent had completed more than 4 years of college. Among fathers, 52 percent had completed 12 or fewer years of formal education, 44 percent had completed either a 2- or 4-year degree, and only one father had completed more than 4 years of college. These rates of educational attainment are relevant to later discussions of educational dislocation among the women whom I interviewed.

The experiences of these women at the intersections of race, class, gender, and sexuality are especially instructive for understanding power relations in sport and society. Additionally, their experiences illustrate the significant cultural space that elite, organized sport occupies as a site for the production of current social arrangements.

SPORT, EDUCATION, AND FAMILIES: A PHENOMENOLOGICAL ANALYSIS

The analyses that follow represent only those interview excerpts that I deemed representative of the political tactics that Latinas utilize in order to navigate the cultural space of softball, families, and higher education. These selections are organized around three broad themes: legacies of educational exclusion, gendered family relations, and a remaking of their culture.

Much of the literature on Latinas in higher education suggests that entry into college is difficult for a number of reasons. In a study by Cardoza, the parents of the subjects made a distinction between aspirations for and expectations of their daughters' education. While parents may *aspire* to support their daughters' educational goals, they often do not *expect* to be able to follow through due to financial limitations. Likewise, Simoniello conducted interviews with eight Mexican women who were employed in various professions. All but one of them stated that, despite receiving genuine support and encouragement for educational achievement, they perceived that parental expectations changed after high school. Similarly, Yolanda, a former Division I student athlete, offered her insights into the mixed messages that many Latinas receive from their parents about college attendance. Her own experiences as an athlete and a Division I head softball coach have helped her to understand these incongruities: "It's almost like [parents] don't care if you go to college or not. There's two extremes. There's one that says 'All my hopes and dreams [fall on you] because we never went to college, now you have to do it for the family.' Then there's the other extreme that [says,] 'We never went [to college], so what? Get a job somewhere. Work at J. C. Penney's and be happy. You don't need college!' So there's no real middleman. Either 'You gotta do it for the family' or 'No one else did it. Why the hell should we spend all that money on you?' There's no importance. I've seen enough young ladies affected by that."[15]

Yolanda's words underscore the real tensions between what Cardoza refers to as aspirations and expectations.[16] The structural realities facing many Latino families make it difficult for parents to maintain their expectations for their kids to attend and graduate from college. Yet, the early messages these women received suggest that their success in school was important to their parents. Clearly, the value placed on education is a social condition that changes within families and across time, but it is the interaction of this condition with the agency of each woman that evolves into a life of one's own making.

For example, "Bugs" was able to convince her father to enroll her in the local youth softball league, but when she began playing more often and getting serious about elite softball, she realized that she had to regain the support of her family. When Bugs was considering her opportunities to go to college, she had to win over her father in particular: "When I decided I was gonna go to college . . . I showed [my dad] 'this is what tuition costs.' He was finally enlightened to the fact that higher education has a price tag. Because all of us kids went to school because it was free [K–12] . . . I really don't think he knew the meaning of tuition or what it was. So . . . I showed him what it cost to go to college and then showed him that it was being paid for, and on top of that I was gonna get financial aid because of my background. He went out and bought me a car!"

Once Bugs started playing collegiate softball, her family attended most, if not all, of her games. They were not opposed to higher education; they simply had neither experienced it nor seen how it might help improve their life in the United States: "My mother and father never made it to one of my high school games. And that wasn't because they didn't want to—they couldn't. My father had to work, and my mother had to take care of the family. When I was in college, I don't think they missed a game, and that includes postseason, when they were [in other towns and states]. And I can say the same about their parents [indicating J. J. and Kim, the other interview participants]. I don't think they ever missed a game."

While various structural inequalities interact with Latino families, they do not mandate a particular Latino response. Many of the women I spoke to told me that at some point they learned that their fathers did not really want them playing softball. Yet, for varied reasons these women were able to continue playing and in many cases recapture their fathers' encouragement. Micaela could not understand her father's disinterest in her desire to take advantage of an opportunity to earn an athletic scholarship for college. After accepting a scholarship at a prestigious Division I institution away from home, Micaela learned that her father's cool attitude was attributable to her older brothers' failed attempts to attend and graduate from college. She described his indifference in this way: "I'm the first one. [My brothers] quit halfway through, and my dad was working, like, days and nights to kind of help them through and pay for all their expenses, and they kind of dropped out, so my dad, after that, and those were the two oldest men, or boys, whatever you call it. So, after that there was, like, there was a gap of six of us or something."

Micaela continued:

> And my dad had really, you know, he really didn't care if we went to college, he kinda expected us not to go to college. He didn't want to push us, I guess, but he's also very negative about it, you know, because he had been hurt really bad by my two brothers. I had mentioned it to him before, like, before I became a senior that I wanted to go to college. And he had had a lot of problems, not discouraging me, but telling me I'd be just like my brothers or, you know. So, in a way it was hard to prove to him that "No, I'm not going to be like my brothers." And he actually— he would always tell me that he has no money to send me to college— he has no money to send me to college. And so . . . a week before I came to [school] to move in, [he told me]. . . . I mean, I hurt a lot, you know, I had a really hard time kind of accepting that when he actually told me.

The experiences of both Bugs and Micaela point again to the difference between their parents' aspirations and expectations. While both Bugs and Micaela found ways to move past what seemed like indifference to higher education, they also learned about their fathers' particular experiences—or lack thereof—with higher education. For Bugs, it was a matter of putting her educational aspirations into a framework that reflected her father's concern for the family's financial stability. Micaela came to realize that her older brothers' failure in college had forever jaded her father's perspective on the value of higher education. Thus, for both women, a seeming ambivalence about higher education turned out to be related to their fathers' concerns for economic stability rather than a distaste for education.

Not entirely unlike the experiences of Bugs and Micaela, Mickey had to get beyond the ambivalence about softball that her mother seemed to have.

Although her mother was gainfully employed, as a single parent of two daughters, she was often concerned about finances. Mickey had been playing elite softball for several years, despite the fact that her mother did not wholeheartedly approve of the time she had to devote to it. Mickey had worked part-time throughout her high school years to pay for extracurricular activities such as cheerleading and softball. When it came time for Mickey to go to college, her mother felt that work and education were enough to focus on and that softball was an unnecessary and time-consuming (however enjoyable) activity.

This disregard for the sport changed, however, when Mickey took her mom on a recruiting visit to a four-year university and a Division II softball program that she wanted to transfer to from her community college: "It was really funny 'cause, [during] my first year at [community] college, it was a battle, and then, like, once she came down to the recruiting trip with me and stuff, she goes 'You know, you don't have to work next year.' I've always had a job. I've had a job for the last six years, and last year was the first year I didn't have a job. Like a part-time job—it's not like I had a full-time job. She goes, 'You don't have to work. I have money.' Now that my tuition's paid for, my books are paid for, and I get a little extra, she goes, 'You don't have to work now!' And she was really cute about it. So, now I mean she loves it that I play. She knows that it makes me happy."

Despite her strong feelings about the futility of softball, Mickey's mother never stopped her daughter from competing. While this is certainly not a ringing endorsement for involvement in sports, it was an open door. Moreover, in the same way that her divorce effected a significant change in the family structure, so too did the increased availability of scholarship funds and financial aid resources bring about a major change. These alterations interacted with and shaped Mickey's mother's beliefs about the importance of collegiate athletic involvement.

These examples illustrate the fact that Latinas may often have to deal with a complex blend of social conditions within families in order to gain both emotional support and financial resources to attend college. The experiences of each of these women underscore the reality that many social factors come together to shape family systems. The fact that these women continued on their path to collegiate softball reveals their individual agency in shaping their lives. They are at once both products and agents of change within particular family environments. Thus, seeing the meaning behind the outward ambivalence was an enabling condition for them. They developed skill in navigating multiple cultural settings, and this same ability helped guide the majority of the women I interviewed.

In *Gendered Transitions,* Pierrette Hondagneu-Sotelo presents an analysis of the gendered experiences of immigration among Mexican women whom she came to know in Northern California. In my own work, although my informants are not immigrants in the traditional sense of the word, they are moving back and forth across cultural borders in their experiences of collegiate softball and gendered institutions. Most significantly, the mothers and daughters are weaving the new with the old in a transition toward a reconstituted, increasingly fluid *mujer* (woman).[17]

In an eloquent essay called "A Letter to My Mother," Claudia Colindres reveals the depth of what is likely a common bond among women in families. Throughout the essay Colindres describes her experience in a predominantly white college as masculinizing and isolating. Her rich description depicts the intersection of race, class, and gender through her obvious struggle with being a woman and una mujer in an extended family that historically denied an education to her own mother: "It was in my senior year of high school that I saw your true colors. You were my ally, and you stood by me, when Father tried to do to me what your father did to you, he was trying to keep me home, because I am a woman, *una mujer.* It was great to see you talk to him, scream to him that I had a right to pursue an education. It was invigorating! You were strong and powerful. You urged me to go away and continue my education even when you knew that I am a woman and therefore in your eyes also *mujer.*"[18] Glenn underscores the fact that Latina mothers, like all mothers, are not simply oppressed within their own families, but they also "act to assert their own standards of mothering and to attain the resources necessary to sustain their children's lives."[19]

According to the women with whom I spoke, the work of their mothers went beyond the traditional gendered roles of mothers in families. Nearly all of the interviewees suggested that their mothers had provided strong messages about educational and professional progress as a means to individual, familial, and community enrichment. Concern for individuals and communities is not uncommon among women of color. As Collins argues, "For women of color, the subjective experience of mothering/motherhood is inextricably linked to the sociocultural concern of racial-ethnic communities—one does not exist without the other."[20]

For example, Micaela described a very distinct message that she received from her mother about her role as a member of larger community: "A lot of it stems from my mom. She's the one that said, 'Do for the rest of us.' You know? And 'the rest of us' didn't mean, like, my family, it was just, like, the other women in my whole family. . . . And so when I was growing up, my mom would kind of encourage all of us to look ahead, and look ahead, 'Don't quit here,' and stuff. And 'Do it for the rest of us who didn't have this opportunity to go on.'" Micaela thus relates that women of color often teach their children to value not only individual but also collective achievement.

Moreover, her example refutes conventional claims that Latinas do not socialize their daughters to achieve in dominant social institutions, thus placing them in a conflicting position between family values and personal goals for education and professional development. Collins argues that "conflict actually lies outside of the households as women and their families engage in collective enterprise to create and maintain family life in the face of forces that undermine family integrity."[21] Micaela's example suggests that she is at once entrusted with representing Latinas who went before her, yet her status as a college student and athlete separates her from her community of origin. By virtue of doing what others were denied, she is distinct from the very women who have propelled her toward higher education and athletics.

Nicole talked about receiving support from both of her parents and, in particular, receiving meaningful messages from her mother about making choices in her life: "Oh, my parents, they pushed me. They wanted the best for me and my sister. They were always giving me little talks, how important it was for me to go to college, and when I got out of college to get a good job, and stuff like that. My mom was, 'I don't want you to be in the place where I was, you know, a housewife. I want you to have something better for yourself, not for you to depend on [someone else].' She was right."

Nicole reflected on her mother's message about independence and personal progress not only with regard to individual achievement but also as part of her duty to her sister. Nicole and her twin sister were both going to be in college at the same time; thus, Nicole's academic and athletic achievements were not only about her but also about increasing the family's ability to support two daughters in higher education. To make the situation even more complex, Nicole was aware that she possessed the requisite skills to earn a scholarship and to succeed in college, so she took her own role and her mother's message seriously. Nicole and others point to the fact that mothers and their children come to understand each other's position and rely on each other's strengths to become empowered.[22]

Although Karin's father went to college and was an athlete at a Division I institution, he still had difficulty letting go of the oldest of his three daughters as she made decisions about her own collegiate career. Karin, now a fifth-year senior at a Division I institution, reflected on her interactions with her parents regarding these major determinations: "He didn't really want me to go 'cause he didn't want me to be that far away. Still, to this day he wants me to get my credentials at [California] State because that's so close to home. But my mom told him, 'You've gotta let her do what she wants to do. If she wants to live down there, let her do it because, if you make her come back here, she will resent you if she doesn't like it.' And I feel moms see that easier than the dads do."

Karin's remarks reflect the reality of women's experiences as oppressed people in various social institutions. At the same time, her mother's firm belief in enhancing Karin's choices with regard to higher education illustrates the power of women to affect each other's circumstances. Karin's mother may have felt constrained by her own parents as a young woman, and now she has a chance to renegotiate the patterns of interaction in her own family. Whatever her reasons, she exemplifies what Collins refers to as "collective enterprise" among women and their children.[23]

In a similar vein, Lucy shared the following about the social significance of her participation in collegiate softball, especially since it is in stark contrast to her mother's opportunities for postsecondary education: "I think it's a big step. It kind of can break the stereotypes that there's not a lot of Latinas out there doing much or that they're home, you know, working or whatever, helping the family. You know, stuck at home. That's, I think it breaks that 'cause my mom went through that. I mean, her dad wouldn't let her go, and she had a scholarship to go to San Diego State. He didn't want her to [go] 'cause it was too far. She had to drive every day to UC–Santa Cruz because he didn't want her to live in the dorms."

Support for involvement in softball was perhaps an avenue by which mothers could encourage their daughters to create their own independent lives. Nicole's mother persuaded her to go on to college, make her own way, and not become dependent, presumably on a man. For each of these women, their experiences in softball may have provided their mothers with a glimpse into the lives they might have chosen for themselves, had they been given the opportunity.

The third broad theme of this analysis is the remaking of culture. The women I interviewed for this research were becoming aware of the risks of entering a pervasively white, middle-class context of education and sport. For example, in his study of Native American college scholarship athletes, Simpson found that various structural and cultural conditions contributed to typically abbreviated collegiate careers. Billy Mills, an Olympic gold medallist and member of the Pine Ridge Reservation, shared the following with Simpson about venturing away from his home: "There's no way to return to the old way, spiritually and economically. . . . If you go too far into society, there's a fear of losing your Indian-ness. There's a spiritual factor that comes into play. To become part of white society you give up half your soul."[24]

The experiences of these women represent a larger understanding that many Latinas share. They yearn to excel, but at the same time they want to preserve their Latina identity while immersed in a middle-class environment of higher education. These struggles between subjectivities make middle-class notions of upward mobility inapplicable to the experience of women of color. The concept of upward mobility or racial uplift implies an escape from one's culture and community of origin. Investigating Latino families reveals the ways that families link individuals to their cultures of origin and simultaneously act as support systems for accessing previously unattainable social spaces.

Latinas who venture into higher education and collegiate athletics must cope with the complexity of what Zavella refers to as "culture in process." The concept of culture in process articulates the "dialectics of how the social structure and culture provide a context for the ways that Chicanas construct their identities." Zavella focuses on diversity among Chicanas, but I contend that her scholarship applies to diversity among Latinas of varied ethnicities, generational statuses, regions of settlement, social classes, and sexualities. The seeming incongruity of moving on and yet remaining an active member of one's family is not only about physical presence but also about political and social connections, as Alma explained: "After I went to school, it was 'Oh, here comes the educated one.' I think [that,] when my mom used to say it, it was because I had come out of the traditional Latina thinking and I had broadened my horizons. And that was very difficult because her thinking was just her mother's thinking, and for me to have my own mind compared to the family mind was very hard for her to accept . . . but it was funny, too. When I went to school, my pride in my family and being Puerto Rican was only enhanced, and it made me more political. And the political side was something she was proud of."[25]

Miranda talked about how playing softball on teams that were predominantly white led to a departure from the culture with which she had grown up. "I think my separation [from family culture] began before college. I think it really began when I started playing softball because I didn't really hang around Latinos. I hung around mostly white people. So, I kind of basically did my own thing. I mean, when I went home, it was different, but we really didn't talk about it."

At the time of our small-group interview Yolanda had recently lost her grandfather. Thinking about what she stood to lose because of his death, she talked about how her Mexican identity is closely tied to who her grandparents are and about how this somehow relates to her more Americanized life today: "Both my grandparents, both sets don't speak a word of English. So when I walk in there I am forced—I am asked to speak Spanish. I love speaking Spanish. I speak Spanglish. I understand everything. But it's a presence—I don't have to go outside and have somebody ask me 'Are you Mexican?' or whatever. My family knows. I walk in [to my grandparents' home]—it's the neatest smell. It's the neatest atmosphere in the world. And now he's gone. And I go into my house, and my house is very Americanized, which is fine. I still speak Spanish with my parents, but it's not the same without my grandparents, and that bothers me."

Alma explained how going to college led to a dichotomy between her own beliefs and those of her family: "My opinion was very different from my family's, especially my mother's. She was very traditional, grew up in the fifties, 'Latina, be quiet, don't say nothing, just be happy that you're in America.' And for me to have my goals in a career, it was just like night and day. To this day we are not allowed to speak politics in the house. We are not allowed to speak religion because, when I went to school—I mean growing up Latina, religion is like your lifeline—every Sunday, you're there. And when I started questioning my religion when I went to college, that was a big separation, too."

Julie illuminated the process of creating culture and moving among various cultural contexts. For her, the experience of being "Hispanic enough" changed over time, and her interactions with neighborhood peers reflected their changing lives. Her education at an elite, predominantly white university was a significant influence on her interactions with folks in her home community. Julie's comments underscore the constant work of maintaining ties to one's family, neighborhood, and culture despite the social consequences that often accompany any embrace of values that fall outside of white middle-class standards. Moreover, Julie's comments illustrate the fact that culture is lost and remade all of the time.[26] As a U.S.-born Latina, elite softball athlete, graduate student, and educator, Julie sees that her values and way of life are continuing to change and are diverging more and more from those of her parents and perhaps many of her peers in the old neighborhood:

> When I was in school, I felt like my Hispanic friends were always trying to be white. I always felt like, because I came from a very traditional Mexican family . . . they kind of would look at me . . . [and] then kind of . . . [think] that 'Oh, you're Mexican' or whatever. But now those people—now that I've been mainstreamed through a primarily white institution—you know at school and everything, I do feel sometimes that I've left my roots. I really do. I feel like I've lost part of my culture. Now those people who used to kind of act white and make fun of me because of my ethnicity are—in fact, they just teased me the other day because I didn't know something in Spanish. They were, like, 'What are you? Mexican or white?' I do wish I knew more about my culture, and I wish, I really wish I could speak Spanish. I don't even know how to speak Spanish.

Clearly, Julie is situated "inside in an outside way."[27] Despite her entrance into the predominantly white, middle-class world of collegiate softball, she is still a marginal member. Likewise, her changing sense of herself as a middle-class Mexican woman, especially one who does not speak a distinguishing language, situates her outside the margins of her home community. She is constantly having to display credentials in both the white, middle-class context of elite softball and the working-class, Mexican-identified community in which she grew up.

Sometimes the push-and-pull of foundation and mobility was centered on friends who were not necessarily leaving the neighborhood but moving toward different extracurricular activities. For example, Josie spoke about the experience of moving between particularly situated groups of friends and teammates. Her experiences also cut across race and class as she maintained ties to her home community as well as her athletic teams:

> See, my friends were all cheerleaders. I was the only athlete in high school. They used to say, "You know, [Josie], you can't play softball forever." And they never understood 'cause I'm a—you see, nobody really gets scholarships where I live. They'd be like, "[Josie], what are you gonna do with it?" And I'd just be like, "I know what I'm doing. I know what I'm doing." They used to be like, "[Josie], why don't you do other things? Why don't you get a job after school? Why don't you do that?" I'm like, "because if I get money here, it's just, like, [the] fifteen hundred dollars that I'm getting is like having a part-time job and helping me pay for school." I think it was just—I didn't really have a problem fitting in, but I was just really different from my friends. I couldn't relate to them [pause] in a lot of [respects]. I always felt closer to my friends on the weekends than I did to the girls that I grew up with the entire time and went to all the basketball games with and all the dances with. That was hard.

Josie's comments illustrate yet again the work that many women do to bridge friendship groups, but this is especially important work among women of color since they are often singled out as racial and ethnic minorities in sport settings.

Lucy talked about how much she enjoyed high school but also about how softball separated her from her friends as they became less and less interested in school:

> I liked high school. It was fun. A lot of my, um—It kind of got weird after a while 'cause after, like, my sophomore year, a lot of my friends who were Latina were [pensive pause] in trouble. You know, they stopped going to class. They just didn't want to, and I was like the straight-and-narrow one. You know, always telling them, "Come on, let's go. We gotta go to class." And they just, you know, they decided to do different. And so they would go on to, like, the secondary high school or the continuation high school. . . . It was kind of weird, but, um, there was still a big core of friends that we used to hang out with. Most of 'em were the

guys, but they were just always there for me, you know? And I had a friend. You know, I had plenty of friends, but those that I had grown up with, you know, middle school, were, you know, gone.

The experiences of these women as members of multiple communities illustrate the difficulty of valuing their home communities while venturing out into new ones. Anzaldúa talks about the varied situations in which Latinas find themselves while crossing these borders in their lives.[28] Pesquera and de la Torre have also discussed the struggles of working-class Chicanas in higher education who wish to retain their Chicana working-class identities while continuing to progress in the largely white middle-class world of academia.[29] Similar struggles exist for Latinas who choose to compete in collegiate athletics, which are both white and middle class. In fact, many of the women I interviewed were constantly shifting between differing cultures, structures, and identities. This fluidity of identities, the valuing of multiple cultures, and the ability to cross borders both enabled and constrained them as they made their ways to collegiate softball. For example, messages from their mothers seemed to fortify them in their quest for various types of achievement through softball. Yet entry into the elite, pervasively white middle-class context of softball also distanced these women from the very communities that lifted them up to begin with.

CONCLUSIONS

Despite my attempt to present a neat and tidy analysis of the sport experiences of a select group of Latinas, these interview excerpts actually illustrate the incredible complexity of venturing into collegiate softball. The women whom I interviewed clearly articulate the types of strategies that have aided them in navigating these varied cultural spaces. While they may take comfort in their families, they also experience discomfort in moving away from the "family mindset." Additionally, they had to convince the same fathers who supported their early sport involvement to continue to back them when softball threatened to take their daughters away from home. This is, of course, as symbolically meaningful as it is geographically real. Ironically, it is the mothers who have gone to bat for their daughters and ensured for them an opportunity to experience independence and create a life of their own design. Several of the interviewees talked about how their mothers or older sisters convinced their fathers to let them play sports and move away to attend college. This is significant power in families that may eventually emerge out of a gendered legacy of exclusion. These mothers were not going to let their daughters miss an opportunity to experience the world beyond their familia and their local community.

Not surprisingly, it was also the mothers who were the most influential in keeping these women tied to la familia and the local community. However, it was clearly the work of each individual woman to navigate the constantly shifting space between maintaining and remaking their culture of origin. That is, these women were continually enacting new subjectivities and refusing categorization. They were neither passive child members of families nor reticent "scholarship girls" in their collegiate settings—they were active agents in their own life events.[30] What is most instructive in this analysis is the focus on the intermingling of the cultural spaces of family, education, and sport. For Latinas, the legacy of exclusion, coupled with the legacy of determination, produces an almost inherently political experience of collegiate sport. Additionally, though mostly the product of a white, middle-class imagination, the image of the passive, fatalistic Latina is annihilated when the diversity of their responses to varied social conditions is affirmed. Participation in collegiate softball is not the answer to social problems that most affect Latinas today, but it is one of many ways in which they may challenge and modify deficient generalizations.

NOTES

1. L. Emery, "From Lowell Mills to the Halls of Fame: Industrial League Sport for Women," in *Women and Sport: Interdisciplinary Perspectives,* edited by D. M. Costa and S. R. Guthrie (Champaign, Ill.: Human Kinetics, 1994), 107–21.

2. C. A. Oglesby, ed., *Encyclopedia of Women and Sport* (Phoenix: Oryx Press, 1998), 256–57; Emery, "From Lowell Mills to the Halls of Fame," 116–17.

3. P. Dickson, *The Worth Book of Softball: A Celebration of America's True Pastime* (New York: Facts on File, 1994).

4. Title IX is a federal law that was passed in 1972 prohibiting sex-based discrimination in any educational institution that receives federal funds. Athletics has been the cultural space in which the law has been the most widely tested.

5. U.S. Bureau of the Census, *Statistical Abstract of the United States: 2000* (Washington, D.C.: U.S. Department of Commerce, 2000).

6. V. L. Abell, "Opportunity Knocking: Women's Softball Experiencing a Growth Spurt—Both in the United States and around the World," NCAA News: News and Features (Mar. 1998), http://www.ncaa.org/wps/portal.

7. B. McCall, "The Economics of ASA Softball," *Balls and Strikes Softball* (1999), 32–33.

8. Abell, "Opportunity Knocking."

9. R. V. Acosta, "Hispanic Women in Sport," *Journal of Health, Physical Education, Recreation, and Dance* 70(4) (1999): 44–46.

10. Women's Sports Foundation, "Minorities in Sport: The Effect of Varsity Sports Participation on the Social, Educational, and Career Mobility of Minority Students" (Aug. 1989) (East Meadow, N.Y.: Author).

11. R. V. Acosta and L. J. Carpenter, "A Longitudinal Analysis of Women in Leadership Positions in Sport," unpublished manuscript (1988); National Collegiate Athletic Association, "1997 Division I Graduation Rates Summary," document no. 11889 (Overland Park, Kans.: June 1997); J. J. Coakley and P. L. Pacey, "The Distribution of Athletic Scholarships among Women in Intercollegiate Sport," in *Sport and the Sociological Imagination: Refereed Proceedings of the Third Annual Conference of the North American Society for the Sociology of Sport, Toronto, Ontario, Canada, November 1982*, edited by N. Theberge and P. Donnelly (Fort Worth: Texas Christian University Press, 1984), 228–41.

12. K. M. Jamieson and M. Baca Zinn, "Latinas in Sport," in *Encyclopedia of Women and Sport*, 180–82.

13. B. Gregorich, *Women at Play: The Story of Women in Baseball* (San Diego: Harcourt Brace, 1993).

14. U.S. Bureau of the Census, *Statistical Abstract of the United States: 2000*.

15. D. Cardoza, "College Attendance and Persistence among Hispanic Women: An Examination of Some Contributing Factors," *Sex Roles* 24(3) (1991): 133–47; S. Nieves-Squires, *Hispanic Women in Higher Education: Making Their Presence on Campus Less Tenuous* (Washington, D.C.: Association of American Colleges, 1991); F. I. Ortiz, "Hispanic American Women in Higher Education: A Consideration of the Socialization Process," *Aztlán* 17(2) (1988): 125–52; K. Simoniello, "On Investigating the Attitudes toward Achievement and Success in Eight Professional U.S. Mexican Women," *Aztlán* 12(1) (1981): 121–37.

16. Cardoza, "College Attendance and Persistence among Hispanic Women."

17. Pierrette Hondagneu-Sotelo, *Gendered Transitions* (Berkeley: University of California Press, 1994).

18. C. Colindres, "A Letter to My Mother," in *The Sexuality of Latinas*, edited by N. Alarcón, A. Castillo, and C. Moraga (Berkeley: Third Woman Press, 1993), 73–79.

19. E. N. Glenn, "Social Constructions of Mothering: A Thematic Overview," in

Mothering: Ideology, Experience, and Agency, edited by E. N. Glenn, G. Chang, and L. R. Forcey (New York: Routledge, 1994), 1-29.

20. P. H. Collins, "Shifting the Center: Race, Class, and Feminist Theorizing about Motherhood," in *Mothering,* 45-65.

21. Ibid.

22. Ibid.

23. Ibid.

24. K. Simpson, "Sporting Dreams Die on the 'Rez,'" in *Sport in Contemporary Society: An Anthology,* 5th ed., edited by D. S. Eitzen (New York: St. Martin's, 1996), 287-94.

25. P. Zavella, "Reflections on Diversity among Chicanas," in *Race,* edited by S. Gregory and R. Sanjek (New Brunswick, N.J.: Rutgers University Press, 1994), 199-212.

26. Ibid.

27. G. H. Cuadraz, "Experiences of Multiple Marginality: A Case Study of Chicana 'Scholarship Women.'" *Association of Mexican American Educators* (1992): 31-43.

28. G. Anzaldúa, *Borderlands/La Frontera: The New Mestiza* (San Francisco: Spinsters/Aunt Lute, 1987).

29. B. M. Pesquera and A. de la Torre, *Building with Our Hands: New Directions in Chicana Studies* (Berkeley: University of California Press, 1993).

30. Cuadraz, "Experiences of Multiple Marginality."

INVISIBLE IDENTITY
Mexican American Sport and Chicano Historiography
SAMUEL O. REGALADO

Chicano historiography has made great strides in recent years. Now considered a vital part of the U.S. historical collage, "the least known, the least sponsored, and the least vocal large minority group in the nation" labels, as educator George I. Sánchez described the contingent in 1950, no longer apply to Mexican Americans.[1] By 2000 the Mexican enclave had seen not only an extensive leap in overall population figures but also increased political clout. Today, for instance, Mexican Americans hold many of California's most distinctive posts in the legislative arena. This, of course, represents a far cry from the late 1940s, when Edward Roybal stood as the lone candidate of Mexican heritage to win a seat on the Los Angeles City Council—and any other office in that state. Much the same occurred, too, at the national level as the number of Mexican Americans in federal positions grew. Similar advancements in the media also occurred. In the 1970s the introduction of cable television and advancements in computer technology added to the increase of a Hispanic presence in the mainstream. But other factors predated this newfound visibility.

To be sure, the movements of the 1960s, along with the emergence of César Chávez, whose crusade for migrant workers won him international recognition, inspired Chicano scholars to—for the first time—critically

233

analyze the Mexican American past. Until the early 1970s, only Carey McWilliams, an attorney and liberal activist during the late 1940s and 1950s who authored the pioneering *North from Mexico,* offered any serious history of Mexicans in the United States. In 1972, however, two academically published narratives made their appearance: Matt S. Meier and Feliciano Rivera's *The Chicanos: A History of Mexican Americans* and Rodolfo Acuña's *Occupied America: The Chicano's Struggle toward Liberation.*[2] The former presented a general overview of Mexicans in the United States, while the latter took a more Marxist perspective from a New Left school of thought.

In the 1980s, the Mexican past in the United States became less invisible. Scholars such as Arnoldo De León, Mario T. García, Albert Camarillo, and Richard Griswold del Castillo scrutinized Mexican American history through a stronger lens. Soon topics such as the Chicano family, immigration, nationalism, and, of course, the impact of social activism became key components in the reconstruction of the past.[3] Still others, like David Weber, Vickie Ruiz, David Gutiérrez, and Ramón Gutiérrez, took on borderland issues, gender dynamics, internal community divisions, Native Americans, and the impact of race.[4] Yet, as scholarship on Mexican Americans expanded with an abundance of attention focused on social activism, a glaring omission remained: the impact of sport.

Professional, semiprofessional, and amateur athletes, recreational leagues, and local media coverage of sports competition often did more to galvanize Mexican American communities and undermine preconceived negative stereotypes than any other activity beyond the scope of this athletic arena. Sport fueled notoriety and bridged important gaps between people of Mexican heritage and the U.S. mainstream. Of equal importance, however, sport also played an instrumental role in shaping the identities of people living in rural colonias and urban barrios. And yet, despite these effects, Chicano scholars turned a blind eye to this topic. For example, although he spent considerable time describing the activities of the Chicano residents of Los Angeles, George J. Sánchez wrote not a word about any athletic events or personalities in his 1993 award-winning book, *Becoming Mexican American: Ethnicity, Culture, and Identity in Chicano Los Angeles, 1900–1945.*[5]

Interestingly, even a scant overview of Southern California's leading Spanish-language newspaper, *La Opinión,* reveals that, during the period of Sánchez's history, ethnic Mexicans there paid considerable attention to events in the boxing arenas and on the baseball diamonds. Six years later,

Manuel G. Gonzales, too, in his *Mexicanos: A History of Mexicans in the United States,* included in his bibliography not a single article dealing with any relationship between sports and the Mexican American community.[6] That same year, Zaragosa Vargas, who edited an anthology titled *Major Problems in Mexican American History: Documents and Essays,* included more than one hundred entries on every conceivable topic—except sport.[7]

These oversights thus begged important questions: Did people of Mexican descent have no viable relationship to sport? Were athletics of no value to Mexicans living in any rural or urban community? Did they identify only with those from the exclusive circles of union leaders, social and political activists, and pedagogical crusaders? The historical record, it turns out, reveals otherwise. The fact of the matter is this: Throughout their history as a people, Mexican Americans have proudly displayed their contributions and achievements in sport. Their love of and involvement in athletic competition has been universal. From the larger urban barrios to the rural agrarian regions and from vocal social activists to migrants working quietly in the grape fields, sport was of paramount importance. Boxing, baseball, football players, and institutions (and even distance runners) took center stage in several communities that sought a larger and more defined presence in the U.S. mainstream. Sport was not simply a factor in the identity of those who labeled themselves Mexican Americans along with groups who trumpeted "Chicanismo"; it was an *essential* aspect in the construction of that identity. And for intuitive scholars, it has provided a window through which to clearly view the evolving dynamics of Mexican America. Contrary to the generally accepted studies of the Mexican American past, therefore, sport was anything but invisible.

The story of the Tarahumaran foot runners, who belonged to a tribe in Mexico's Sierra Madre range, marks an early bridge between sport, identity, and visibility. Having captivated the borderlands and many of the world's track aficionados in the 1920s with their remarkable endurance, the Tarahumaras became, arguably, the highest-profile Mexicans of their day. But, as historian Mark Dyreson points out, the seeming positive promotion was one of duplicity. "Commentators in the United States," said Dyreson, "alternately lauded the Tarahumara for their pristine lifestyle and satirized them for their uncivilized customs." Not surprisingly, demeaning misconceptions of Mexicans in that same era were reinforced in many circles of U.S. society. In the burgeoning movie industry, for instance, Hollywood launched a series of "greaser" films, which portrayed Mexicans as a primitive, unsophisticated society.[8] That ethnic Mexicans could succeed in anything, let alone the field of play, many believed, was not so much attributable to their prowess as strategists but, in the case of the Tarahumaras, to their "extreme primitivism." Still, their athletic achievement was undeniable and, given the media attention they received, surely carried weight in Mexican America. In an era in which most preconceived notions of Mexicans were condescending at best, the Tarahumaras' success, however small in mainstream circles, ironically loomed large as the Mexican community in Texas sought to create bonds in their quest to establish a distinct identity.

Still, the impact of sport on ethnic groups in the United States is not news. Nineteenth-century newcomers to the country, for instance, quickly identified the value of athletics as a means to assimilate into their new environs. "Sports," argues historian Benjamin Rader, "could both ease the transition of ethnic groups into a new society and aid them in protecting their identity."[9] Moreover, as Michael T. Isenberg states, "In the sporting arena the outsider could be brought inside, even if only for a little while."[10] This was not unimportant to Irish immigrants of that era, for instance, most of whom idolized boxer John L. Sullivan. They saw in Sullivan not only the epitome of athletic success but also an achiever whose appeal to a national audience did not come at the expense of his Irish identity.

These principles easily fit the early career of Rodolfo "Corky" Gonzales. Gonzales, a principal player in the movimiento of the 1960s, initially became recognized because of his success in the boxing ring in the late 1940s. Apart from his better-known contentious image, which came later (in the 1950s), the Denver press presented a clean-cut image of Gonzales. Victorious in the ring, easy to interview, and entrepreneurial in opening his own restaurant business, Gonzales was the picture of Anglo-American virtues. In certain respects, the assimilated boxer's Mexican roots, to many mainstream Denver whites, were simply incidental.

But as he gravitated in the direction of social activism, Denver journalists deconstructed their earlier portraits of Corky Gonzales and repainted one of a confrontational dissident. No longer the cover boy of the Denver mainstream press, Gonzales—and his agenda—had, by the mid-1960s, become "too ethnic" and thus unacceptable to the earlier proponents of assimilation. With Gonzales no longer a pillar of the Denver sporting scene, Americans elsewhere came to know him as the poet who penned the movimiento anthem "I Am Joaquín," the founder of the Crusade for Justice, and the lead organizer for the 1969 Denver Youth Conference. However, as writer Tom Romero states, Gonzales's story as a "multifaceted" symbol of America, one in which the elements of assimilation and identity clashed, came as result of his notoriety in the ring. His success and visibility as a sports figure became the building blocks for proponents of assimilation and accommodation, but they also made him a lightning rod of controversy as he channeled his fame to advance his Chicano identity.

Gregory Rodríguez's interpretation of the topic of identity exhibits an interesting point of view. Arguing that "hybrid unities" were formed through boxing, he suggests that this sense of being Mexican was a continuum of "fashioned identities" relevant to the "evolving realities" of the larger world. A Mexican identity thus had no borders and, in some cases, was culturally, not ethnically, driven. In the Los Angeles Mexican subculture of boxing, ethnic identity was a badge of honor one might attain through achievement in the ring. For that reason, Mexican American and Mexican boxing aficionados in the 1960s bestowed the label of "honorary Mexican" on several fighters of other ethnic groups with whom a relationship had developed both in and out of the ring.

Class, too, was a major factor in the development of these hybrid communities, and allegiances often crossed cultural lines. Not surprisingly, ethnic Mexicans adopted black, Cuban, and Greek boxers into their circles. Non-Mexican athletes, to be sure, did not abandon their cultures, but the socioeconomic circumstances that juxtaposed similar elements found in the Mexican enclaves helped to forge relationships that came together in the boxing arena.

Rodríguez's analysis successfully expands the parameters of the Mexican American identity. Boxing, in this case, was the magnet that drew non-Mexican people into the ethnic Mexican enclave and became the centerpiece of their identity. That is, their commonalities outweighed their physical characteristics. Mexicans in the boxing subculture could relate far more to boxers of a similar class than to other ethnic Mexicans whose societal and/or activist positions were far removed from their own.

Interestingly, Rodríguez's "evolving realities" hypothesis has a connection to the principles discussed in Katherine M. Jamieson's analysis of Latinas and their families in relation to collegiate softball. For Jamieson's case studies, the transition from home to college life as a result of athletics marked a period in which they experienced a "culture in process." Already having challenged the status quo within the social context of the Mexican family unit by playing competitive softball, Latina women, once in college, forged a new kind of hybrid identity in which the role of family culture was recognized to a lesser degree. Moreover, in contrast to previous generations, culture—to the Latina college woman of the 1990s—was in constant flux. "This fluidity of identities, the valuing of multiple cultures, and the ability to cross borders both enabled and constrained [these women] as they made their ways to collegiate softball," argues Jamieson. Culture and identity were not lost. They had simply evolved.

Baseball, too, was part of the pulse of the Chicano world and was highly visible in the land of Aztlán. Both at the professional and amateur levels, Mexican Americans identified with a sport that, as in the United States, had a long and distinguished history in Mexico. At the beginning of the twentieth century, Mexican baseball at the professional level was such that major league teams routinely visited that nation for exhibition contests. By the late 1940s the Mexican baseball hierarchy, led by Jorge Pasqual, even briefly challenged U.S. big leagues for baseball supremacy in North America. But the game was of equal value to campesinos in the country's hinterlands. Small pueblos took great pride in the fortunes of their ball teams. Indeed, it was from these impoverished ranks that Fernando Valenzuela rose to become, in the early 1980s, a transnational hero. The game's transnational components and impact on community bonding found replication inside the barrios and colonias of the north.

Baseball, for instance, had a comfortable and important home in Mexican agricultural communities that found themselves far north of the borderland regions. "People socialized and discussed community issues at the games and strengthened their sense of racial and ethnic solidarity," claims historian Richard Santillán.[11] The local baseball diamond on a Sunday afternoon was not unlike the Jewish kitchen, which, author Irving Howe states, "was the one place where immigrants might recall to themselves that they were not mere creatures of toil and circumstances, but also human beings defined by their sociability."[12]

As in other ethnic communities, sports clubs and recreational centers were the epicenters of activity. In the East Los Angeles barrio, for instance, during the 1950s and 1960s the Los Angeles Forty-sixty (baseball) Club was "an organization designed to contribute to community affairs; one that promoted fellowship, good will and brotherhood along the lines of other traditional American organizations such as the Elks Club, YMCA, and others."[13]

Baseball was a communal activity. Migrant workers, industrial proletariats, Catholic churches, and young women all played the game. Players and coaches constructed their own fields, and many of their spouses "made the bases by sewing anew work-out pillows."[14] The baseball clubs also provided a support system for newcomers. To a degree, these organizations took on the role of the late nineteenth-century *mutualistas* (mutual benefit societies). Whereas cultural identity ranked as the sole criterion for mutual aid support, by the twentieth century those factors—along with a love for the game—eased one's transition into a new region.

Baseball was a vital part of the Mexican American routine of life, and success in the game was a badge of honor that both strengthened community cohesion and reinforced a sense of cultural identity in a transnational context. Baseball in Mexican Los Angeles during the 1920s and 1930s, Douglas Monroy has observed, "was one way the various people from south of the border forged an identity as Mexicans, a way for Mexicans to garner respect in the eyes of the americanos, and a public reinforcement of the traditional manly family values of forceful, dynamic activities."[15]

The game had other implications as well. During the Great Depression, for instance, Mexican American ballplayers in Corona, California, participated in the sport to satisfy their athletic appetites. The games also drew a handful of players who channeled and networked their ideas regarding union activity in the area's labor force. Moreover, as José Alamillo points out, through many of their sports clubs, citrus growers, reformers, and laborers all used the game to advance their social, labor, and political agendas. The Corona Athletics Baseball Club, in particular, recruited support for its struggles with citrus employers, and, in a period in which local police routinely harassed labor meetings, the club granted the use of its field for these gatherings.

"Mexican residents created their own leisure spaces and formed their own sport clubs, which assumed a heightened political role during times of labor-management conflict," Alamillo reveals. That several players from the Corona Athletics, the area's most popular team, climbed into the majors added to the prestige of Mexican American semiprofessional baseball. The Corona Mexican ballplayers and their aficionados also built their own diamond in part to offset the discrimination they experienced at public facilities. In short, "For Corona's Mexican working-class community, the Athletics' baseball field represented an important cultural space," states Alamillo.

Baseball's popularity also drew ample attention from journalists of the

Spanish-language press. In the construction of ethnic identity, the role of the local media and their relationship to sport in their communities had always been strong and often encouraged their readers to participate in and support athletics. In the period before World War II, Japanese American journalists fully recognized, according to publisher James Sakamoto, that "competition must be had to give life to the community."[16] Indeed, dailies that represented other ethnic enclaves (e.g., *Chicago Defender, Pittsburgh Courier,* and other black papers) were not shy about promoting the feats of the Negro League stars. "For the black fan," says historian Donn Rogosin, "the sports pages of the *Defender* or *Courier* were a lifeline to the rest of black America."[17] Even the Jewish press trumpeted the endeavors of their own athletes in the professional ranks. The *American Hebrew, Jewish Exponent,* and *Jewish Voice* all routinely ran stories about Jewish ballplayers in the major leagues. Of course, comments such as that of Pittsburgh shortstop Jim Levey, who told the *B'nai B'rith Messenger* that "You tell . . . everyone else who cares to know that I am a Jew . . . and mighty proud of it," were always a cause for celebration.[18]

Since the late nineteenth century, journalists who were Mexican nationalists in residence in the United States have also recognized the power of the press. Ultimately, they assumed the mantle as crusaders to present a positive image of Mexicans to their readers. To these writers and others who gravitated to them, the unifying theme of "La Raza" became a banner around which they could rally to both survive and advance themselves in the land of Aztlán.[19]

The Los Angeles–based *La Opinión* took the lead in this regard. Stories about the homeland were interwoven with issues relevant to Mexican residents in the United States. At the same time, sport was not ignored. Boxing, of course, was popular, and the paper did a good job in reporting on the many amateur clubs in the semiprofessional ranks and municipal city leagues that were prevalent in the Los Angeles basin. Though relatively few Mexicans played in the major leagues during the twentieth century, *La Opinión* nonetheless highlighted their achievements with weekly articles.

The fortunes of their brethren in the major leagues were always illuminated, and this was not unimportant. While boxing captured the attention of a Mexican audience on both sides of the border, *La Opinión*'s baseball coverage offered its readers an opportunity to keep tabs on the skills of mexicano players who were competing against mainstream U.S. players in a national forum.

Nearly a century after Mexican journalists declared their commitment to advancing a positive image for Mexicans in the United States, Fernando

Valenzuela's thunderous 1981 arrival into the major leagues was akin to striking oil. His appeal was threefold: He was obviously appealing to Mexican nationals, a magnet to Mexican Americans, and a brown version of Horatio Alger to the U.S. mainstream. That he rose from an impoverished background also enhanced his reputation. Valenzuela, a transnational hero who remained a Mexican citizen, enlarged the concept of being Mexican and strengthened Mexican Americans' sense of identity.

Apart from the national spotlight, sports other than baseball sometimes won the day. Far from the Southwest, Mexican workers, feeling culturally displaced, found solace in soccer as early as the 1940s. In and around the Great Lakes region and in urban barrios, they played the game and formed athletic institutions that helped them maintain a sense of cultural identity. Through the development of these clubs, players competed not only against other mexicanos but also against other ethnic communities on an equal basis.

Victories on the soccer field, however, were only part of the story. Many of the soccer clubs also held an importance that transcended the arena of play. In Chicago and Detroit, for instance, two of the soccer clubs there "became authentic community centers for Mexican families in the urban landscape and responded to their desire to articulate a commitment to reside permanently in the United States," states Juan Javier Pescador. The clubs became the forum that Pescador refers to as the community's "social space," in which political, racial, transnational, and ethnic identity might be defined and promoted to the world outside that of the barrio. It was there and in clubs where other sports were played that Mexicans living in the United States could forge what George J. Sánchez has referred to as a "new cultural identity."[20]

Contrary to the popular notion that only through professional sport could social mobility be attained, Mexican Americans in post–World War II Texas, Alex Mendoza observes, drew their inspiration from an unlikely source: distance runners. Prior to that time and unnoticed by scholars, tejanos amassed an impressive list of accolades as high school runners. The same might be said, in part, of those who participated in athletic competition in the Texas colonias. Mexican American distance runners there provided important inspiration. For tejanos in need of local heroes, the distance runners of the 1950s, all of whom earned scholarships to college, attained prominence in the small colonias and barrios they called home.

As they opened the door for those who came in later generations, many of the athletes who ran in the 1950s returned to their communities as teachers and coaches. One, Ricardo Romo, went on to earn a Ph.D. in history from the University of Texas. Indeed, as Alex Mendoza states, the tejanos who ran in the 1970s pointed to the previous generation of runners as role models who not only stimulated their interest in running but also served as gatekeepers for others like themselves. "I started to see that I represented a group of people and that my success could motivate others from the Hispanic culture to strive to do the same," said Roland Reina.

The high school football scene in the Lone Star State was no less important for ethnic identity and cultural bonding. Located in southeastern Texas just north of Brownsville and next to the Rio Grande, the little hamlet of Donna was one of many isolated towns almost entirely inhabited by Mexican Americans and Mexicans. And in a state in which football reigned, especially in small communities, Texas pigskin aficionados never considered Mexicans to be on par with Anglo athletes at the high school level. Nonetheless, the 1961 Donna High School Redskins were a championship football team that turned heads as far away as Dallas.

Beyond the scope of their athletic victory, the team also shot holes in the long-standing theory of Mexican inadequacies as a people. The Donna Redskins won recognition in an arena that mainstream Texans held in high regard. The reverberations of that success, according to historian Jorge Iber, "permitted many of the valley's Mexican American youth to envisage goals which previous generations could not." For small towns like Donna, Texas, the Mexican boys who played high school football, states Iber, "provided the Valley's Spanish-speaking population with a focal point of pride and self-esteem."

Fighting negative stereotypes, of course, was nothing new for Mexican athletes in Texas (and arguably beyond). In the early 1930s, Everado Carlos ("E. C.") Lerma won such acclaim on the high school gridiron that Texas Christian University offered him an athletic scholarship. However, the announcement of the award did not escape some mainstream Texans, who believed that the scholarship should have been given to a "real American." Nonetheless, Lerma went on to compete at Texas A&I and earned a degree. His notable success, which chipped away at the then popular perceptions of Mexican inadequacies, paved an important path for others such as football star Bobby Cavazos, who not only earned a scholarship to Texas Tech University in 1950 but also led the Red Raiders to a Gator Bowl victory against Auburn University in 1954.

Still, fighting negative stereotypes was only part of the story. The case of the Donna Redskins, Iber states, reveals that, for ethnic Mexicans, their traditions and economic circumstances proved to be factors as difficult to overcome as the prejudices they contended with outside of their ethnic circles. In short, rather than the perceptions of Mexicans held by Anglo educators and journalists, it was the approval of their parents to pursue athletics that was, for many young athletes, the primary challenge. To the parents of these budding sports competitors, the chief concern was not the touchdowns but instead the difficulties of sustaining life in a poverty-stricken environment. In this regard, the Mexican American experience in Donna, Texas, Iber states, magnified that of the ethnic Mexican experience on a larger scale. Rising to the challenge of social discrimination was thus not always the initial step in the development of identity and acceptance. For most, reckoning with poverty lay at the beginning of that task.

Sport in Mexican America indeed offers to historians a picture of "everyday life and organizational life" that, at the very least, is on equal footing with other aspects of the community they have previously analyzed. Mexican American competitive sport has crossed class and regional lines, stimulated hybrid and fluid identities, and enhanced a transnational culture. Ethnic Mexican sports stars have won fame in small locales, as well as in the national spotlight of the U.S. mainstream. As a badge of honor to aficionados, their success stimulated hope in those who sought opportunity for themselves and their people. Opportunities that were realized through sports both challenged family traditions and symbolized the virtues of others. Athletic clubs and institutions in the colonias and barrios in many cases reinforced masculine pride and in other cases emboldened young women to redefine their own cultural roles.

Yet, in spite of overwhelming evidence, the topic of sport within the ethnic Mexican world in the United States has, apart from a handful of professional and lay historians, remained largely invisible and unrecognized by scholars who have studied that group. The chapters in this book not only tell us about the history and everyday life of Mexican Americans but also explain the meaning and importance of their athletic accomplishments as they relate to the Mexican American experience overall. There is nothing secret about the connections between sport and ethnic Mexicans. The only secret is seen in the absence of that story within the general histories of the Mexican American people. Yes, Chicano historians have made great strides in advancing the historiography of their community, but, to complete the picture, still greater strides are needed.

NOTES

1. In Carey McWilliams, *Brothers under the Skin* (Boston: Little, Brown, 1951), 13.
2. Carey McWilliams, *North from Mexico: The Spanish-speaking People of the United States* (New York: Lippincott, 1948); Matt S. Meier and Feliciano Rivera, *The Chicanos: A History of Mexican Americans* (New York: Hill and Wang, 1972); Rodolfo F. Acuña, *Occupied America: The Chicano's Struggle toward Liberation* (San Francisco: Canfield, 1972).
3. Arnoldo De León, *They Called Them Greasers: Anglo Attitudes toward Mexicans in Texas, 1821–1900* (Austin: University of Texas Press, 1983); Mario T. García, *Desert Immigrants: The Mexicans of El Paso, 1880–1920* (New Haven, Conn.: Yale University Press, 1981); Albert Camarillo, *Chicanos in California: A History of Mexican Americans in California* (San Francisco: Boyd and Fraser, 1984); Richard Griswold del Castillo, *La Familia: Chicano Families in the Urban Southwest, 1848 to the Present* (Notre Dame, Ind.: Notre Dame University Press, 1984).
4. David J. Weber, *Foreigners in Their Native Land: Historical Roots of the Mexican Americans* (Albuquerque: University of New Mexico Press, 1973); Vickie L. Ruiz, *Cannery Women/Cannery Lives: Mexican Women, Unionization, and the California Food-processing Industry, 1930–1950* (Albuquerque: University of New Mexico Press, 1987); David G. Gutiérrez, *Walls and Mirrors: Mexican Americans, Mexican Immigrants in the United States* (Wilmington, Del.: Scholarly Resources, 1996); Ramón A. Gutiérrez, *When Jesus Came, the Corn Mothers Went Away: Marriage, Sexuality, and Power in New Mexico, 1500–1846* (Stanford: Stanford University Press, 1991).
5. George J. Sánchez, *Becoming Mexican American: Ethnicity, Culture, and Identity in Chicano Los Angeles, 1900–1945* (New York: Oxford University Press, 1993).
6. Manuel G. Gonzales, *Mexicanos: A History of Mexicans in the United States* (Bloomington: Indiana University Press, 1999).
7. Zaragosa Vargas, ed., *Major Problems in Mexican American History* (Boston: Houghton Mifflin, 1999). Vargas's book was designed to "invite readers to see Chicanos in their everyday life and in their organizational life," xv.
8. Samuel O. Regalado, *Viva Baseball!: Latin Major Leaguers and Their Special Hunger* (Urbana: University of Illinois Press, 1998), 68.
9. Benjamin G. Rader, *American Sports: From the Age of Folk Games to the Age of Televised Sports,* 4th ed. (Englewood Cliffs, N.J.: Prentice-Hall, 1999), 69.

10. Michael T. Isenberg, *John L. Sullivan and His America* (Urbana: University of Illinois Press, 1988), 45.

11. Richard Santillán, "Mexican Baseball Teams in the Midwest: The Politics of Cultural Survival and Civil Rights," *Perspectives in Mexican American Studies* 7 (2000): 131–52.

12. Irving Howe, *World of Our Fathers: The Journey of the East European Jews to America and the Life They Found and Made* (New York: Simon and Schuster, 1976), 172.

13. Samuel O. Regalado, "Baseball in the Barrios: The Scene in East Los Angeles since World War II," *Baseball History* 1(2) (Summer 1986): 55.

14. Santillán, "Mexican Baseball Teams in the Midwest."

15. Douglas Monroy, *Rebirth: Mexican Los Angeles from the Great Migration to the Great Depression* (Berkeley: University of California Press, 1999), 46–47. Researchers interested in the topic of baseball and its transnational impact might also explore Alan M. Klein, *Baseball on the Border: A Tale of Two Laredos* (Princeton, N.J.: Princeton University Press, 1997).

16. Samuel O. Regalado, "'Play Ball!' Baseball and Seattle's Japanese-American Courier League, 1928–1941," *Pacific Northwest Quarterly* 87(1) (Winter 1995–1996): 29.

17. Donn Rogosin, *Invisible Men: Life in Baseball's Negro Leagues* (New York: Atheneum, 1985), 89.

18. Peter Levine, *Ellis Island to Ebbets Field: Sport and the American Jewish Experience* (New York: Oxford University Press, 1992), 123.

19. Gutiérrez, *Walls and Mirrors*, 36.

20. Sánchez, *Becoming Mexican American*, 12–13.

LIST OF CONTRIBUTORS

JOSÉ ALAMILLO is assistant professor in the Department of Comparative Ethnic Studies, Washington State University. Alamillo's publications include *Making Lemonade out of Lemons: Mexican American Labor and Leisure in a California Town, 1880-1960* (forthcoming from the University of Illinois Press) and "More than a Fiesta: Ethnic Identity, Cultural Politics, and Cinco de Mayo Festivals in Corona, California, 1930-1950," in *Aztlán: A Journal of Chicano Studies* 28(2) (Fall 2003). In addition, he is currently working on an article titled "The Making of a Mexican American Sporting Culture in Los Angeles, 1920-1945." His areas of research interest include race, gender, and American sport and Chicano/a and Latino/a studies.

JORGE IBER is chair of the Department of History, Texas Tech University. Iber's publications include *Hispanics in the Mormon Zion, 1912-1999* (College Station: Texas A&M University Press, 2001); *Hispanics in the American West*, coauthored with Arnoldo De León (Santa Barbara: ABC-Clio, 2005); "Digging the 'Richest Hole on Earth': The Hispanic Miners of Utah, 1912-1945," coauthored with Armando Solórzano, *Perspectives in Mexican American Studies* 7 (Spring 2001). His essays have also appeared in *Journal of the West, Southwestern Historical Quarterly,* and *International Journal for the History of Sport.* His areas of research interest include Chicano/a and Latino/a history and ethnic groups and American sport.

KATHERINE M. JAMIESON is assistant professor in the Department of Exercise and Sport Science, University of North Carolina-Greensboro. Jamieson's publications include "Reading Nancy López: Decoding Representations of Race, Class, Sexuality, and Gender," *Sociology of Sport Journal* 15(4) (1998); "Beyond the Racial Binary: Stacking in Women's Collegiate Softball," *Women in Sport and Physical Activity Journal* 11(1) (2002); and "Occupying a Middle Space: Toward a Mestiza Sports Studies," *Sociology of Sport Journal* 20(1) (2003). Her areas of research interest include physical activity in the lives of adolescent Latinas in North Carolina and positional segregation in NCAA Division I softball.

ALEX MENDOZA is assistant professor in the Department of History, University of Texas-Tyler. Mendoza is a recent graduate of Texas Tech University, and his research interests include race relations in the South, historical memory, and nineteenth-century U.S. history. In addition, he is an avid distance runner.

JUAN JAVIER PESCADOR is assistant professor in the Department of History, Michigan State University. Pescador is the author of *The New World inside a Basque Village: The Oiartzun Valley and Its Atlantic Emigrants* (Reno: University of Nevada Press, 2003) and coauthor (with Ida Altman and Sarah Cline) of *The Early History of Greater Mexico* (Upper Saddle River, N.J.: Prentice Hall, 2003). He has done extensive research on the lives of Mexicans in the Midwest and earned a faculty fellowship with the Great Lakes Culture Institute at Michigan State University (2001) and an NEH summer fellowship at the Chicago Historical Society (2002).

SAMUEL O. REGALADO is a professor in the Department of History, California State University-Stanislaus. Regalado's most recent publications include *Viva Baseball!: Latin Major Leaguers and Their Special Hunger* (Urbana: University of Illinois Press, 1998); "Sammy Sosa Meets Horatio Alger: Latin Ballplayers and the American Success Myth," in *Baseball and the American Dream: Race, Class, Gender, and the National Pastime,* edited by Robert Elias (Armonk, N.Y.: M. E. Sharpe, 2001); and "Incarcerated Sport: Nisei Women's Softball and Athletics during the Japanese Internment Period," *Journal of Sport History* 27(3) (2000).

His research interests include sport and its relationship to U.S. ethnic populations and Latin America.

GREGORY RODRÍGUEZ is assistant professor in the Mexican American Studies and Research Center, University of Arizona. Rodríguez is a graduate of the University of San Diego, where his dissertation was titled "'Palaces of Pain': Arenas of Mexican-American Dreams: Boxing and the Formation of Mexican Identities in Twentieth-century Los Angeles." His research interests include popular culture for the mobilization of ethnic groups and gender identities within communities of Mexican Americans and Mexican nationals.

MARK DYRESON is associate professor of kinesiology at Penn State University. His research interests focus on the role of sport in the creation of modern societies. He has published a book, *Making the American Team: Sport, Culture, and the Olympic Experience* (Urbana: Illinois University Press, 1989) and numerous articles in journals such as the *Journal of Contemporary History, Journal of Sport History,* and *Peace Review.*

TOM I. ROMERO II is assistant professor of law at Hamline University School of Law in St. Paul, Minnesota. A graduate of the University of Michigan School of Law, he also received a Ph.D. from the University of Michigan's Department of History. His dissertation, "Of Race and Rights: Legal Culture, Social Change, and the Making of a Multiracial Metropolis, Denver 1940–1975," examines the relationship of the law to race relations and civic identity in a major U.S. city. Prior to his appointment at Hamline, Romero served as the Western Legal Studies Fellow at the University of Colorado's Center of the American West, Law School, and Department of History. His research interests include the legal history of the American West, social movements, and racial formation in law and society.

INDEX

AAGBL (All-American Girls Baseball League), 216
Abell, V. L., 215
Acosta, R. V., 215
Acuña, Rodolfo, 234
Adame, Homero, 191–92, 196, 197, 203
Adame, Humberto, 191, 196, 197, 207n9
Adams, David Wallace, 3, 125
African Americans: baseball story, 63; newspapers, 240; sports research, 3, 146; Texas Western basketball impact, 136–37
Aguirre, Bobby, 198
Aguirre, Enrique C., 24, 28
Aguirre, Hank, 59
Alamillo, José M.: chapter by, 50–72; comments on, 11, 147, 239
Alice, Texas, 190
All-American Girls Baseball League (AAGBL), 216
All-American runners, 191

Allen, Forrest "Phog," 37
Allen, Robert, 103
Almada, Baldomero "Melo," 54, 60–61
Almada, Mel, 75
Alma (softball player), 225–26
Alou, Felipe, 146, 152
Alou, Jesus, 152
Alou, Mateo, 152
Alta California newspaper, 151
Alvarado, Raul, 136, 141–42n27
Alvarez, Isabel, 216
Amateur Athletic Union (AAU), 92–94
Amateur Softball Association, 214–15
American Dry Cleaners, 57
An American-Mexican Frontier (Taylor), 127–28
Amoros, Sandy, 150
Anaya, Frank R., 110
Anzaldúa, G., 229
Aragón, Art, 180, 182
Arbena, Joseph, 42n17
Arias, Randy, 212n71

251

Asian Americans, sports research, 3, 125
assimilation activities: company baseball teams, 52–54, 68; Midwest soccer clubs, 80–81, 84–85; play reformers generally, 53, 72*n*39
Athletes Remembered (Longoria), 9, 126
Atlante soccer club, 76
Austin American newspaper, 193
Austin Statesman reports, Tarahumaran racers, 27, 28, 29, 30–31, 32, 36–37
Austin Sunday American-Statesman, 35–36
auto racing, 1–2
Avery, Louie, 124
Avila, Alfredo, 136, 141–42*n*27
Avila, Oscar, 133, 134, 135, 136, 141–42*n*27
Avila, Richard, 130, 134, 136, 141–42*n*27
Avila, Roberto Francisco "Beto," 75, 150

Backus, Billy, 175
Badeaux, Johnny, 141–42*n*27
Baillet-Latour, Henri, 24
Balderas, Tony, 66
Baltimore Orioles, 152
Barba, Marcelino, 56
Barker Motor Company, 29
Barnett, K. S., 98
Barrera, Fabian, 132, 135, 141–42*n*27
baseball: as assimilation activity, 52–54, 68; as community activity, 58–59, 82–83, 238–39; company teams, 52–54, 62, 68; dominance of, 74–75; and ethnic pride, 7, 61–62, 238–39; language barriers, 192; literature reviews, 6–9, 146–47; major league barriers, 50, 54, 60–61; in Mexico, 51–52, 54–55, 61, 75, 238. *See also* Corona Athletics Baseball Club; softball participation; Spanish-language newspapers
Basilio, Carmen, 180
basketball, collegiate, 136

Bavasi, Buzzie, 153
Baylor University, 142*n*38, 205
Becerra, Joe, 176
Becoming Mexican American (Sánchez), 234
Bedford, Texas, 210*n*47
Beezley, William, 6
Bellmont, L. Theo, 24, 26, 35
Benavides, Abel, 130, 133–34, 136, 141–42*n*27
Benyo, Richard, 190
blacklisting, baseball players, 61
Bogardus, Emory, 53
Bonkowski, Jerry, 1–2
Border Olympics, 191
border spaces, soccer clubs as, 74
Boston Red Sox, 75
Bowie High School, 190
boxing: Gonzales career, 92–98, 170–71; sports research review, 5. *See also* raza boxing
Boyle, Robert H., 175
bracero program, 163
Brady football, 131
Brannan, Charles F., 103
Brooklyn Dodgers, 60
Brownsville Pace High School, 202, 204
Brownwood High School, 123
Brumley, Bill, 141–42*n*27
Buchanan, Olin, 124
Buda, Texas, 34
"Bugs" (softball player), 219, 220
Bustos, Crystal, 215
Butts, Leon, 136–37

Cahn, Leonard, 95–96
California Angels, 153
California Fruit Growers Exchange (CFGE), 52
Callahan, Mushy, 177
Campaneris, Dagoberto "Bert," 152
Campanis, Al, 155

Cantú, Inocensio, 191, 195, 207n9
Carberry, Jack, 96–97
Cardinals baseball team, 82–83
Cardoza, D., 218–19
Carmona, Erubey "Chango," 172–74
Carroll High School, 123
Cashion, Ty, 122, 126–27
Casino Monte Carlo, 80
Castillo, Fernando, 136
Castillo, Ysora del, 216
Cavazos, Bobby, 125–26, 242
Cepeda, Orlando, 146, 152, 154, 159n38
Chagnon, Remi, 60
Champions (Stowers and Evans), 190
Chandler, A. B., 61
Chapin, Eudibiel Guillen, 172–74
Chávez, Mary, 106
Chicago National Soccer League (CNSL), 78
Chicano, definition, 14
Chicano movement. *See* newspaper coverage, in Denver
The Chicanos (Meier and Rivera), 234
Clemente, Roberto, 145
Cleveland Indians, 61, 75, 150
Club América, 77
Club Atlas, 76
Club Deportivo Necaxa (in Mexico), 78
Club Guadalajara, 77, 82
Club México, 75
Club Necaxa (in Chicago), 78–81, 83–84
Club Necaxa (in Mexico), 76
Club Social y Deportivo México, 82–84
coaches, distance running, 197–98, 204–205, 209n25, 212n67, 241–42
Colindres, Claudia, 222
Collins, P. H., 222–23
company teams: baseball, 7, 52–54, 55, 62, 68; Mexican soccer, 75–76; women's softball, 214
Conde, Carlos "Cuco," 175
Contreras, Chevo, 192
Contreras, Gilberto, 201

Contreras, Irene, 63
Contreras, Mark, 203
Cooke, Jack Kent, 179
Cope, Myron, 122–23
Corky's Corner, 98–99
Corona Athletics Baseball Club: overview, 51, 68–69; as community activity, 58–59, 238; and ethnic pride, 58–59, 61–62; family opposition, 59–60; formation of, 55; as major league source, 51, 60–61; as masculine culture, 57, 62–64; as non-agricultural opportunity, 55–57; segregation barriers, 57–58, 61; sponsors/funding, 57, 59; union activity, 64–65
Corona Cubs, 64
Corona Foothill Company, 64, 65
Corona Independent, 67
Corpus Christi Caller, 130
Corpus Christi schools, 136
Correa, Manuel, 78
Cortez, Natividad "Tito," 56, 57, 60, 61, 63
cross-country. *See* distance runners
Cruz, Carlos "Teo," 171
Cruz, Manuel, 66
Crystal City, Texas, 193, 201, 202, 210n47
Crystal City High School, 123
CSD México, 82–84
Cuban Stars, 216
Cuellar, Miguel, 152
culture change theme, softball study, 225–29
Currigan, Tom, 106, 109–10, 111
Cuzarare, Juanita, 31–32
Cuzarare, Lola, 31–32, 37

Dalevuelta, Jacobo, 22
Dallas Morning News, 23, 124, 134, 136
Dark, Alvin, 154, 159n38
de la Fuente, Mario, 9, 126

de la Garza, Raul, 132, 135, 141–42*n*27
de la Torre, A., 229
de León, Arnoldo, 11
Delgadillo, Ray, 60
del Rio, Dolores, 149
Denver Post reports: activism of Gonzales, 110–11; antipoverty programs, 108–10; boxing, 94–95, 96–98; Mexican American community, 101, 112; trial of Gonzales, 103–104
Detroit soccer club, 82–84
Detroit Soccer League, 82, 83
Devine football, 131
Díaz, Al, 160, 161
Dickson, P., 214
distance runners: as coaches, 197–98, 204–205, 209*n*25, 241–42; community support, 202–203; as ethnic representatives, 203–205; family support networks, 200–202; literature review, 189–90; during the *1950s*, 191–93; during the *1960s*, 193–95; during the *1970s*, 197, 199, 209*n*36; during the *1980s*, 198–202, 209*n*36, 210*n*47; during the *1990s*, 202–203, 205, 210*n*47, 211*n*51, *n*55; during the early *2000s*, 206, 212*n*71; successes summarized, 189, 190–91, 198, 206*n*2
Don Campbell's Texas Football magazine, 123–24
Donna High School football: championship game, 124, 132–33; coaching style, 130–31; community impact, 133–36, 242; cultural/social setting, 128–29; participation barriers, 127–28, 243; regular season, 129–31; team members, 141–42*n*27
Doyle, William E., 103
drinking behavior, 63
Du Bose, H. B., 27, 31, 36–37
Dyreson, Jodella K., 6

Dyreson, Mark: chapter by, 19–49; comments on, 10–11, 235–36

Eagle Pass, Texas, 129, 202–203
Eaton, Aileen, 172, 179, 181
Ebihara-Torres bout, 160–61
Edinburg High School, 197, 205–206, 212*n*63
education exclusion theme, softball study, 218–21
Edwards, Fred, 133, 141–42*n*27
El Campo, Texas, 191
El Paso, Texas: distance running, 197, 198, 201, 210*n*47; football, 123
El Paso Shoe Store Club, 7
El Paso Times, 198
endurance running. *See* Tarahumaran *indios*
Enríquez, Gilbert, 56
Escoto, S. B., 190
ESPN, NASCAR article, 1
Estrado, Alberto, 190
Estrellas Cubanas, 216
ethnic pride: basketball participants, 136; football participants, 133–34, 135; runner perspectives, 192–93, 203–206; and soccer clubs, 78–79, 81, 82, 83–84; softball study, 225–29; sports research, 124–26, 137, 146–47, 225. *See also* baseball; raza boxing
Evan, Wilbur, 190
Excélsior reports: baseball players, 61; Tarahumaran racers, 25–26, 28–29, 33–34
Exchange Lemon Products team, 62

Falfurrias High School, 194–95, 197, 202, 209*n*25
fans. *See* spectator/fan responses
Federación Mexicana de Fútbol (FeMexFut), 76–77
Fernández, Gigi, 216

Fernández, Lisa, 214, 216
Fernández, Mary Jo, 216
Fidler, David P., 147
Fitten, Jimmy, 179
Fitzpatrick, Frank, 136–37
Flores, Jesse, 54, 59–60
football, high school: appeal of, 121–23; championship distribution, 123–24; classification systems, 138n3, n9; and ethnic pride, 135, 242; extra points system, 143n43; literature reviews, 5, 8, 9, 125–27; participation obstacles, 127–28, 130, 243. *See also* Donna High School football
football, professional, 126
Foot Locker Cross-country Championships, 210n47
Foster, Jack, 101
four minute mile, 194, 200, 208n19
Fox Tech High School, 192–93
Franks, Joel S., 3, 125
Frederick, Charles R., Jr., 121
Furbeck, J. Nelson, 28
Furillo, Bud, 171

Gallegos, Ricardo, 193–94, 195–96, 201, 202
Gallegos, Ricky, Jr., 201, 210n47, 211n55
Galvani, Luís, 94–96
García, Ceferino, 179
García, Matt, 4–5
García, Rodolfo, 145, 149–50, 153, 154, 155, 172
Gelber, Steven, 56
Gem, Gerald R., 3, 125, 134
Gerstle, Gary, 91
Gibbs, Joe, 2
Gil, Miguel, 40n2
Gilliam, Phillip, 99
Glenn, E. N., 222
globalization and raza boxing, 164–65

golf, 216
Gómez, Andres, 210n47
Gómez, José Luis "Chili," 54, 75
Gómez, Vernon "Lefty," 75
Gonzales, Eulalia, 216
Gonzales, Manuel G., 235
Gonzales, Rudolfo "Corky": anti-poverty program leadership, 105–109; boxing career, 92–98, 170–71; as Chicano movement leader, 90, 107, 109–12; community activities, 99; lawsuit, 89; on media power, 89; newspaper coverage summarized, 90–91, 111–15, 236–37; political activities, 99–101, 104–105; post-boxing newspaper image, 102–104, 111–12; restaurant business, 98–99; trial of, 103–104
Gonzales, Rudolfo "El Gato," 174
González, Joe, 132–33, 134, 136, 141–42n27
González, Roberto: as coach, 197, 198, 209n25; college competition, 196–97; on ethnic representation, 203; high school competition, 194–95; on Romo, 208n22
González de Echevarría, Roberto, 147
Goodman, Cary, 53
Gordon, Jeff, 2
Gossage, Eddie, 1, 2
Graziano, Rocky, 92
Graziano, Tony, 175–76
gringo, defined, 143n53
Guerrero, Jess, 50, 63
Guerro, Roberto, 2
Guillén, Rene, 202–203, 204, 212n63
Guttmann, Allan, 5

Halimi, Alphonse, 176–77
Hall, John, 170
Harasta, Cathy, 134, 136
Hardy, Stephen, 39

INDEX **255**

Hart, Bill, 123–24
Haskell Indian School, 29
Hayden, Jessie, 52–53
Heinrich, Bernd, 40
Heller, Walter, 105
Henry, Lawrence, 103
El Heraldo de México, 148
Hernández, Juan R., 78
Hispanic, definition, 15
Hodgkin, G. B., 52
Hollywood Stars, 150
Hondagneu-Sotelo, Pierrette, 222
Hooper, Verle, 141–42n27
Houston, Kathleen, 36
Howing, Irving, 238
Hoyt, Palmer, 89–90, 101
Huerrera, Joseph, 110
Hulme, Jim, 141–42n27
hybrid unities. *See* raza boxing

Iber, Jorge: chapters by, 1–18, 121–44; comments on, 12–13, 125–26, 242, 243
I Like You, Gringo—But! (de la Fuente), 9, 126
El Imparcial, 56
indigenismo, Tarahumaran symbolism, 21–22, 38
El Informador, 151–52
International Boxing Club, 180
Isenberg, Michael T., 236
Italian Americans, sports research, 125

Jackson, Howard, 94
James Bowie High School, 123
Jameson Company, 64, 65
Jamieson, Kathy: chapter by, 213–32; comments on, 14, 237–38
Jarrett, Ned, 2
Jay High School, 188, 189, 198–200
Jewish newspapers, 240
Johnson, Lyndon, 105–106
Jones, Anita, 81

Josie (softball player), 227–28
Journal of Sport History, 5–6
The Joy of Sports (Novak), 121–22
Julie (softball player), 226–27

Kanner, Jack, 98
Kansas Relays, 37
Karin (softball player), 224
Keefe, William McGregor, 96–97
Kelleher, James, 109
Kieran, John, 27–28
King Ranch Cowboys, 8–9, 126
Kinney Cross-country Championships, 200, 210n47
Klein, Alan, 147
Kleinman, Bill, 29
Krugel, Mitchell, 122
Kyle, Texas, 31

labor unions, 52, 64–68, 76
La Habra Citrus Association, 52–53
Lanier High School, 123, 192
Lansing, Michigan, 82–83
Lantz, Harry, 130, 141–42n27
La Prade, Bennie, 130, 135
Lara, Michael, 210n47
Laredo, Texas: baseball, 192; distance running, 191, 197, 201, 203, 204, 210n47; football, 123, 129
Laredo Times, 133
Lasorda, Tommy, 155
Latina participation. *See* softball participation; women in sports
Latino, definition, 15
Leal, Rick, 135
LeCompte, Mary Lou, 6
Lennon, Jimmy, 160, 173
Lerma, Everado Carlos (E. C.), 125–26, 242
"A Letter to My Mother" (Colindres), 222
Levey, Jim, 240
Levine, Peter, 3, 125

Liga Mexicanan de Football Amateur Association, 75
literature reviews, sports research, 3–6, 124–26, 146–47
Longoria, Mario, 9, 126, 208*n*20
López, Danny "Little Red," 176
López, Donovan, 8–9, 126
López, Ernie "Indian Red," 176
López, Goyo, 203
López, Marcelino, 153
López, Nancy, 216
Los Angeles Angels, 150
Los Angeles Colored Giants, 63
Los Angeles Dodgers, 145–46, 150, 152–56
Los Angeles Forty-sixty Club, 238–39
Los Angeles Nippons, 7
Los Angeles Times reports, 160–61, 171, 182
Lozano, Ignacio, 148–49, 155
Lubbock football, 123
Lucy (softball player), 224, 228–29
Lule, Jack, 113
Luna, Memo, 150

Macías, Raúl "Ratón," 176, 177, 179
Major Problems in Mexican American History (Vargas), 235
maquila manufacturing, 163–64
Marcano Guevara, Arturo J., 147
Marichal, Juan, 146, 152, 154
Marrero, Mirtha, 216
Martínez, Bernave, 209*n*25
Martínez, Conchita, 216
Martínez, Homero: as coach, 197, 198, 204–205, 212*n*67; college competition, 196; on ethnic representation, 203, 204–205; high school competition, 194–96; on role models, 197, 208*n*22
Martínez, José, 198
Martínez, Tony, 210*n*47
Masters of the Marathon (Benyo), 190

McCarthy, Marvin, 95
McCoy, Babe, 179
McCoy, Jackie, 169–70, 174
McDonnell, John, 199
McNabb, Dave, 124
McTaggart, Brian, 124
McWilliams, Carey, 234
Medina, Heliodoro, 66
Medina, José, 212*n*63
Meier, Matt S., 234
Mejía, Zeke, 56, 57
Menchaca, Richard, 192
Mendoza, Alex, 210*n*47
Mendoza, Alexander: chapter by, 188–212; comments on, 14, 241
Mercedes football, 129–30
Messner, Michael, 62
Mexican American, definition, 14
"Mexican Baseball Teams in the Midwest" (Santillán), 6–7
Mexican League, 61
Mexican National Baseball League, 75
Mexicanos (Gonzales), 235
Mexican Soccer Federation, 76
Mexico: baseball, 51–52, 54–55, 61, 75; soccer, 75–77. *See also* Tarahumaran *indios*
Meyer, Doris L., 148
Micaela (softball player), 219–20, 223
Michaelson, Frank, 103
Mickey (softball player), 220–21
Midwest soccer. *See* soccer clubs
Mills, Billy, 225
Miranda (softball player), 226
Mission, Texas, 200, 206*n*2, 208*n*19
Mitchell, Arden H., 104
Monroy, Douglas, 6, 7, 238
Montes, Javier, 190, 206*n*2
Montes, Lee, 190
Montez de Ocas, Rosalie (later Parnassus), 178
Moody, Dan, 30
Mormino, Gary Ross, 3, 125

Moynihan, Neal Patrick, 99
El Mundo, 151
Murphy, Frank, 190
Murray, Jim, 178, 179, 182

Nabokov, Peter, 48*n*93
Nacogdoches, Texas, 190
Nápoles, José Angel, 175-76
NASCAR racing, 1-2
Native Americans, sports research, 3, 124-25, 225
Navarro, José, 204
NBC television, 75
Necaxa club (in Chicago), 78-81, 83-84
Necaxa club (in Mexico), 76
Neighborhood House (San Diego), 53-54
Neighborhood Youth Corps (NYC), 105, 106
Nelson, Chet, 93
Nelson, Cordner, 189
newspaper coverage: baseball players, 54, 60-61, 126; boxing, 149-50, 160-61, 171, 172-73, 186-87*n*33; high school football, 124, 130, 133, 134-35; labor strikes, 65-67; runners, 193, 198, 203; soccer, 79; Tarahumaran racers, 22-23, 24-26, 27-29, 30-31, 33-36
newspaper coverage, in Denver: activism of Gonzales, 110-12, 236-37; antipoverty programs, 106-107, 108-10; boxing, 91-98, 236; Chicano nationalism, 90-91, 110-11, 112, 113-15; Mexican American community, 101-102; political activity of Gonzales, 102-103; racial/ethnic distinctions, 95-97, 113-15; trial of Gonzales, 103-104
newspapers, Spanish-language, 147-49, 151-52, 240. *See also La Opinión* newspaper

Newton, Quigg, 99
New York Times reports, 23, 27-28, 186-87*n*33
New York Yankees, 75
Nicole (softball player), 223-24
Nixon High School, 197
Norris, Jim, 180
Novak, Michael, 121-22

Oakland Athletics, 152
Occupied America (Acuña), 234
Olympic Games: Mexico's expectations/hopes, 21, 24, 25, 34, 37-38; Mexico's hosting, 77; running competitions, 188-89, 202, 206*n*2; softball, 215, 216; women's races, 37-38, 48*n*92
La Opinión newspaper: baseball coverage, 7, 61, 145-46, 150, 152-56, 240-41; boxing coverage, 149-50, 161, 172-73; founding of, 148-49; promotion of baseball, 54-55; sports coverage generally, 149-50, 156-57; union activity coverage, 66
Ordaz, Gustavo Díaz, 180-81, 186*n*33
Ortega, Phil, 153
Ortiz, Alfonso, 65
Ortiz, Manuel, 170
Osif, Philip, 29

Paciencia, Juanita, 31-32
Padilla, Nick, 131, 136
Paredes, Américo, 184*n*4
Park, Roberta J., 3, 125
Parnassus, George, 177-82
Parnassus, Rosalie Montez de Ocas, 178
Patton Park, Detroit, 82
Pedraza, Luz, 130, 132-33, 136, 141-42*n*27
Peña, Federico, 112
Pennington, Campbell W., 41*n*9
Pérez, Bobby, 60

Pérez, Migdalia, 216
Pérez, Román, 82
Pescador, Juan Javier: chapter by, 73–88; comments on, 11–12, 241
Pesdquera, B. M., 229
Philadelphia Phillies, 75
Phillips, Bum, 121
The Pigskin Pulpit (Cashion), 122
play reformers, 53, 68, 72*n*39
Practice! Practice! Practice! (López), 8–9, 126
Prefontaine, Steve, 189–90
La Prensa, 149
La Prensa Libre, 152
Prieto, Jorge, 9, 126
Prlia, Leo, 173
Pro México, 40*n*2
punts, football, 132–33, 143*n*43

Quanah Indians, 124, 132–33
The Quarterback Who Almost Wasn't (Prieto), 9, 126

Racine Bells, 216
Rader, Benjamin, 236
radio programming, 80, 145–46, 152–53
Ramírez, Aaron, 200, 206*n*2, 208*n*19, 211*n*51
Ramos, Armando "Mando," 170–74
Ramos, Rudy, 65, 67
Ramos, Ultiminio "Sugar," 176, 181
Rancho Sespe, 52
Rarámuri Indians, 41*n*9. *See also* Tarahumaran *indios*
Ratliff, Harold, 133
raza boxing: fan riots, 160–61; Halimi and fans, 176–77; and intergroup communication process, 174–75, 237; McCoy's role, 169–70, 174; Mexican American dominance, 161–62, 186–87*n*33; Nápoles and fans, 175–76; Parnassus' role, 177–82; Ramos and fans, 170–74; as reflection of culture change, 162–69, 182–84; theoretical approaches, 166–69
Rebirth (Monroy), 6, 7
"Recent Chicano Historiography" (Saragoza), 4
Refugio football, 131
Regalado, Samuel O.: chapters by, 145–59, 233–45; comments on, 3, 6, 13, 58, 125, 135, 147
Reina, Eileen, 199, 200–201
Reina, Emily, 199
Reina, Janice, 199
Reina, Ralph, 199, 200–201
Reina, Randy, 198–99, 203, 210*n*42
Reina, Reubén: college competition, 200, 206*n*2, 208*n*19, 211*n*51; on ethnic representation, 204; high school competition, 198, 199–200, 202, 210*n*47, *n*48; Olympic competition, 188–89
Reina, Roland, 198–99, 200–201, 204, 210*n*42, 242
Reyes, Alfonso, 38
Richardson, James Perkins, 138
Rickard, Tex, 28
Riess, Steven A., 3, 125
Riley, Charley, 92, 98
Rio Grande City football, 129–30
Rios-Bustamante, Antonio, 4
Rivera, Feliciano, 234
Riverside Daily Press, 65
Riverside High School, 198
Roberson, Jackie, 141–42*n*27
Rocky Mountain News, lawsuit, 89
Rocky Mountain News reports: activism of Gonzales, 110–11; antipoverty programs, 106–107, 108–109; boxing, 91–95, 96–97; civil liberties editorial, 90; Mexican American community, 101–102; political activities of Gonzales, 102–103; trial of Gonzales, 103–104

Rodríguez, Alice, 67
Rodríguez, Gregory S.: chapter by, 160-87; comments on, 13-14, 149-50, 237
Rodríguez, Luís, 176
Rodríguez, Tomás, 26, 36-37
Rogosin, Donn, 146, 240
Rojas, Alex, 82
Rojas, J. Fernando, 33-34
Rojas, Raúl, 170-71, 172, 182
Rojas, Salvador, 82, 84
Romero, Tom I.: chapter by, 89-120; comments on, 12, 237
Romo, Henry, 196
Romo, Ricardo: college competitions, 194, 196, 208nn19-20; high school competitions, 192-93; as role model, 194, 204, 208n22, 241; in sports books, 190; on work ethnic, 196
Romo, Vicente, 153
Roseboro, Johnny, 154
Ruck, Rob, 146
Ruiz, Frank, 62
Ruiz, Vicky, 84
running competitions. *See* distance runners; Tarahumaran *indios*
"Running Reinas," 198-201
Ryun, Jim, 189-90, 194, 208n20

Sabates, Félix, 2
Said, Edward, 183
Sakamoto, James, 240
Salazar, Alberto, 190
Saldívar, Vicente, 181, 182, 186-87n33
Salido, Augustín, 31, 32, 36
Salzer, Morris, 95-96, 98
San Antonio, Texas: distance running, 192-93, 210n47; football, 123
San Antonio Express, 24, 29, 30
San Antonio Express-News, 9, 126
Sánchez, George I., 233
Sánchez, George J., 59, 78, 84-85, 234
Sánchez, Luís, 201-203

Sánchez-Vicario, Aranxta, 216
San Diego Padres, 150
San Francisco Giants, 146, 150-51, 154, 159n38
San Miguel, Leoncio, 19-21
Santa María, Gabriel, 201, 204
Santillán, Richard, 6-7, 75, 84, 147, 238
Saragoza, Alex M., 4
scholarships: distance running, 196-97; football, 242; softball, 219-20
Scott, Earl, 129-31
Sepulveda, Sonia, 205, 212n67
Shank, Reuben, 92
The Silence of Great Distance (Murphy), 190
Simoniello, K., 218
Simons, William M., 3, 125
Simpson, K., 225
Simpson, O. J., 171
Singletary, Wes, 3
Smith College, 214
soccer clubs: Chicago, 78-81; as community centers, 73-74, 82-84, 241; Detroit, 81-84; Mexican, 75-77; Midwest beginnings, 74-75, 77-78
soccer participation, research review, 5
softball participation: as assimilation activity, 53-54; culture change theme, 225-30, 237-38; education exclusion theme, 218-21, 224, 229-30; family support factors, 218-25, 229-30; gender role theme, 222-25, 229-30; growth of, 57, 214-15; participation barriers, 215; research methodology, 216-18
Southwest Conference (SWC), 142n38
Spalding, Keith, 52
Spanish-language newspapers, 147-49, 151-52, 240. *See also La Opinión* newspaper
spectator/fan responses: auto racing, 1-2; high school football, 121-24, 131, 134-35; Tarahumaran racers, 19-

20, 29, 30, 31–32, 33–34. *See also* raza boxing
Sports (Guttmann), 5
Sports Illustrated, 175, 181
sports research, literature reviews, 3–6, 124–26, 146–47
Stone, Tommy, 135, 141–42n27
Stowers, Carlton, 190
strikes, labor, 65–67
Sullivan, John L., 236
Sul Ross State University, 196
Sunkist, 52
Sweeny High School, 131

Tarahumaran *indios:* homeland, 21, 42n15; Mexico race, 19–21; as national heroes, 34, 37; news coverage, 22–23, 24–26, 27–29, 30–31, 33–36; Olympic races, 38, 48n93; promotional uses of, 21–22, 24–25, 34–35, 36–37, 38–40, 42n17, 235–36; spectator responses, 19–20, 29, 30, 31–32, 33–34; travel to U.S., 25–27; U.S. races, 10–11, 30–33, 37, 46n69
Taylor, Dora, 2
Taylor, Paul S., 127–28
El Tecolote, 151
tejano, definition, 17n19
television coverage, 75, 77
tennis, 216
Texas A&I University, 196, 199, 242
Texas Christian University, 242
Texas Football Trilogy (Krugel), 122
Texas Outlook, 127–28
Texas Relays, 24–25, 27, 29, 32
Texas State University, 212n71
Texas Tech University, 242
Texas Western basketball, 136
They Called Them Greasers (de León), 11
They Call Me Super Mex (Trevino), 9, 126
Thompson, Wallace, 51
Tobin, John W., 30, 32
Torres, Joaquín, 210n47

Torres, José, 32–33, 37, 38
Torres-Ebihara bout, 160–61
transmigration and raza boxing, 163–64
Trevino, Lee, 9, 126
Tucson Cowboys, 61
Tulpetiac, Mexico, 20
Tygiel, Jules, 146

UIL (University Interscholastic League), 189, 206n2, 209n36, 210n40
United Cannery Agricultural Packing and Allied Workers of America (UCAPAWA), 64–65
United High School, 197
El Universal newspaper, 28–29, 33
University Interscholastic League (UIL), 189, 206n2, 209n36, 210n40
University of Arizona, 200
University of Arkansas, 142n38, 199, 200, 210n42, n45
University of Texas, 24–25, 29, 191–92, 194, 204, 209n9, 212n63
Uribe, Charles, 66
Uribe, Jess, 59
Uribe, Louis, 60
Uribe, Marcus, 56, 57, 65–66

Valdez, Bernard, 106
Valenzuela, Fernando, 145–46, 154–56, 240–41
Vargas, Zaragosa, 235
Vásquez, Laura, 205, 212n67
Vázquez, Mike, 2
Victoria Junior College, 191

Waco football, 123
And the Walls Came Tumbling Down (Fitzpatrick), 136–37
War on Poverty, 105–108
Washington Park, Lansing, 82–83
Weslaco High School, 136
Wichita Falls football, 123

Williams, Charlie, 123
women in sports: Olympic Games, 37–38, 48*n*92; as spectators/supporters, 57, 85; Tarahumaran *indios,* 10, 31–32, 37. *See also* softball participation
Wood, Gordon, 123
World Boxing Country (WBC), 179
A World of Its Own (García), 4–5

Yolanda (softball player), 218, 226
Yoseloff, Anthony A., 3, 125
Yracheta, Ricardo, 212*n*63

Zafíro, Tomás, 21, 25, 30–33, 34
Zavella, P., 225
Zieff, Susan G., 3, 125
Zurita, Juan, 179